"Elkind brings us along for the walk of a lifetime and shows us that adventure doesn't have to end when we reach a certain age. *To Walk It Is To See It* is an honestly written, compelling story of perseverance. Like all great travel literature, it makes us want to take a leap and travel immediately. An inspiring read for anyone thinking of undertaking a physical challenge, as well as for those who like to read about them."

—MARIANNE C. BOHR, author of *The Twenty:*
One Woman's Trek Across Corsica on the GR20 Trail

"Movingly inspiring, *To Walk It Is To See It* tells the story of a journey of 1,400 miles—a journey of a marriage, a journey toward self-awareness. This book is lyrically personal and highly engaging. It says something significant about facing the unexpected, persevering, and cherishing the world around us and the worlds within."

—JUDY GOLDMAN, author of *Child: A Memoir*

"Kathy Elkind takes readers on an honest, unfiltered, real-time journey of discovery, exploring the constantly changing landscapes of Europe, of being a woman, and of a marriage in midstream. *To Walk It Is to See It* is a delightful reminder to appreciate and celebrate every moment of life's adventures."

—BETH JUSINO, author of *Walking to the End of the World:*
A Thousand Miles on the Camino de Santiago

TO WALK IT
IS TO SEE IT

TO WALK IT IS TO SEE IT

1 COUPLE, 98 DAYS,
1400 MILES ON EUROPE'S GR5

KATHY ELKIND

SHE WRITES PRESS

Published 2023
Printed in the United States of America

Print ISBN: 978-1-64742-525-8
E-ISBN: 978-1-64742-526-5
Library of Congress Control Number: 2023904917

For information, address:
She Writes Press
1569 Solano Ave #546
Berkeley, CA 94707

Interior design and layout by Katherine Lloyd, The DESK
Map of the GR5 by Sam Elkind
Lyrics by The Grift reprinted with permission by Clint Bierman

She Writes Press is a division of SparkPoint Studio, LLC.

For Jim
who walks with me through life.
And for our children, Kate and Sam.

"If you want to go fast, go alone;
but if you want to go far, go together."
African Proverb

AUTHOR'S NOTE

Throughout the book I have used the metric system when talking about distance. I'm guiding you through foreign countries and part of the experience is dealing with difference.

Here is an easy way to calculate in your head. Ten kilometers is 6 miles. So 30 kilometers is 3 times 6 or 18 miles.

For meters: 100 meters is 300 feet or 1,000 meters is 3,000 ft. When I say we trudged up 80 meters, we trudged up 240 feet.

In a few places I have consolidated events to keep the narrative flowing. As with all memoirs this is my story. Others may remember things differently.

CONTENTS

Map of the GR5

PROLOGUE

SHIFTING INTENTIONS

I peel off my sticky sun shirt, hiking shorts, and dusty wool socks, and step into the sandy shallows. The surprisingly cold June river flows over my tired feet, shifting my intentions of diving in. The sun on my pale skin is glorious. Iced feet and warm air caressing my body are all I need.

"I'm just going to forest bathe," I call to Jim, my husband, who is knee-deep in the River Doubs, about to plunge in.

"Oh, come on in. You can do it," he says, turning to look at me, his silver hair shining in the late morning sunlight.

"Yes, I know I can do it, but I don't want to. It feels invigorating and refreshing just to be naked in the forest air. I don't want to dive into this cold water," I say. I take a deep breath and exhale slowly, tilting my face to the sunbeams. *Why do I still have to be assertive to get my desires heard? After twenty-seven years of marriage, why can't he hear and accept?* For now, I let the irritation float away in the current.

Today is our fifty-third day on the Grande Randonnée Cinq (GR5), a little over halfway on our grand adventure. In many ways, we have been continuously forest bathing—focusing our attention and bringing awareness to what we see, hear, feel, and smell—for nearly two months as we've walked through meadows, forests, and villages of the Netherlands, Belgium, Luxembourg, and now France.

The River Doubs is the boundary between France and Switzerland, though I see no signs of a different country; the wispy birch, sturdy spruce, and Queen Anne's lace on the opposite bank are identical to the flora on this bank. We stopped at a narrow sandy beach on this slow-moving part of the river to skinny-dip. But I'm content free of clothes and wrapped in sun.

Beech trees stretch their almond-shaped leaves out over the river, shading the shore in dappled shadows. The elegant breeze sets the shadows in motion and adds harmony to the sound of the river rushing down around the bend. Where I stand, the sun dries my sweat, leaving miniature salt crystals clinging to my skin.

I splash water on my fair, freckled, and sun-spotted face. I scoop up another handful and pour it on the back of my neck. The water trickles between my shoulder blades, sending a shiver of wakefulness to every skin cell. In contrast, the sun on my bare white chest and belly is relaxing yet rapturous. I've always loved skinny-dipping and sunbathing in the nude. The sensual and loving feelings from experiences stored in my DNA over a lifetime release, and I feel alive.

I place my hands on my belly, stretching my fingers to hold the smooth round roll released from the waistband and snaps of my shorts. My pinky fingers graze the top of my graying pubic hair. No one told me that my pubic hair would turn gray. I have not seen many naked older women. My hands hold the three dimensions of stomach, uterus, and vagina. The fourth dimension is what this area has accomplished over time: birthed two children, digested and nourished me daily, and aroused my sexual pleasure—some would say the essence of what we women have been put on this earth to accomplish. I've checked all the boxes. *Am I done? Is there more?* In the society I've grown up in, women over a certain age become invisible and irrelevant. Youth is idealized, but there is change in the air. Strong older women are beginning to be valued. I'm not done. I have another third of my life to live if I'm lucky. I will not be invisible and irrelevant. *How will that look?* I do not know yet. This adventure is a search for how I want to show up for the last third of my life.

My belly and the organs it protects do not get the positive and loving attention they deserve. Closing my eyes tenderly, I consciously send loving-kindness through my hands to the core of my body. Like a print pulled from a fixer in a darkroom, an image of pulsating energy emanating from my heart and running along my arms and out my hands to my belly develops under my eyelids. Breathing deeply, standing still, I rest in the presence of the divine feminine, my higher spirit. A whiff of fragrance from a blossom I can't identify rides the current and whispers in my nostrils, *You are you.*

Jim wades back to shore, dripping wet and grinning big. "The water is really refreshing. Do you want a hug?" he asks, holding his arms out wide playfully.

"No, get away from me," I say, putting my hand up to stop his advance. "I'm glad you had a good swim," I add.

I used to be the one who jumped in cold water, but I don't want to anymore. I know he is kidding about hugging me, but what I hear in his voice is that he is hardcore and I'm not anymore. I hear disappointment in his voice. It is hard in a marriage of twenty-seven years to know whether I am correct about what he is thinking or if I am just inferring it.

Looking back, I see he was sad that I did not share the swim with him. Maybe it is hard to have a partner not want to dive in anymore when they once dove in all the time. Maybe he was worried that there were other things I would give up. Our relationship was born out of being hardcore in nature. I have been hardcore for many years, but I don't want to be hardcore any longer. Maybe flexible core. Some days, diving in gives me pleasure. Other days, like today, I find joy and comfort being naked in the forest air.

Jim and I are outdoors people. He grew up backpacking, hiking, and sailing with his family. I grew up camping, hiking, and canoeing in New Hampshire and Maine with my father, brother, and sister. My mother mutinied in the 1970s and decided that camping was not her thing. Standing up to my dad and refusing to go on those trips shifted our family dynamics. At the time, I vaguely understood why she did it. Now, I see it was her way of joining the feminist revolution in the early 1970s. I'm proud of what she did.

My father led these expeditions, and he did not leave room for suggestions from the crew. I appreciate that he took us canoeing through the Okefenokee Swamp in Georgia while many of my friends were on Florida beaches for spring break. I learned how to skim dead mosquitoes off instant chocolate pudding and still enjoy the chemical goodness, to shine a flashlight from the tent platform over the water and see the glowing red eyes of the alligators ten yards out, and to put my younger sister in the bow of the canoe because she saw the snakes hanging from the mangroves before I did. Adventures with my dad were colorful experiences, but I always missed the loving comfort of my mom. That division was not what I wanted in my marriage.

When Jim and I first adventured together in our late twenties, each of us tried to impress the other with our daring and our outdoor skills. On our second date, we cross-country skied through the woods outside of Boston. Our first overnight, we camped in two feet of new snow in the White Mountains of New Hampshire. But I had my limits when it came to adrenaline sports. I would not rock climb and I had no interest in whitewater kayaking, both of which he loved.

One year into our relationship, we backpacked in the White Goat Wilderness Area in British Columbia. We talked loudly or rang a bell all day to warn the grizzly bears that we were in their backyard. I did not sleep well those nights with only a thin sheet of nylon between a potential bear and me. Because I was still trying to impress Jim, I did not tell him how scared I was. I'm amazed at some of the stupid things I did to impress him. We never saw a grizzly, but we did see fresh scat and ripped-up rotten logs where they had foraged.

I've strengthened my voice over the years, thanks to my mom. I will not camp in grizzly country anymore. I'll do black bears, but not grizzlies. And I don't want to carry a heavy pack again. Outdoor endeavors continued to strengthen our relationship, but friction arose after our children, Kate and Sam, left the nest and I was traveling through menopause. I did not want to ski off ice-covered cliffs or backcountry ski in avalanche danger, all pursuits Jim loved. We had to find a middle ground.

Along comes the GR5. She is European refined. She is pampered and pampering. She winds from village to village. Read: hotel to hotel. Read: no heavy packs involved. Read: croissants for breakfast and someone else cooking dinner most nights. Yet, while she is refined, she is not a wimp. To walk the extent of her 2,300 kilometer (1,400 mile) footpath takes strength, determination, and curiosity. She is our new adventure.

Some American kids take a gap year between high school and college. It's a pause in life, a time to find oneself before being sucked into the next inevitable stage. Neither Kate nor Sam took a gap year, but many of their friends did. So, the idea of a hiatus in life was not new to us.

Why can't adults on the edge of sixty take a gap year? We had sold our house of twenty-seven years, the one where we had raised our family. We'd left our community in Harvard, Massachusetts, and our jobs. We'd just moved to the Green Mountains of Vermont to join a new community in the Mad River Valley. I had let go of my fertile body, as all women do. I had transitioned into this new post-menopausal body, testing her out and getting to know her. What could she do at age fifty-seven?

This was the perfect time to pause. This was the perfect time to figure out who we were as a couple with grown children who had flown the nest. We had a shared vision to travel and adventure before our bodies began to fail us. This was a symbolic journey, representing leaving the old life and entering a new one. We would embark on an unknown adventure to find our true selves and discover who we were as a couple entering the last third of our lives.

Many couples give up at this point and dissolve their marriage. Other couples continue without reflection. We decided to walk for ninety-eight days (though at the time we had no idea how long it would take) with only each other as company. We were going to have kilometers and kilometers of time to reflect.

When you travel by yourself, you are the captain of your journey and make all the decisions. As a couple, we were not going to be captain and first mate, the way most couples functioned before the 1970s on adventures and in the household. That was the dynamic that Jim and I were raised in as children. We had made a point in our marriage to work on being equals as most of our contemporaries had. We were a team of equals. We each had our strengths and weaknesses, and after twenty-seven years of marriage, we knew each other's strengths and weaknesses well. Though in new territory, would this still be the case?

There is a saying: An adventure is not worth telling if there are no dragons. In many ways, we had already befriended our dragons. We had done our work, but with any adventure, there are always more dragons.

On the edges of ancient maps, dragons and sea monsters

represent the unknown dangers. Even though it was on an app on our phones, our map still had dragons and sea monsters. *Would we complete the whole GR5? Would Jim get bored and mutiny? Were we crazy to walk for over three months together when we had never hiked more than ten days in a row? Could my body handle walking and walking and walking? Would the snow in the Alps be melted by the time we got there around July 1? What had we gotten ourselves into?*

Standing naked and ankle deep in the River Doubs, I'm beginning to see what we have gotten ourselves into. Miraculously, we have fallen into the grandest journey of our life. We walk through the cathedral of the Earth.

PART ONE

THE NETHERLANDS AND BELGIUM

BIKING TO THE BEGINNING

I *bless my kids, I bless my backpack, I bless my mom, I bless the rest of my family, I bless my knee, I bless my hip, which hurts today.* These are the blessings I repeat over and over to the beat of my footsteps on a practice hike in Sicily. Jim and I never make life easy. We feed on complicated itineraries. Before attempting the GR5 we have spent six weeks building strength and endurance during day hikes in southern Italy.

I've longed for a grand adventure all my life, but the time was never right. What is it about a grand adventure that entrances me? The appeal of being self-sufficient with newness around every corner is magnetic. I read once that infants need stimulation from new objects and it is recommended that parents hang new mobiles to stimulate the infant's brain. *Maybe as an infant in this new stage of life, I need new stimulation for my older brain?* Some people go on long adventures to escape. *Am I trying to escape anything? Or is my longing for adventure a quest for something?*

I chose the GR5, and Jim went along with it. He could see I was bubbling over with excitement. What I did not know was that Jim had some trepidations about the GR5. He kept those to himself. We would be navigating the GR5 and navigating our relationship. Or maybe our relationship was going to be navigating the GR5.

After Italy we now head to Amsterdam. We've already decided to bike this first section of the trip. It is so flat I worried that walking it would bore Jim. Jim is not fun to be around when he is bored. He might mutiny. He loves risk and physical challenge. Luckily, he has embraced the idea of biking the first week of easy miles in the Low Countries.

After we pick up our bikes in the center of Amsterdam, we explore around the edge of a nearby city park, taking in the architecture and all the people sprawled on the lawn in the sun. Outside the modern Van Gogh Museum, a collection of cherry trees planted in diagonal rows blooms in unison. The petals begin to spatter the manicured lawn with pink and white polka dots. The cherry trees' position, adjacent to a glamourous glass wall, creates mirrored optics—twice as many pink-and-white lollypop trees as are truly there. My eyes flash back and forth between real and reflected. The white and pink blossoms on the green grass with the blue sky conjure a more joyous image than in any museum. Little do I know at the time how much I will come to love cherry trees on this adventure.

Back at our hotel room, we reappraise, reprioritize, and repack our belongings, this time for biking. Our mission is to fit our belongings into two panniers each. The rest we leave behind with a note of donation, trusting these discarded objects will find future use.

Truth is, we've been simplifying and letting go of possessions for months, ever since last year when we were preparing to put our home of twenty-seven years on the market. I'm a good shedder. I've had practice. I had cleaned out my father's treasures a few years earlier. He had been a squirrel, and I filled a dumpster. I've read the book about owning only a hundred items. Minimalism has been floating around me like Pig Pen's cloud for the last ten years.

And Jim is a packing wizard. When we used to venture off with the kids for a long weekend, he packed the car with geometric skill. When the kids started to pack their own duffel bags as five- and seven-year-olds—we thought it was important for them to be involved at an early age—Jim created a spreadsheet for packing. Jim's lust for organization irritated me and amused me at the same time, though as time moves on the irritation wanes. If Jim is a spreadsheet all ordered, precise, and full of data, I'm a brainstorm web—erratic, spread out, and colorful.

Down in the hotel's clean and well-lit parking garage where our bikes are parked, Jim rigs up a system of hanging an extra pocket from our packs onto our handlebars for stashing our wallets, phones, and snacks for the day. Finally, I strap my backpack onto the back rack with trekking poles on top. I will not need these until we get to Spa, Belgium.

We pedal south out of the city toward Leiden, which is halfway to Hoek van Holland where the GR5 begins. We are on bike trails and lanes the whole way. It's just us and our bikes carrying our possessions, free to move at our own pace. We are in a state of nirvana, biking in a country that adores bicycles. Gliding by a commuter train station, I see tens of thousands of bikes parked neatly, three levels high, taking up more than a city block. I've never seen so many bikes in my life.

Now out in the countryside, I grasp how flat the landscape is. The blue-and-white sky takes up most of the space, while the foreground is made up of freshly tilled brown earth as we are biking through agricultural lands with some green here and there. Out on the wide-open horizon, the only blips are a few farmhouses and barns; when we come upon tulip fields, the explosion of yellow, apricot, and red shocks my eyes. We see a grass covered dike and ride down it to get a great angle for pictures of the expansive tulip fields, astoundingly brilliant stripes of color racing to the end of the earth.

Tulips have been my favorite flower since I started drawing them at age five. The simple shape, almost the inverse of a heart shape, and the courageous colors speak to me. The economy of a whole nation went from boom to bust because of a global lust for tulips. They are powerful flowers. I had always wanted to experience the tulip fields. Despite all our planning, I had not realized that we would be here when they were blooming. It was not until we were on the plane to Amsterdam and reading about what we might see that I grasped our good fortune.

I'm in heaven to be here, and I did not even plan it! This is a good omen.

The next morning, we wander along the canals in the center of Leiden, eventually searching out an outdoor equipment shop for last-minute items. I buy a knife because I lost my Swiss Army knife in Sicily. We look for a guidebook in English for the northern section of the GR5 but cannot find one.

In the afternoon, while Jim goes to the windmill museum, Molden Valk, and grocery shopping for lunch supplies, I decide to visit Keukenhof with my camera to experience the famous tulip gardens. Even though it is crowded and expensive, I'm rewarded for my decision. My camera and I shoot over two hundred pictures in two hours. I ramble from one garden to the next, no plan, just following the kaleidoscope of colors. It's like being in a candy shop on LSD, colors dancing before my eyes. Going to Keukenhof in your fifties and sixties is the equivalent of doing recreational drugs as a teenager—something everyone should experience, at least people who love gardens.

That night I don't sleep well. We are sleeping on a tiny pull-out sofa at an Airbnb on the edge of Leiden. Every time I turn over, I bump into Jim. In the morning, I'm grumpy but also excited that we will be in Hoek van Holland tonight.

Breakfast is buttered rolls, chocolate sprinkles, and yogurt with fruit. What a cool country to have little yellow boxes of chocolate sprinkles for your rolls or toast! I like this country with its canals, tulips, and sprinkles.

We pack up our bikes for the second time. It's raining lightly, not enough to get soaked but enough to feel damp on the back of our necks. After a day off, it feels wonderful to ride again. We have a short thirty-nine kilometers to ride. Heading south, we ride by more tulip fields, field-hockey fields, and row upon row of greenhouses. Surprisingly, the small country of the Netherlands is the second-largest exporter of agriculture in the world.

We ride through the Hague, home to the International Court of Justice. The bike route Jim plotted lets us slip through the city, going park to park without being on the street with cars. From the parks, we spot impressive opulent building after impressive opulent building. Looking back, I'm not sure why we did not stop and visit a sight or two. At the time, I was so focused on getting to the beginning of the GR5, I did not want to stop for anything, so we said our familiar refrain, "We will have to come back another time."

An hour later, as a church bell rings in the noon hour, I spot a bright orange bench on the sidewalk. We pull our bikes off the bike lane and sit down to bread and cheese. Right next to the bench, I spy an A-frame chalkboard sign that says, "Never underestimate the power of chocolate."

"Wow, do I know how to pick a good lunch bench!" I say, pointing at the sign and then the chocolate shop next to us. "I'm going in to order a hot chocolate to warm up. Do you want one?"

"Do you even have to ask?"

I order two hot chocolates, which are basically melted chocolate bars, the liquid is so viscous. I chat with the owner, a slim energetic man, about chocolate and discover that all the chocolates in his store are sustainably grown in South America.

Jim bursts in to see what is taking so long. We end up talking to the owner for an hour about sustainability. Jim ran a solar company in Massachusetts. It turns out the owner's apartment behind the shop is one of thirty-three in a newly built sustainable housing cooperative. He leads us on a tour of the housing project, which he has co-designed. The outside of the building has beautiful slate and Douglas fir siding. There is a common garden area in the middle with stormwater absorption ponds and a soon-to-be community pavilion for meetings. Solar thermal, solar PV, and air source heat pumps make the apartments all energy neutral.

We are sad to leave our new friend, but with our panniers fuller still with sustainable chocolate bars, it is time to bike on. An orange bench (benches will become very important to us), chocolate, and solar are more good omens.

Two hours later, I stand up on my pedals to see if I can see the North Sea and to give my butt a rest from the saddle, but the grass-covered dunes are too high. The coast here comes down to a point forming one side of a vast opening for Hoek van Holland's enormous harbor, which eventually leads to the busy shipping harbor of Rotterdam.

We decide to stop at a parking lot with access through the dunes to the beach and the ocean before we get to Hoek van Holland's center. We want to baptize our feet in preparation for a 2,289 kilometer (1,423 mile) journey.

I think back to a journal entry I wrote seven years before: "I'm listening to my fifty-year-old body at the end of a fluid yoga class. My tummy is round and gurgling. My body feels like she wants to go on a long walk. I want to walk and walk and walk."

Now it's April 25, 2018; Jim and I walk into the cold North Sea. We are about to walk and walk and walk after we bike and bike.

On the expansive windswept beach, the sand and waves race each other to the horizon. If anyone else were on this Dutch beach in late April, they would think us crazy standing in the shallow frothy surf, the wind howling so much we yell to hear each other. They would see our wool socks carefully tucked into our gray walking shoes placed out of the reach of the waves. They would see a middle-aged couple: him wearing black shorts over an athletic physique, calf muscles bulging and twitching, his gray hair trimmed like the businessman that he had been; her with straight highlighted blond hair and a padded physique of the middle-aged type that she shields under layers of tech wool.

The odd couple skips and jumps in the frigid water, celebrating both the fact that they are about to embark upon the adventure of a lifetime and that all their preparation is behind them. After a long preamble, they have made it to the true beginning of their journey.

But there is no one else on the beach this day to witness our antics. We are alone together.

"I'm getting out. It's too cold for me," Jim shouts.

"I'll be out in a minute. I have a ritual to perform," I say. My second sentence gets lost in the wind. Even though the ice-cold water has stopped the flow of blood to my curled toes, I reach down, scoop up a handful of seawater, and, careful not to wet the cuff of my raincoat, deliver the holy water to my lips. I intend to swallow a handful of the North Sea and carry this liquid with me the whole length of the trail. The first salty swallow burns the back of my throat so much that I gag and spit the rest out. I'm sure I managed to get a few milliliters down.

I have read about the ritual of walkers filling a small bottle of the North Sea water and carrying it with them to the end of the trail at the Mediterranean and then pouring it into the warm sea. I love the idea of the ritual, but my practical nature objects to this. I don't want to carry any extra weight; I need all the energy I have to get me to the Mediterranean. So, I drink the seawater and carry it in my body.

Looking back, I see that I became the vessel, carrying my desires, struggles, and love across the continent of Europe.

THE FIRST WAYMARK

By four o'clock we arrive in the center of Hoek van Holland. Outside the train station, a signpost that most people probably walk by stands tall in a grassy intersection. I have seen pictures of the signpost in blogs and books, and it's a thrill to see in person. My head is buzzing. The wooden post is ten feet tall and adorned with five arrow-shaped boards about two feet long. Two of the boards point northeast and three point generally southeast, like a tall thin woman with five arms pointing.

I focus on the lowest arm. The black paint is worn off, but the words and numbers carved in the wood are still visible: "GR5 Hoek van Holland to Nice 2289K." At the tip of the arrow is a white-and-red rectangle—the waymark to guide us—and a smaller blue square with "E2" printed in bright yellow.

There are twelve European long-distance paths, making up a network of over 70,000 kilometers of trails. The paths are designated by the European Ramblers Association (ERA). ERA was founded in 1969. In 2018 it was made up of fifty-eight walking organizations in thirty-three different European countries representing three million registered walkers. The E2 starts in Great Britain and then comes across to Hoek van Holland. The E2 and the GR5 are basically the same route.

I know none of this history of European walking paths as I stand under the sign. Jim takes pictures of me. I've never been one for stopping and taking pictures of signs like at national parks, but this time is different. This time we are walking and biking, and I want to memorialize the first waymark of the GR5. Every cell in my body is fully alive.

EXHILARATION (DAY 1)

oday is the day. The soft light of dawn floats through the window, knocking gently at my eyelids. My eyes scan the worn hotel room, helping me remember where I am. Jim is sleeping beside me. A painting of crashing waves in a gold frame hangs over faded floral wallpaper. Out the window, I see the steeple of the church.

Last night, I heard the bell chime eleven, twelve, and one. I did not sleep well again. I can't blame it on a small bed because we are in a queen. My legs twitched restlessly and my exuberance to start the trip could not be contained. I felt like a kid on Christmas Eve who cannot sleep. This feeling was more than just nervousness; there was euphoria folded in.

I realize now there was also the feeling of accomplishment—the accomplishment of acting on my dream. The bubbling emotions of exuberance, jitters, and giddiness would not rest in my body. I was like a toddler with too much sugar in her bloodstream.

I had tried to calm myself with meditation, but that did not work. The cortisol was more potent than the dopamine from meditating. I rolled my body back and forth, trying the left side and then the right, over and over. At some point, I dozed off.

I reach for my phone. Six thirty. *Our first day with our new acquaintance, the GR5.* I'm a bit sad that we are not walking with her today. We will be paralleling the GR5 and intersecting her many times but not exactly walking with her. Today we are biking to a town three islands away that the GR5 used to go through thirty years ago.

Back at home, I had gotten so focused on reading *Walking Europe from Top to Bottom*, which was published in 1984, that the name of the island the authors had walked through stuck in my head. When planning the biking route, Jim asked me where we wanted to bike for the first night. I said Renesse, not realizing the GR5 did not go that way any longer. Luckily, on bikes it is not a mistake that matters.

I feel Jim's body roll next to mine. "Morning," he says, his eyes still closed.

"Morning. Today is the day!" I whisper excitedly. My eyes are wide open.

"You need to mellow out. You are going to explode," Jim says, slipping his arm around my waist for a morning cuddle.

"I know. I'm just so happy and nervous. I barely slept at all."

I jump out of bed and dress in yesterday's biking clothes, which I conveniently left in a pile right next to the bed. I pull my thin blond hair into a ponytail and don't look into the mirror. I notice my ears are blocked, and my head feels fuzzy. *I wish I had slept better.*

We make our way quietly down the carpeted stairs to the dining room. It's hard to keep quiet when you are euphoric. We had asked for the earliest breakfast. The young waiter brings us coffee and asks if we want eggs. Yes, we do.

Our stomachs are full of croissants, buttered toast with chocolate sprinkles, scrambled eggs, and fruit salad. We reload the bikes after retrieving them from the shed out back. We will come to find all of the hotels have places to park your bike for the night. I think, *Can you imagine Motel 6s with places to park a bike?*

We bike down to the ferry dock and wait in the cold wind for the ferry to come across the choppy harbor.

On the small ferry, we are the only passengers except for one guy on a beat-up motorbike. The captain takes us close to the shore and points out seals basking in the sunshine on the cold sandy beach. We feel like we are on a private tour.

We pull up to a dock, and the captain motions that this is our stop. We grab our bikes and wheel them off the pier to a large asphalt parking lot edged with massive oil tanks.

"Can this be it?" I ask. We look at the GPS. Yes, this is where we start.

We bike by chemical tanks, more oil tanks, and corrugated metal storage buildings that decorate the landscape. "This is probably why the GR5 was moved years ago. I can't imagine walking through this industrial zone," I call over the wind to Jim.

Twenty minutes later, we leave the industrial complex behind as we cross over a bridge to the next island, made up of beautiful farmland and villages. Because of the harsh coastal winds, spring is not as far along as in Amsterdam. Some of the trees still have buds on them. The villages' houses have well-tended gardens, and I notice espaliered fruit trees and trimmed hedges delineating the gardens' structure. The Dutch take great pride in their gardens.

We find a bench along a bike path next to a potato field to have our lunch. I'm so tired. *Is it from biking or because I have not been sleeping?* I feel weak but I don't want to admit it. I lie on the pavement in the middle of the bike path. We are the only ones biking on this April day. I can feel the gentle warmth of the pavement seep into my back, but it is not enough.

"Are you okay?" asks Jim as he kneels next to his upside-down bike, tightening the crankshaft.

"I just wish I had more energy. I wonder if I caught something on the airplane. How's your bike?"

"I'm hoping tightening it will hold it until we get to Renesse. I checked—there is a bike shop there."

In the afternoon, we have a four-kilometer ride on top of a dike. The giant delta system of dikes and tide-controlled gates were built to keep the ocean water out of the flat land that is probably only a foot above sea level. Up on the dike, the head-winds are vicious. They are called wind hills because biking into the wind feels like you are biking up a hill. The flat land allows the winds to roar across the landscape uninterrupted. And, of course, we are biking right into the wind. I feel like I'm biking in slow motion. I lower my gear, then lower it again.

"I need to draft you. This headwind is too strong, and my energy is low," I call out.

I tuck in behind Jim and draft him. He is a steady rider, and I trust him to bike a straight line. I stay close to his back wheel in the best protection of his body. He is average height and build while I'm slightly smaller than him. Over the years, I have gotten better and better at drafting him. Drafting allows us to go at a faster pace as a couple. His strength plows into the wind, and I follow. I don't know the calculations, but I know that I save energy and go faster when we ride this way. But it takes concentration on my part to stay with him and not hit his back wheel with my front wheel. My gloved hands are always on alert, ready to brake if I need to. Crashing our bikes is not in the plan. Occasionally, I call up to him, "Slow down. I can't keep the pace up this late in the afternoon." He has gotten better and better at listening to me.

About eight years ago, we contemplated buying a tandem bike. We rented one in Walla Walla, Washington, for a three-day biking excursion when we visited Kate at Whitman College for parents' weekend. Tandem biking was a fun new way to bike together through the rolling wheat fields. But on the second day, we rode down a long half-mile hill on a curvy wet road, going faster and faster. The speed caused my eyes to water even with my glasses on, and I could not see. With fear in my voice, I asked Jim to slow down. He could not hear me because of the wind and the speed. We made it to the bottom of the hill. He turned to me and said with a big smile, "We got up to fifty-seven miles an hour."

"That's too fast," I barked at him. "I don't like it when we go that fast. I want control of the brakes." Rage boiled through my body. "I don't ever want to go that fast again. Do you understand me?" He grudgingly said yes.

We never bought a tandem bike. We work better moving in parallel, not tethered together.

Finally, we cross over one more bridge to the third island of the day and wind our way over to the village of Renesse by the sea. We stop at a grocery store and buy garlic, ginger, and lunch for tomorrow. At the hotel, I make ginger tea and swallow quartered cloves of garlic, trying to support my immune system. I crawl into bed and nap before dinner.

Jim visits the local bike shop across town. The friendly owner replaces the crank shaft. Jim's bike is fixed, but I'm not sure my body is fixed so easily.

For two more days we bike into the wind with views of beautiful canals, green fields with sheep, and just-born lambs frisking in the cold sunshine. The bike trail leads us through the city gates of a quintessential Dutch town with drawbridges, cobblestone streets, and boat-filled canals. After riding along coastal bays with shorebirds feeding on nutrient-rich mudflats and giant windmills creating green energy, we finally head east into Belgium. We know we are in Belgium when every village has at least one chocolate shop. The beauty of the landscape sustains me for a few more days though my energy is still low.

Out in the Belgian countryside, we bike by fields and fields of black plastic. We can't figure out what it is. Then we see three men carrying stacks and stacks of plastic crates and a funny look-ing contraption out in the field.

I slow down and get off my bike to inspect. "I'm going to take a look."

Jim slows down and waits for me.

The gray plastic crates stacked next to the red farm truck are filled with white asparagus. It is grown under the black plastic to keep it from photosynthesizing and turning green. I ask if I can take pictures, and they nod their heads.

At three thirty, we arrive at the hotel and settle in. I fall right to sleep, exhausted from another day of biking with a weak body. Every muscle is depleted, not just my legs.

At dinner, I order the white asparagus special with hard-boiled egg and ham in a white sauce, the Flemish way. Jim has the white asparagus with smoked salmon. The tender stalks melt in my mouth with a gentle fresh-grass taste bathed in juicy butter. I'm trying to pretend that everything is well, but my exhilaration is gone.

Laying on the bed after dinner I survey the map and make a radical decision.

"I'm going to bike nine kilometers to the train station in Ant-werp and take the train to Diest. My body needs to rest so I don't get sicker. I can't make the seventy kilometers. I'll meet you at the hotel."

"Are you sure you don't want me to come with you?"

"No, I'll be fine," I say dismissing his support.

I'm not good at asking for support or accepting it. I was brought up to tough it out. And I know Jim will be happier biking. I put his feelings above my own, being the good wife, the way my mother modeled for me in our patriarchal society. *Think about others' feel-ings, not your own.* It makes me sad that after all these years I am still putting his feelings above my own. But I am not fully aware that I am doing it. Being sick and away from home, I am in fight, flight, or freeze mode and I cannot make caring decisions.

DEPLETED
(DAY 4)

Jim sets off early on his bike as we planned. I'm glad he is fulfilling our obligation, but there is a small part of me that wishes he was coming with me to help.

We are a team. He is going to bike while I'm going to take care of my body and rest. This is how I try to convince myself.

I'm scared to bike to the city by myself, but the thought of a short day gives me courage. With weak leg muscles, I pedal slowly and navigate through foreign streets in a gray drizzle to the busy central train station. I'm afraid to lock my bike outside with all my possessions on it, so I roll it in with me as I stand in the ticket line. People look at me like I'm weird, but I feel so depleted that I don't care.

Train ticket in hand, I gaze up at the massive schedule board, searching for my train from Antwerp to Diest. *There it is.* I must get myself and my heavy bike to track seven in eleven minutes.

I'm so focused on my bike and getting the ticket, I haven't taken in my surroundings. Antwerp Central is the most beautiful train station I have ever seen. The domed ceiling is just as ornate as the cathedrals we visited in Italy. Gray marble columns and gilded sculptures frame an elaborate clock high above the central arch to the Train Hall. Instead of an altar to a god or goddess, the building is an altar to time and travel. The expanse of open

26

space held by the arches mutes the sound of hundreds of commuters and travelers moving across the marble floors. I take a few pictures of the magnificent building. I will study them later, as I now have nine minutes to get to my train.

Wheeling my bike down the steep steps to the underground walkway that connects the platforms is arduous. Luckily a petite woman helps me steady the bike on the way down and helps me push it up the steps to track seven.

As we part, she says, "Next time, use the elevator."

"Thank you! I will," I say. *Why didn't I think of that?*

The train is there on track seven. I walk along the platform, searching for the cars that allow bikes. Six cars down, I press the red button to open the electric door and lift my bike up the short step to the train. A man inside reaches out to help pull it and me up. I figure out how to attach the bike to the bike stand with the red cord and sit down on the bench across from my bike. There are three other bikes and three riders sitting across from them. *I guess I'm doing this right.*

Twenty-five minutes later, I'm at my stop to transfer. Google says that I will be arriving at track three and need to get to track one in seven minutes. As I guide the bike off the train, I look for the elevator. This is a small rural train station, and I don't see an elevator. I see the stairs. *How do people in wheelchairs maneuver the underground stairwells to get from one platform to another?*

This time guiding my heavy bike down the stairs, no one offers to help me. The bike is pulling me down the stairs. I feel like I'm going to be launched to the bottom. I have no strength in my arms, and it's all I can do to make it to the bottom. Going up is a bit easier because I have more control, and halfway up, two young men help me push the bike up to the top. I thank them profusely as we run to the train. They hop in the first car with a smile. I keep going, looking for the sign that bikes are allowed. I don't see one. The train is making sounds like it is ready to go.

I press the open-door button on the next car and climb inside to the space between cars. This is not the place I'm supposed to be, but only two people are in the next car. I lean my bike against the wall. There is no place to sit. I'm near the entrance to the toilets. The train lurches forward and I notice my legs are shaking. I could leave my bike here and sit in the car and still see the bike. But the lurching of the train might make the bike fall and block the way to the toilets. I decide to rest against my bike and watch the countryside go by. I feel demoralized. My ears are blocked, and it's hard to hear. But a smile grows on my face as I think about the people who have helped me navigate my bike this morning. Strangers reaching out to help gives me faith in humanity and faith in myself.

An hour later, I'm at our hotel in Diest, a lovely boutique hotel, though I don't have the energy to appreciate it. After parking my bike in the front hall under the stairs, I climb into the clean sheets and fall asleep. My head feels like an overinflated beach ball, and my throat is sore.

The next day is another day of biking/train/biking, but this time I find the elevators. I climb into the next bed in the next hotel in the city of Liège. This is not how I imagined our trip would be.

The competitive side of me is glad that we are still moving along, but there is a vulnerable side of me that wants to stop and get better.

Bang! Bang! Bang!

I wake out of a foggy afternoon sleep. I get up and open the door. Jim stands there grinning, his checks red from exertion. I fall into his arms.

"You don't look good," he says. His smile fades, and his eyebrows rise.

"My ears feel like they are going to explode. The back of my throat feels like sandpaper. I've slept for two hours. The train and biking were easier today. How was your bike ride?" I ask. He hugs me tighter. Then I slip out of his arms and back into bed. Jim unpacks his belongings and his tales of the day.

"The biking reminded me of upstate New York. Rolling hill farms, cherries, apples, hay, and potatoes. It was extremely windy and ridiculously slow uphill into the wind. It was a good thing you were not with me feeling the way you do. But the sky was dramatic with dark clouds. There are paved bike trails that cut right through the farmland. They go on for miles and are in beautiful shape, better than the roads in some places." He pauses his story, faces the wall, places both hands on the wall, and leans in to stretch his calves. "I thought I might see more World War II pillboxes guarding the canal like yesterday but didn't."

I snuggle deeper under the quilt. I love hearing his descriptions of the countryside. I wish I had the energy to be out there riding with him, but I'm relieved I was on the train watching the images of Belgian countryside flicker by like an old-fashioned movie.

My earlier concern about him being bored has floated away. I can hear in his voice the excitement of discovering historical sites and natural beauty.

"I'll go out and get some food for dinner. Do you want anything special?" he asks.

"Soup and salad would be good. Maybe we should take tomorrow off?"

"Okay. That's probably the right thing to do. I'm feeling a little off too, and I don't want to get what you have. Maybe you should go to the doctor tomorrow? I'll stop at the desk and change our reservation."

"I could use a full day of rest. And this city looks like a nice place for you to explore." I ignore his talk of doctors. I don't like going to doctors. I want to heal myself. "I was looking at the map and the topography, and it gets hillier going all the way to Spa. I'm not sure I can make it up those hills the way I'm feeling, and our bikes are heavier than we thought they were going to be," I say.

"All right, let's take a day off and only go halfway to Spa. You find a place to stay halfway, and when I get back, I'll email the bike shop and get them to pick up the bikes wherever you decide."

I knew Jim wanted to keep going but was being considerate and caring. A friend once said, "Jim is intellectual, competitive, and generous. And you can see his mind turning as he tries to keep all these wheels in gear." I see this happening now as he enlarges the generous gear and minimizes the competitive gear. Jim is not competitive with others, just himself.

For the next thirty-six hours, I drink buckets of ginger tea. Jim delivers a green smoothie, which soothes my throat. I stay in bed the whole next day, coughing. My right eye waters, and when I look in the mirror, I see red streaks on my white eyeball. I have pinkeye too! *I just want to be home in my own bed.*

I finally give in and look for a doctor on Google and call one, but it's a holiday, Labor Day, May 1, and the offices are closed. I think about going to the emergency room at the hospital, though after reading a few reviews online, I decide I don't want to wait hours at a hospital and risk catching something else.

Sleep helps. Jim heads out to the museum of metallurgy and industry and then plans to go to the sculpture garden, but because of the holiday, they are closed too. He ends up with a flat tire, and due to a series of mishaps, it takes him three hours to get it fixed.

In the morning with the sun shining, I have some energy; a full day in bed has helped. We bike out of the city of Liège along L'Ourthe River. I get a foggy sense of all the places I did not get to see, but at this point I'm just focused on getting my body to the next town.

As we leave the flatland, we encounter our first small hills of the Ardennes. My energy lowers as the day goes on. I pedal slowly. I seem to be okay on the flat after the hill. But we encounter a second hill after lunch. I get off my bike and walk it. We only have two more kilometers. On the final hill, I get off my bike again. Jim also gets off his bike.

"I'll take your bike," he says and walks both of our bikes up the longest hill so far. I feel grateful for his kindness. It is not steep or long. I might have refused his help on a different day, but I'm too tired now.

How did I get to this point where my husband is walking my bike up the hill? What should I be doing differently? What is my body trying to tell me?

BIRTH OF A WALKER (DAY 7)

Ten minutes later, we push our bikes up a short driveway to a small white cottage, an Airbnb I booked yesterday. Our hosts, Phillips and Anne, greet us. He works from home on computers, and she is a nurse. Phillips can speak a tiny bit of English. We use Google Translate and hand gestures to learn they have two children the same age as ours. One is in college, and the other works in Antwerp. Phillips shows us to our room on the first floor and shows us how to use the lock on the front door. He tells us there are two restaurants in town.

We empty our bike panniers for the last time just as Anton, the bike shop owner, shows up with his wife. We chat about our trip. He loads our bikes into his white van. They drive the four hours back to Amsterdam. It's discouraging to think we have been biking for eight days (I've been biking for six days) and it is only a four-hour drive by car. They took the highway's direct route, and we meandered the Delta and Flanders regions.

It's a short walk into town, and right away, we see a white-and-red GR5 rectangle on a telephone pole. Tomorrow the real walking trip begins. I'm super excited even though I'm still not feeling a hundred percent or even fifty percent. I'm amazed at how the exhilaration of the trip keeps me going.

The only open place in town is a bar with a small menu. We order soup and spaghetti Bolognese, which warms my insides.

Back in our room it's time to pack our backpacks. I wish I had more energy for packing, as I love packing. The bikes have carried our possessions. Now we will carry them ourselves, getting closer to being snails and turtles carrying our houses on our backs.

In Vermont just before we left, I folded my belongings in orderly piles on our queen-size bed: two wool T-shirts, two sun shirts, raincoat, rain pants, puffy jacket, lightweight wool hat, four pairs of socks, four pairs of underwear, three bras, one pair of capris, one pair of walking pants, one skirt, one pair of black leggings that can also substitute as long johns, t-kit (toothbrush, small wooden hairbrush with three hair bands on the handle, aspirin, a small container of face cream, lip balm with sunscreen), first-aid kit (moleskin, band aides, Pepto-Bismol, curcumin, and Advil), emergency Mylar blanket, two emergency energy bars, charger, iPad Mini, felt hat, good camera, nine inch tripod, one battery, extra pair of prescription glasses, sunglasses, silk sleeping sheet, backpacking towel, water filter, mini travel purse for passport and money, bathing suit, two water bottles, black Allbirds shoes, and a small fold-up shopping bag. Our bed looked as though it was covered in a three-dimensional quilt.

Spread out it seemed like a lot, but I worked hard on sticking to my central goal: to carry as little as possible. Simplify. Simplify. Maybe this is why I was so intrigued by walking the GR5, as it was another form of playing with minimalism. After shedding so many of our possessions, it was time to take it to higher level. One set of clothes for walking, one set of evening wear, and some warm and waterproof layers? Would that work?

Also on the bed were three pieces of paper with the words "Mindfulness," "Self-Compassion," and "Contentment" written in large letters as if I were going to hang them up in a second-grade classroom. Mindfulness to help me stay grounded. Self-compassion to use when the journey gets difficult. Contentment to help me accept things as they are.

I didn't physically pack the paper with the written words. I took a picture of my piles of clothes and the three terms laid on the bed. I will carry three items that weigh nothing but take the most effort to use: mindfulness, self-compassion, and contentment.

Jim carries a folder with a copy of a treaty from 1949.

When we were planning, Jim worked on deciding if we needed a visa since we would be in Europe for so long. We filled out the lengthy twenty-four-page application and got finger-printed at the Montpelier police station. Then we drove three hours down to Boston to the French Embassy and—surprise— the official there said we do not need a long-term visa. He said there is a treaty from 1949 that allows Americans to visit the Schengen countries for up to ninety days and then be in France for another ninety days. We were skeptical. He said that if the border patrol asked, we should push hard and explain about the treaty. At home we googled the treaty and found nothing. We put Jim's sister, an environmental historian at San Diego State, on the task. In less than twenty-four hours, she sent us a copy of the treaty that she found in the Library of Congress. We printed it out and placed it in our special papers folder. This paper is worth its weight to carry.

Jim also emailed the French Consulate in Washington, DC, asking six questions about the treaty. He got back one line: "Yes, the treaty is in good standing." We added this to the physical folder and an electronic folder. We had done our homework.

Here in Belgium, all my possessions are in colorful nylon stuff sacks in categories: underwear and socks in light blue, evening clothes in orange, rain gear in navy blue. One guideline to pack-ing is to place the items I use the most during the day close to the top and the items I won't need until evening at the bottom.

I'm tired, so I slide the colored stuff sacks into my pack after placing my iPad close to the frame in the bottom to keep it safe. My Osprey pack is thirty-six liters, which is not big. When we were shopping for equipment, Jim found auxiliary side pockets. I attach a pocket to each side of my pack, making it wider than it is tall. It doesn't look right to me. My goal for the next few weeks is to shed more stuff so that I can get rid of the side pockets.

After putting warm compresses on my ears and eyes, trying to heal myself the old-fashioned way, I climb into bed before the sun sets. Even though Anne is a nurse, I don't ask her for advice about my sickness. For one thing, she does not speak English, and I feel like a failure coming to her house sick.

I can see now that I was in denial. I didn't listen to my body. I kept telling myself, *I'll get better soon.* It was as though the part of me that yearned to walk was so strong, it overrode everything else. I couldn't pay attention to anything else going on within me.

I also see that to commit to this epic adventure in a foreign land, I had to don my tough-woman skin. It was a mindset I had to drop into, a belief and faith that I could do it. Admitting I was sick would have dissolved the tough-woman skin, and without the skin I might have failed.

The GR5 is two hundred meters from our bed. I can hear her calling, *See you in the morning. I've been waiting for you.*

Over a breakfast of yogurt, pastries, and coffee, Phillips convinces us that we need to see an amazing allée of trees. He looks up English words and phrases to try to explain it to us. If we understand him correctly, this allée is a short drive, and then he will walk with us to the GR5.

We squish the backpacks into the trunk of their small blue

sedan, and Jim and I fold ourselves into the back seat. It turns out this will be the last car we are in for three months.

So much for walking down into town and joining the GR5, where we saw the waymark last night. Part of me does not want to get into the car. But this opportunity has presented itself, and we will take it. *Trust*.

Anne drives us out of town up a country road for two kilometers to a mansion. Phillips leads us across an expansive lawn and down a garden path. At the end is the entrance to the allée. We peer down the green tree tunnel. Phillips tells us the *charmille* is 570 meters. I calculate in my head that it's more than 1,500 feet, the length of five field-hockey fields. On the sign, we read that the allée was built in 1885 so that women could walk outside without getting the sun on their tender skin. It is made up of 4,500 beech trees meticulously pruned and trained to grow together at the top to create an archway—a giant parasol. In 1979, it was declared a national monument, and in 1985 it was restored, but still, 70 percent of the trees are over a century old.

The birds are cheering us on this sunny May morning. We take our first steps into the 1,500-foot verdant bower. Jim and Phillips walk silently, side by side on the worn dirt path. I walk behind, through emerald light. I see this is where we are born onto the GR5. Phillips is our midwife, showing us the way through the topiary birth canal.

I stop and examine one of the 4,500 trees. The gnarled stocky trunk has been pruned and shaped year after year to grow in the form of a candy cane. The leafy branches from both the trees on the left and on the right unite overhead, forming the canopy roof of our passage.

I gaze back at the opening for a moment, pausing to question going back, like an infant stalled in labor, but the child always crowns. I turn and stroll forward, now pulled through the green tunnel by the light at the end.

We come out on the other side to full sun. I'm not like the women in the 1800s; I love the feel of the sun kissing my skin. It is an impressive architectural garden feature built for women. I wonder, did the woman of the house have it commissioned, or did her husband? It's beautiful, but also, in some ways, a prison. If women could only walk in the shade, they were confined to just 570 meters.

We follow Phillips on a path that takes us to a vista of the Belgian countryside, a patchwork of meadows and wood lots, fifty shades of green. The three of us absorb the view in silence. Then Phillips points south and says half in French and half in English, "Follow that track, and you will come to a village. At the village, you will see a GR5 sign."

He holds out his hand to me, clasps mine in his, and shakes. His hand is soft and warm. He does the same to Jim.

"Thank you for hosting us last night. And for walking the allée with us. It's a beautiful way to start our walk," I say, looking him directly in his eyes.

He says, "I'm happy to walk this morning." He pauses. "I should walk more. You make me want to walk more." He pauses again and looks out at the view with a faraway look in his eyes. "Good luck on your journey."

This is the beginning of the real trip. We are fledgling walkers. We check the GPS to make sure what Phillips told us is accurate, and it is. We walk down the forest track and enter a small village. Right away, we see a white-and-red rectangle GR5 waymark on a phone pole with an arrow headed up out of the village. "Our first waymark," I say putting my hand on the small sign to make sure it is real.

VISIT TO THE DOC (DAY 9)

By the time we walk into the town of Spa and find our apartment, I'm feeling dreadful again. My ears, throat, and eyes are on fire. I shed the tough-woman skin and give in. I email Phillips and ask if Anne knows a doctor in Spa, since she works here. He responds immediately. Anne makes an appointment with Phillips's doctor for nine the next morning. The address is three blocks away from our apartment, off a side street from the city center. I thank him profusely.

Jim changes the reservations so that we can stay in Spa for two more days.

The next morning, we sit in a quiet, crowded waiting room. We wait for over an hour, but I'm relieved to be here. I don't care how long I have to wait.

There have not been many times in my life when Jim has sat in a waiting room with me. We're lucky in that respect. We sat together before ultrasounds for each baby and for Kate's first check-up, but that's it. I don't think I've ever joined him for one of his health appointments. Waiting rooms are thick with uncertainty, nervousness, and fear. But here, I feel hopeful, safe, and nurtured.

The nurse comes into the waiting room and stands there. I'm beginning to figure out this Belgian health system. The patients in the waiting room keep track of whose turn it is. If it is your turn, you get up and go with the nurse. The problem is I did not figure out the system until ten minutes ago, and I have not been paying detailed attention to who was here when I got here and who came after I arrived. By nature, I am an observer of people, so I feel it could be my turn, but I'm not positive. I scan the room with a quizzical look at the other patients sitting side by side around the perimeter. They all nod at me that it is my turn.

"Do you want me to come with you?" Jim asks.

"No, thanks, I can handle it."

I follow the nurse into a bright, sunny doctor's office with floor-to-ceiling windows that look down on the main street. The white molding and wood floors make me think this might have been a parlor a hundred years ago. Two female doctors sit at a modern conference table. One has long, thin blond hair and an angular face. The other has bobbed brown hair and a round face. They are both in their late thirties and wear street clothes. I could be coming in for a job interview, except off to the side is an examination table and cupboards that contain medical supplies. The doctors stand up in unison, and we greet each other with handshakes. Then they beckon me to sit down.

"Do either of you speak English?" I ask, looking at one then the other. I can't figure out who is in charge.

"A little bit," says the brown-haired one tentatively.

I pull out my phone, where I have created an extensive list of my symptoms and an explanation that we are walking the GR5 all translated into French. I hold the phone up as a gift, but I'm not sure who to give it to.

The blond doctor reaches across the table and takes my phone. She reads the list and then hands it to the other doctor, who might be in training or a scribe. It's hard to tell.

They confer in French. Then the senior doctor says, "*Asseyez-vous sur la table d'examenet je vais vous regarder.*" She extends her arm and points to the examination table.

The senior doctor carefully lifts my hair and looks in my right ear and then the left. In a serious tone, she says something in French. The doc-in-training takes notes on a laptop back at the conference table. I can tell the way the senior doctor is talking that she has seen something. I hear the word *rouge*.

Then the doctor asks me to say "ahh." Ahh is the same in French or English.

She nods her head and sort of says, "Whoa." The other doctor nods and continues taking notes.

The soft hands of the senior doctor on my glands, which I know are swollen because they have been bothering me for days, are comforting—a healing touch.

A small tear forms in my right eye. I wipe it away quickly. *Finally, I'm being taken care of.* Not that Jim had not tried, but he was ill-equipped. I feel like I did when I was young and had had a bad day at school, held it together all day, and cried when I got home because I felt safe within the sphere of my mother.

Now, I am in safe hands and can let my guard down. The worry that I had been carrying for days about being sick can finally be released. I take a deep breath and slowly exhale.

The doctor then listens to my heart with her stethoscope after warming it with her hand.

"*Prends une profonde inspiration*," she says as she takes a deep breath to show me. I take another deep breath and slowly release it as she listens to my lungs.

When I reflect on this experience, it strikes me how the French word for *breath* is *inspiration*. When I slow down and breathe deeply, I breathe out what I do not need and then breathe in new thoughts and insights. No, more precisely, the act of breathing in and out clears the clutter of thinking—what some people call the monkey mind—and exposes the insights and wisdoms that are already there. Like clearing the snow off of a frozen pond and exposing pond weed and fish slowly swimming, insights appear below the surface. I will discover this as I walk and breathe over and over in the days, weeks, and months to come.

Finally, she beckons me back to the conference table. She taps away on her laptop. They converse with each other. The junior doc asks, "Where are you staying?"

"Just a few blocks from here. We are staying in Spa for the next two days."

She says, "We have three prescriptions for you: one for amoxicillin for your ears and throat, one for throat spray, and one for eye drops. The pharmacy is on this same block down on the main street." She points out the window and to the right. She continues, "Your lungs are good. You don't have . . ." she pauses, searching for the word, ". . . pneumonia."

The senior doc hands me three pieces of paper fresh from the printer. I thank them profusely. "*Merci beaucoup, merci beaucoup.*" I want to hug them, but that might not be appropriate in this culture.

Back in the waiting room I rejoin Jim. I already paid the nurse 25.50 euros when I arrived, so we walk out the door. I lean into him and say, "I have double ear infections, strep throat, and conjunctivitis if I understood them correctly. The communication was a little sketchy. But they were very nice, and I feel relief already. Let's go to the pharmacy. It's just around the corner."

"You go back to the apartment to rest. I'll get the prescriptions," he says.

When he returns, I immediately take all three medications. I lie on the overstuffed couch in the overstuffed apartment and nap for the rest of the day.

I realize that exhilaration for the trip had interrupted my sleep for many nights. Even more, I'd been unaware that over-excitement had hijacked common sense and allowed the illness to progress so far. Now I know to honor the euphoria but also be aware how powerful it can be. *With that awareness, can I now listen better to signals from my body?*

We are taking two days off. Will we make up the time? Being sick was not in our plan. Our plan, not well defined, is basically to arrive at Lake Geneva where the Alps begin before July 1, because the snow should be melted out of the passes by then. Our friends Margo and Todd are planning to meet us there and hike with us the first week in the Alps. Margo and Todd are old friends who are amazing hikers.

Back in Vermont, I had roughed out a schedule gleaned from *Walking Europe from Top to Bottom* by Susanna Margolis and Ginger Harmon. Even though the book was over thirty years old, I loved the maps of each region and the corresponding tables presenting the number of kilometers walked and the hours it took for each day. These tables were extremely helpful in planning with the one wild assumption that we would walk roughly at the same pace as they did. I took a picture of each map and table and stored them in my phone.

Using the information, I figured that we would walk through Belgium, Luxembourg, and Lorraine in May, walk the Vosges and the Jura in June, and arrive at Lake Geneva before July 1. Right now we are making reservations only a few days ahead because we still don't know our pace.

I'm reminded that I can plan and plan, but I cannot control life.

When I wake up from my nap, I feel much better. It makes cosmic sense that I waited to get to Spa to heal from my illnesses. For centuries people have been coming to Spa to drink the so-called curative waters. Jim has collected mineral water from the spa's source. Its minerals and effervescence tingle my lips.

We eat soup and salad that we prepare ourselves. Then we venture out to a park for a short evening stroll. The park is made up of expansive green lawns interrupted by giant common and copper beech trees. The vibrant new leaf colors are intoxicating as I bend my head back and rest my chin on the trunk of the beech and gaze at the evening sky above. The copper beech leaves in May are pink—not neon pink or rose pink, but a sunlit ruby pink. That color against the sapphire evening sky gives me hope. I hug the copper beauty, my cheek resting on the smooth milky-gray bark, my arms not even wrapping halfway around its diameter. I will the new ruby-pink leaf energy to seep into my body and help heal me. The antibiotics, the spa waters, the tree energy, and the gift of another day of rest are all doing their best to get me well.

DANDELIONS IN BEER COUNTRY (DAY 11)

Two mornings later, after cleaning the apartment, we are all packed up and ready to walk. Exhilaration reenters my body, but I take a mindful breath and set the intention to work *with* the exhilaration, not let it overpower me.

We walk side by side down the quiet streets of Spa. Tulips and pansies bloom outside the casino, rowdy with color. European towns and villages are densely populated at their centers, but it does not take long for us to reach the edge of town and begin walking into a hemlock forest. The soft earth gives with each footstep. The route is well marked with white-and-red way-marks. After fifteen minutes of gentle climbing, off to the left we see a modern house made of glass. And through its view we get a glimpse of the buildings of Spa down in the valley.

"How are you feeling today? You seem chipper again," Jim says as we climb higher.

"I feel almost a hundred percent better. My ears are still blocked some of the time, but I have my energy back." I adjust my pack, tightening the waistband and loosening the chest strap.

As the GR5 moves on to a forest track, the land flattens and I adjust my pace. After a kilometer of flat woods, we enter an expansive plateau, Fagne de Malchamps, a huge area of protected bogland. It seems weird to have wetlands up on a plateau.

A boardwalk cuts across the bog, passing sedges, bilberry bushes, and heathers. I pull out my phone and record a short video. Being able to create videos and post them on YouTube is a support to me. The need to share what I'm witnessing is fulfilled by connecting to my small audience. Making videos is a form of keeping a journal. In the evening I edit the videos in iMovie, a new skill for me to keep stretching my brain. My goal is to make and post a video once every two weeks.

At the end of the boardwalk, we climb a lookout tower with glorious green views over the Ardennes in every direction.

After walking downhill for an hour, we enter a tiny village of stone buildings with a paved road. A bench in the shade next to a prattling stream and a bocce court is the perfect place for lunch. As we eat our cheese and bread, we watch bikers race by. Lilacs and apple blossoms permeate the clear May sunshine. "Did you bring the bocce balls?" I say, leaning into Jim and giving him a quick kiss on the lips.

On the tree providing shade, a new form of the waymark is painted on the bark. There is the white-and-red rectangle and underneath, on the right side, is a shortened white-and-red mark. This indicates we turn left. The path to the right has white-and-red slashes forming an *X*, which indicates to not go that way. I feel comforted by all these waymarks directing us. We begin the gentle climb, and I slow my pace as part of my body digests lunch. I want to have enough energy for the whole day of walking.

The last gradual descent into Stavelot is spectacular with woods on the right and open pastures to the left. Arriving at two thirty, we have enough time to visit the Abbey Museum. The abbey, founded in the seventh century, has a long history of gaining, losing, and regaining territory. Extensively detailed exhibits span the centuries, and after two hours my brain is as tired as my body. After a lovely alfresco dinner, we sleep. Our first full day of walking is complete.

The next morning, up on a plateau, Belgian dandelions stretch as far as the eye can see. The rolling fields are not green but yellow—a sun yellow that goes on and on to the indigo horizon. I'm no expert on cows, but in just two days, we have seen three varieties of cows, if the color of cows determines the variety: dirty off-white, creamy brown and white, and black and white—*like a description of chocolates*, I muse to myself. These cows look sturdier than Vermont cows, with short legs and muscular bodies. Vermont cows seem to wear black-and-white dresses that are too big, their leather hanging from their bones. These Belgian cousins come to the edges of the barbed wire fence, say hi to us, and then go back to eating the prolific dandelions. *Does eating dandelion greens make their milk healthier—dandelion-fed milk?*

In the afternoon, we encounter kilometers of hot pavement. We cross over a highway. The cars zip by so fast it hurts me—I can barely look over the guardrails at the speeding cars, as it gives me a stomachache. We have slowed down from biking pace to walking pace—a human being's natural pace. Twenty minutes later, we are away from the noisy highway and back to the dandelion fields.

"I need to stop and check a hot spot on my left foot," I say. There have been benches all morning, but just when we need one, there are none. We plop into the dust on the side of a dirt lane. I peel my sweaty sock off my puffy pink foot.

"You should check yours too," I say as I focus on the red circle on the side of my big toe. "It's not a blister yet, but it will be if I don't cover it with that SecondSkin."

I pull the small plastic box out of my pack and open it to find squishy material the size of a small Band-Aid. I peel off the back and place it carefully over my hot spot, making sure the edges do not rub to make more hot spots.

"Oh, I have two full-on blisters on my right foot. Pass me the box." Jim says, his bushy eyebrows furrowed and his head bent over, examining his feet. What would a passerby think seeing two adults sitting in the dust inspecting their feet? "And on my left, I have one blister. I need to keep checking more often. You're better at taking care of your feet," he says and begins tending to his feet.

Three more days of inspecting our feet as if they were newborns pays off; we no longer have blisters. All the walking books warn of blisters. I've read adventure books where blisters take people down. In other adventure books the heroine keeps going with blisters. I'm not that tough. Blisters form when your feet are not broken in. Blisters form on your hands when you are new to rowing or chopping wood. Now that our feet are broken in, our blisters are gone.

Meanwhile, I'm getting over my emotional blisters from traveling to a new place every day. That tiny bit of anxiety or wariness is healing over. I'm settling into the flow of daily walking. During the week of biking and sickness, I mostly endured. Now towards the end of this first week of walking, I trust the GR5, trust my feet, trust my body, and trust the experience. The sunshine, the cows, and the dandelions have been my second skin.

The dandelion carpets turn from yellow to white fluff and blow away, revealing green again.

Our last night in Belgium, we sit on the deck of a small country hotel looking at horses in a pasture and cows grazing on the distant hillside. I sip a cold beer with an image of a wolf on the label. We are in beer country. Somewhere along the GR5, we will cross over an invisible line into wine country and vineyards will replace wheat fields, but not yet. We drink a different beer each evening. I wonder if the wheat fields we walk by are grown for this beer. We have not seen hops growing, only wheat.

Jim has his iPad out and writes in his journal.

"Have you written your haiku today?" I ask. He set a goal of writing a haiku a day on this journey.

"Working on it now."

"Can I hear it?"

"Footsteps and bird songs
Wind whispers wheat, pastures
Languid eyed cows."

"I love the 'Wind whispers wheat.'"

The hotel proprietress, who is short, lean, gray-haired, and has the energy of a ten-year-old, dashes onto the deck. In her hand is my tripod. "Did you forget this yesterday?" she asks.

"Yes," I say as my cheeks redden. "Thank you."

"The owner of the hotel you stayed in last night found it in your room, and her son drove it here," she says.

"Wow, thank you so much," I say, receiving the nine-inch tripod into my hand.

She retreats into the bar.

Jim laughs, leaning his head back. He knows I tried to leave the tripod in the room so I would not have to carry it. I decided it was not worth its weight.

"I guess I'm not supposed to leave this behind," I pause. "That was so nice of the hotel owner from last night. How did she know where we were staying?"

"Remember? She helped me find this place, as I could not get through on the phone. They are all helpful. Even when you don't want their help," he says with a grin.

"I guess I always have to leave a note with discarded items."

That night at dinner, the hotel proprietress is everywhere. She is the bartender, the waitress, the hostess. Her movements are efficient and graceful like those of a conductor. She makes sure everyone has a beer or wine within ten minutes of sitting down.

But she does not return to ask for dinner orders for half an hour. I watch the clientele fall under her spell. American clientele would raise a hand and demand service.

Her husband is the cook. We have learned from four nights of staying in small Belgian hotels that the hotels are all family-run, and they all work hard. The hotel restaurants have one seating. Dinner is from seven or eight in the evening until nine or ten—not like in the United States, where restaurants greedily compact in as many seatings as possible. Here, slow eating, slow drinking, and a relaxed pace are obligatory.

The dining room is muted even though every table is full. There is soft conversation like a meditative retreat, which I enjoy in contrast to the loud laughing permeating so many restaurants in the States. Jim and I sink into this quiet pace. I used to look at older couples who ate dinner together without talking and think, *I will never do that.* But here it is okay not to talk all the time. I still struggle with wanting to fill the void with chatter. But the dark wooden walls and the candlelight support me in my desire to rest my tongue. It's like the struggle with meditation. *Can I just be here at the table and enjoy the peace?*

An accepted silver silence floats between us over the maroon tablecloth. The food is nothing special, but the atmosphere is restorative and nourishing and soaks into our bodies the way the beauty of the countryside has. Tomorrow we will leave Belgium and walk into Luxembourg.

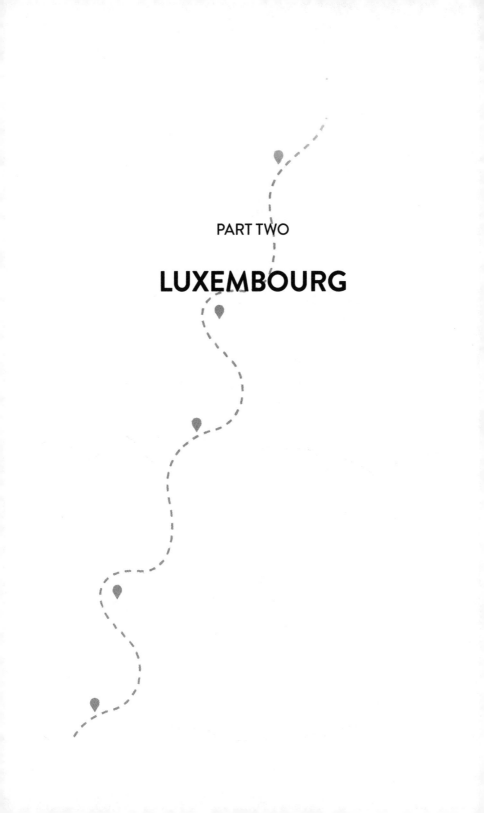

PART TWO

LUXEMBOURG

DAY OFF
(DAY 18)

Three days later, I wake up in the morning to rain dancing on the roof of the trekker's cabin. A comforting thought floats into my awareness. *Tomorrow, we are taking a day off.* It's the first day off since I was sick. I feel so much better, but my ears are still blocked. Jim will go shopping for new boots tomorrow because the treads on his boots are wearing down and they just don't fit him well. He found a store for outdoor equipment in Trier, Germany, a bus and train ride away.

I will have a day to myself, a luxury. Jim and I have been getting along fine—no big arguments. One of the reasons we have been getting along so well is that at home we argue about how to load the dishwasher and where I put the tape measure. But here on the trail we each have our own equipment. There is no communal equipment except for an emergency battery for our cell phones that Jim carries. Another luxury is that we'll get to spend two nights in the same hotel.

Lying on the top bunk, my face is eighteen inches from the roof rafters. Jim sleeps on the top of the other bunk a few feet away. A shiver runs up my back. Not an emotional shiver, just a candid physical shiver. I'm cold. I assumed sleeping on the top bunk would keep me warm through the night. This trekker's hut is a cute little cabin in a campground, but there are no blankets. We have our silk sleeping sheets but no sleeping bags. We had read that all the mountain refuges have blankets, so all you need is a sleeping sheet. I'm wearing my warm wool layers, my puffy jacket, and my hat, and I'm still chilled.

Even with the rain and cold I'm excited to get going. We have splurged and reserved a nice room in a hotel for our day off. The sooner we walk, the sooner we will get there. The trekker's hut is a perfectly adequate place to shelter for a night, but I would not want to spend my day off here. I don't mind walking in the rain and, so far, when we have started off walking in the rain it has usually stopped by midmorning. I have this internal trust that the weather will clear up.

The campground restaurant is not fancy. In the empty restaurant, we eat a simple breakfast of bread, croissants, coffee, and bananas, the only fruit they can find in the kitchen that morning.

Two nights ago, we stayed at our first trekker's cabin at a campground overflowing with German motorcyclists and families. That evening at the campground restaurant, while eating another dinner of white asparagus, the waiter handed us an order form and told us to pass it in by 8:00 p.m. The white slip of paper listed six varieties of bread and ten different pastries. It was fun to come back to the restaurant at 8:00 a.m. and see everyone picking up their bread orders. One grandfather walked away with six baguettes and six raspberry pastries, his grandson carrying two round loaves of bread in a white plastic bag. Where in an American campground can you order fresh bread and pastries, not to mention dine on white asparagus?

Since entering Luxembourg, the waymarks have changed from the familiar white-and-red rectangles to yellow discs on a blue square. We don't know why Luxembourg does things differently. But the trail is well marked and easy to follow.

Today, we cross a stone bridge into the picturesque village of Gilsdorf. No shops are open, and the cobblestone streets are empty. We climb a hill, leaving the village behind.

My heartbeat rises, thumping faster against my ribs. My breath quickens. This hill is too early in the day. I'm out of breath too soon. I slow down my pace as my socks soak up the water from the knee-high grass. Sometimes the trails through the fields have been mowed, and sometimes we wade through the waist-high grass. The rain tapers off as I had faith that it would, my socks wetter than my raincoat.

Radiant red poppies greet us at the top of the hill. Their color is exuberant against the gray-green landscape, and they cheer me along. We walk the broad, open ridge with giant wind turbines in the distance. We pass young wheat and yellow rapeseed fields for three kilometers, then we walk through another small village seeing no one.

In the afternoon, we glide through glorious beech woods. The fledgling green leaves are like emeralds shining in the sun, but with no sun out. The forest is like a striped flag—a lofty vibrant green layer of leaves, a silver-gray layer of muscular trunks and branches, and finally a brown layer of duff and last year's dead leaves. It's a tidy forest with no underbrush. The woods go on and on like the fields had gone on and on in the morning. I'm feeling pensive. I pull out my phone and my earbuds, which I've safely stored in the top pocket of my pack. It's time to experiment with walking and listening to a book. I listened to many books when training in Vermont, and I have a long list of books for listening. *Think how much I can learn and experience while still walking.*

I had started listening to *My Brilliant Friend* when we were in Naples. It is about two friends growing up in Naples in the 1950s. I only have a few more chapters.

Through my earbuds, the author describes the dusty, narrow, sunlit cobblestone streets of Naples. I look around and see the moist deep-green forest. I remember reading that the Grand Duke of Luxembourg held lots of forest land. I wonder if he owns this land. It feels like it has been the same for hundreds of years.

The trees with their smooth silver bark are gigantic and majestic, like sentries guarding a magical kingdom.

Oh, wait, what is the author saying? I've been distracted by the scenery. Maybe I could listen to a book about Luxembourg, but Naples is not working.

I put the iPhone away. So much for listening to books while I walk. Even though these beech woods go on and on, I don't want to be in Naples. I want to be here now in these woods. The birds singing in the upper branches are the authors I want to listen to.

I learn later that beech leaves are edible when young. Beechwood burns for many hours with a bright but calm flame. Female and male flowers appear on the same branch. They work as a team, just like Jim and me. In the past, I've had a fondness for oak trees. The musky scent of split oak is reassuring, as all the houses I've lived in were heated by woodstove.

But beech trees are beginning to take over the ecosystem of my heart.

We arrive in the town of Beaufort and check into the hotel, a bright yellow stucco building with large plate-glass windows, located on the outskirts of town. I see a container of knobby wooden walking sticks in the corner of the lobby. Walking sticks instead of umbrellas—I like the hotel immediately.

Even though we are taking a day off tomorrow, we begin our ritual of washing socks, underwear, and wool T-shirts by hand in the sink. And because we are taking tomorrow off, I also wash my capris. I love the warm water on my hands after a day of walking outside. I carry a small bottle of shampoo, which I also use as detergent, except when the bathroom has shower gel. Sometimes there is no stopper for the sink and I stuff a sock in the drain to hold the water. This hotel has a heated towel rack, so our laundry will dry easily. We get very creative hanging socks and underwear on light fixtures and shower stalls. Occasionally if they are still damp in the morning, we hang our socks off the backs of our packs to get them fully dry. We each do our own laundry. Laundry, shower, check email, figure out dinner.

Tonight, standing on the main street, Jim and I argue about which restaurant to eat in. He wants to eat in a Portuguese restaurant because the menu looks good. I think since we are in Luxembourg, we should eat in a Luxembourg restaurant. But hunger encourages me to give in. I say "give in" because, with Jim and I at the end of the day, little decisions become a power struggle.

It turns out many Portuguese people emigrated to Luxembourg in the 1980s. And Jim is right. The red wine is excellent, and so is the rich, earthy tomato-based sauce on the pasta.

The next morning at eight thirty, I wake up with a big smile on my face when I realize we do not have to walk today. I can stay in this soft bed all day if I want. Jim has gone off on his errands. I listen to the last few chapters of *My Brilliant Friend*. Now I'm enjoying my mind being in Naples when my body rests in Luxembourg.

At ten, I wander into town and stop in the *farmacia* to buy some herbal nasal spray that the pharmacist says will unclog my ears. After paying for my purchase, I saunter down to the castle and the castle museum. Part of me feels like I should go into the museum, but I just don't feel like it. A few days ago, we walked through an abandoned castle, and in Vianden Jim went to the iconic castle and museum and enjoyed the history. I skipped it to write emails and write in my journal. Castle history is all about war strategy, weapons, and dungeons. I have no interest. Men recorded medieval history about men. Women and their stories were neglected and abandoned. I take a few photos of the castle framed by weeping willows. The rounded towers and curved fortress walls are a wonder of architecture. I stroll back through town, stopping at the church, but the door is locked.

I end up back at the hotel where I need to be, resting. I don't want to deal with the fancy hotel restaurant, so I eat the leftovers from last night for lunch: cold, soggy salad and cold spaghetti. The flavors fill me up.

I slide back into bed and check my email. Kate graduated from nursing school yesterday, and I missed it. Part of me feels like a bad mother, and I'm sad to miss a meaningful celebration of her life, but I've witnessed all the other milestones. It's okay to be on an adventure for me and us. My nephew sent a video of my mother pinning Kate. Because of our absence, the rest of my family stepped in, and Kate ended up having seven devoted relatives cheer her on.

Jim and I have made it a point to FaceTime or call Kate and Sam at least once a week. Sam lives in Denver and works for an educational software company. I also check in with my mother, and Jim checks in with his parents. Technology keeps us close even when we are far away.

I surrender to sleep, feeling safe and grateful for my faithful family.

At four o'clock, I wake up as Jim returns from his expedition. Success. He has found boots that fit.

"I bought you a present." He tosses a tan safari sun hat onto the bed. "It is one of those dorky hats you don't like."

"Thank you, that will work," I answer with a smile.

"Are you sure it is not too dorky for you?" he laughs.

"No, I'm finally ready to accept function over style. I hate to leave my colorful striped hat from Sicily, but it just does not work in the wind." I continue, "And I'm going to leave my felt hat, also. It's too warm to wear. I want my pack to be as light as possible. I've shed enough clothes and reorganized my pack, so I don't need the extra pockets. How about you?"

"I'm getting there."

We decide to eat dinner at the hotel restaurant. It's a tired, elegant room with tables covered in white linen set around the edge, looking out the large plate-glass windows into the untended gardens surrounding the hotel. Such neglect is surprising because most of Luxembourg has been well kept. The dining room is not busy. The waiter tells us it will be full every night in a few weeks, as the walking season will have begun. There is a fixed-price menu, and we enjoy a dinner of trout, roasted potatoes, and red cabbage. Jim tried the Luxembourgian Black Pudding, or blood sausage, and for dessert, vanilla ice cream in a meringue shell. It was all good food but nothing special—elegant but no soul. Last night's Portuguese dinner had soul; you could taste the sunshine in the tomato sauce.

Even after my three-hour nap, I fall right to sleep.

LANGUAGES
(DAY 20)

As we begin walking on this sunny May day, I feel a little stiff from yesterday's day off, like a rusty hinge on a gate closed all winter, although I'm happy for the spring weather again. We have a twenty-six-kilometer day ahead of us. We are in an area known as Petite Suisse Luxembourgeoise (Little Switzerland, Luxembourg). It looks nothing like Switzerland but is dramatic in its own way. We walk through a wooded gorge with pock-marked sandstone cliffs rising on both sides of us. The sandstone looks like the back of a braille card that a blind giant might read, the holes in linear layers. A bubbling stream winds between the towering blocks of sandstone, reflecting the filtered sunlight and harmonizing with the ever-present chorus of birds. Moss and ferns blanket the ground, drinking in the humid air. Little wooden bridges cross over the stream, and we do not stay on one side long.

This is a popular walking area. We have seen more people walking today than we have on the whole trip. We come across a group of middle schoolers who are way out ahead of the rest of their group. The teachers do not seem to care that the students race ahead a kilometer. I hear no teacher calling for them to slow down. In the United States, every child would have to be with an adult. I like that these kids can walk on their own. The teachers are training their children to be walkers.

The GR5 eventually climbs one of the sandstone ledges. The first group of kids stands on a walkers' balcony overlooking the expansive rolling countryside, drinking from their water bottles. We sit on a bench and eat chocolate and nuts, sharing the view with the students. From this precipice, one of the students points north and chats with her friends in French. I follow her arm and realize we can see where we started this morning. Then she points south. That must be where the day ends. Climbing high allows us to get an overall perspective. The meandering gorge below is like a maze, small, detailed, and tunneled like our lives can be. Sometimes we need to climb up and gain perspective. The GR5 supports me to view the expanse of my life.

"Are you on a school trip?" I ask in English, a smile building on my face.

They all smile faintly, a little embarrassed. They look at one another to see who is going to answer.

Finally, one of the boys in a crisp white shirt politely says, "Yes, we come here every year to walk."

"Do you study English in school?" I ask. "Your English is good."

"Yes, and we study Luxembourgish too," he says. He squirms and turns to his friends.

Luxembourgish is a Germanic language. It is one of Luxembourg's three official languages, along with French and German. Maybe they have been speaking Luxembourgish. My brain cannot distinguish the two languages.

I'm jealous and impressed with their language abilities.

Stumbling around with the French language reminds me of my frustration with my first and only language, English. I love reading now, but I used to hate it.

I was a regular kid, happy riding tricycles, climbing trees, and playing TV tag until first grade. At recess on the cement playground, I ran around with all the other girls skipping rope, playing tag, and hand clapping, "Miss Mary Mack, Mack, Mack, all dressed in black, black, black . . ." I was one of the cool girls on the first-grade playground in public school in the 1960s. But in the classroom at reading time, curiously, Mrs. Richardson called me up with three boys to sit at her table. My friends were in two other reading groups, comprised of all girls. I don't remember understanding that they could read, but I do remember feeling left out. My heart was crushed. *Why wasn't I with my friends in the bluebird group?* I felt isolated and different. I began to question my confidence.

At the spring parent-teacher conference, my mother was told that I was not learning to read, and that maybe I was "retarded"—a word we'd be horrified to hear in any school today but which was commonly used fifty years ago. My mother knew I was smart. I was her oldest. She was married at twenty-two and at twenty-three gave birth to me. She had never stood up to authority, being a good girl of the 1940s and '50s, but she knew I was not stupid, and she did not believe this teacher. She moved me to a small private school for second grade, where I had to get to know a whole new group of girls who had all attended first grade together. I was not so confident this go-round. I did eventually make friends out on the swings, running around the field, and building fairy houses in the pine grove. But I continued to struggle in the classroom, except for math.

More parent-teacher conferences. It was decided that I should stay back a grade. My mother took me for testing at Massachusetts General Hospital in Boston, and I was diagnosed with dyslexia.

I was privileged to live in the Boston area where there were so many medical and educational resources. I was also lucky to have a mom who cared and a father who earned enough that I could go to private school and get extra tutoring. So many other children lacked these resources and did not receive the help and compassion they needed. They were labeled and demeaned because they could not read. Many acted out.

The statistics on dyslexia are interesting. In the general population, ten percent of people have dyslexia. Sixty percent of people in prison have dyslexia. Thirty-five percent of entrepreneurs have dyslexia.

These statistics, to me, point towards a pattern. If a person with dyslexia comes from white privilege or has someone to advocate for them, they have a good chance of becoming an entrepreneur. But without diagnosis, attention and support they are more likely to become frustrated, discouraged, and hopeless—more apt to act out repeatedly and even to end up in prison.

The second year of second grade was not any better. On the first day, I sat at my wooden desk in the third row next to the window. The walls were covered with the same pictures and posters from last year. My favorite part of the room was the pull-down map of the world in the back of the classroom. I could study the rivers, oceans, and mountains all day even though I couldn't read one name on the map.

Mrs. Kenny, who knew me from last year's second grade, introduced me to the class. "This is Kathy. She is joining us for second grade."

"She is staying back because she is stupid," said George, squatting on his chair and pointing at me.

My face turned rouge. My heart beat faster. Like a good girl, I looked straight ahead and ignored George's declaration, but the words pierced my heart, and a seed of shame began to grow.

"Sit down, George," said Mrs. Kenny.

She went on talking about what would happen in second grade. She ignored George's words too. Her inaction pierced a second and bigger hole in my heart. She did not protect me. She did not explain to the class that I'm smart, but my brain is wired differently—words my mother told me over and over.

Who should I believe, my mother or George? How could I explain to George that I'm smart when I'm not moving on to third grade with all the other kids my age, my friends from last year? I see now how grief was present in my second-grade classroom. There was no way I was going to speak up for myself. I kept my mouth shut and silently burned inside. Plus, I knew that kids who stayed back were dumb; all the sitcoms on TV told me so.

After lunch, Mrs. Kenny walked up and down the desk aisles handing out corrected spelling tests. She put most of the papers face up, but when she got to me, she placed mine face down. I grasped one corner and slowly flipped it over, when what I really wanted to do was crumple it up and run out of the room. The white paper with thin blue and dashed lines had more red lead than my black lead scrawl. Ten out of ten wrong, and these were words we'd studied last year. My tentative misfit words were strangled and shamed under the red web of authority.

On a good week in second grade, I got seven wrong and three correct even though I studied. My struggles with school work continued.

I have extraordinary respect for the Luxembourg students on the cliffs looking out over the view.

We say good-bye to the trilingual students and drop down into the sandstone chasm again, where the air is cooler. The striated sandstone is now covered with moss everywhere. The GR5 takes us through narrow passages where my shoulders just slide through. One gigantic boulder has a tree growing on its crown, the exposed roots clinging to the dimpled formation. Green caverns hold secrets where water eroded passageways thousands of years ago. The trail climbs up and over dramatic formations for a few hours. The middle schoolers are going to love this part. Occasionally, I hear a cry of delight behind us. I wonder how many of those middle schoolers struggle with learning. At least today they can enjoy themselves on the playground of the GR5 and so can I.

COMMUNICATION (DAY 20)

In the late afternoon, we arrive at Hotel Gruber in Steinheim. The small hotel backs up on the Sauer River. In halting English, the proprietress says that the restaurant will not be open tonight because of a death in the family. She explains that we can take a bus back to the city of Echternach, which we walked through about an hour ago. She explains half in English and half in French how to flag down the hourly bus.

I'm discouraged that we have to backtrack to Echternach; if we had known, we could have eaten there and then walked here. On the other hand, I respect and appreciate the way these family-run hotels keep surviving. It's easy to have compassion for these family-owned businesses.

Two hours later, we stand on the corner diagonally across from the hotel. "Did she say how much the bus is?" Jim asks.

"No, I don't think so."

"When I went to buy my hiking boots, I just held out my hand with a collection of coins so the driver could take what they needed."

Just then, the electric bus rolls up and quietly stops in front of us.

"*Bonjour. Á Echternach, s'il vous plaît,*" Jim says, holding his hand gently in front of the driver.

The driver picks out a one-euro coin and two ten-euro cent coins. Then nods.

I watch over Jim's shoulder. Jim is very comfortable traveling and asking for help or figuring out life on the road. I have this old inner need to do everything right and not cause a commotion. I excelled at pretending in elementary school. I wanted so much to be seen as normal and to fit in. Pretending seeped into my bones. But I don't want to pretend anymore.

When I was in fourth grade, during library time my friends each checked out a tall stack of horse books and began to read them voraciously. I wanted to be like everyone else, so I checked out four horse books from the library. I didn't even like horses, but peer pressure was strong, and my confidence was weak. I settled myself onto a big pillow and cracked open a horse book. Tables and big pillows had replaced wooden desks in 1970. My school was experimenting with open classrooms.

I didn't try to read the horse book, but I pretended to read it. I forced my eyes to follow the black words on the white page to the end of the line and then start over again and over again. When I felt enough time had passed, I turned the page. *Was I turning the pages too fast? Too slow? Would someone find out that I was pretending?* It took a lot of work to pretend to read—to pretend to be normal.

I was good at pretending. But it was scary. *Who was going to find out? When would I be exposed as a non-reader? How long could I keep this up?*

Pretending was exhausting. It emptied my heart. At the same time, the shame kept growing. Shame is emptiness.

At night I would go home and eat to soothe myself. I'd have a snack in the kitchen with my younger brother and sister, and I would feel better for a short time. Later, alone, I would find Chips Ahoy! cookies or graham crackers in the pantry and sneak them up to my room and eat them in bed in secret. I tried to fill my emptiness with food. But the cookie crumbs scattered over my bedspread just became sharp edges of more shame scattered over my heart.

Home and food were a refuge. But even at home, there was a giant neon sign that I was not like others. My brother, Rob, two and a half years younger than me, could read better when he got to first grade than I could in third. My mother tried not to make a big deal of this, and my brother never teased me about it, but I felt outside the natural order of things.

I finally learned to read in the seventh grade, though I was not on grade level. I was slow and still stumbled with multi-syllabic words.

The absolute worst was reading out loud. In the eighth grade, I never made eye contact with my teacher during literature time. I tried to be invisible, slinking low in my chair. When called to read *Romeo and Juliet*, my stomach froze up and became lead. Now that I think about it, maybe it was my heart and soul that froze. My face turned red hot. Pools of sweat formed under my arms. I struggled through the lines, skipping words and guessing at words, trying not to hear the other students' giggles and snorts. It was excruciating.

I was so relieved when my turn was over, but to no avail. I still felt embarrassed, exposed, and raw. It was a festering wound that never healed.

My mother continued to try to heal my wound. "You are a smart person. You have a high IQ. You have amazing comprehension. When I read out loud to you, you remember every detail. You are a great math student."

The late afternoons scoring goals as a left wing on the green field-hockey field helped heal my wound. But the next morning, it would be ripped open again. Now I was exposed to my peers as the girl who could not read.

I never talked with anyone about the pain and shame I felt. I barely acknowledged it myself. *Hide, hide, hide. Pretend, pretend, pretend.*

As the years went on, I caught up with my peers as a reader with tutors' help through high school and with great determination. Romance and sex were great motivators. One of the first books I read on my own was *Little Women*. I thought it was written in Old English because it was so difficult to read but years later when I reread it, I was surprised to see it was just plain English. I kept reading because I wanted to find out if Jo and Laurie were ever going to kiss. I was devastated when she refused him. I also remember reading every word of *The Joy of Sex* at the house where I babysat. After putting the kids to bed, I cautiously pulled out the big white book from the bookcase and read while eating a bowl of ice cream, enjoying two guilty pleasures by the light of a 60-watt bulb with the dark night all around.

Later I learned the square root rule from the book *The Dyslexic Advantage*. If it takes a regular person nine hours to learn something, it takes a dyslexic three times as long, so twenty-seven hours to learn something new. This means people with dyslexia need lots of patient people to support them. I was lucky; I had my mother.

I could read my textbooks in college, but I was slow. I finally asked for help at the writing center, and I worked long hours on my papers with support in graduate school. I became an elementary teacher and reading tutor. I empathized with struggling readers. I could get inside their brains and see where they needed help. I was patient with their struggles.

I taught second grade for four years before moving on to fourth grade. So essentially, I was in second grade six times. By teaching phonics over and over, the structure of the English language finally seeped into my brain. We teach what we need to learn.

I read books out loud to my second graders more than any other teacher in the school and became known as the read-aloud teacher. When other teachers showed movies before vacations, I read chapter books out loud for two hours to my students, and in the process, I transferred the love of books and reading to them. Stuart Little, Mrs. Piggle Wiggle, Beezus, Ramona, Wilbur, and Charlotte all jumped from my heart to theirs.

Dyslexia has a positive side to it. I discovered that I'm a big-picture thinker. I'm creative and a great planner—valuable skills for this adventure. My struggles with dyslexia also have a silver lining: I'm good at reading people. As a struggling reader, I searched the teacher's face for clues to what the answer was. People express so much in their faces and in body language. Three times a week for twelve years, while being tutored, I got to practice reading body language. This ability has helped on our journey.

Jim and I sit on black metal café chairs on the edge of a pedestrian street at an outdoor restaurant a few blocks from where the bus let us off. A bubbling fountain mutes the traffic noise from a few streets over. At seven o'clock, the May sun is still warm. The menu lies open between us. Jim has his phone out and is using his camera in Google Translate to read the menu—the wonders of technology. This is a touristy restaurant with a simple menu of pizzas and salads. Echternach has a famous Benedictine abbey that we saw this afternoon from a view up high on the GR5, and we got a glimpse of it from the bus just coming into town.

We decide to split a pizza and order a salad each.

The waiter, a tall thin man with just a fleck of gray in his sideburns, stands stiffly by our table and looks directly at Jim. He asks in French if he can take our order.

Jim asks, *"Parlez-vous anglais?"*

"No," he says with a stone face.

Jim says, *"Nous voudrions une pizza et deux salades."*

The waiter replies with a long monologue in French, going on and on.

Jim and I both have blank faces.

The waiter tries again with the same words, but this time, he uses hand gestures. He raises two fingers. I hear the word "special" a few times.

I lean over to Jim. "He is saying there is a special of a salad and a half pizza, and we should order two of the specials."

"*Oui, oui,*" I say to the waiter.

We point on the menu to the caprese pizza and spinach salads we want. And the waiter walks away.

"How did you know what he was saying?" Jim asks. "I could not follow him at all. He was speaking so fast. I couldn't translate his words."

"I'm not sure, but I watched his whole body language, and I heard the word 'special' a few times. I don't know what else he was saying. But I just felt he was trying to tell us about the special."

"You're amazing," he says, looking at me with a confused look.

Jim has always been the academically smart one. But being away from business, and especially on this trip, he is seeing there are other forms of smart. I let the compliment soak in. Jim is focused and sees the trees. I can see the whole forest.

After our stomachs are full, we saunter back to the bus stop at the edge of a walking park along the Sauer River.

"Do you want to walk back to the hotel? It's about five kilometers," Jim asks with a smirk on his face.

"No, thanks. But if you want to, you can. Twenty-six kilometers was enough for me."

"No, I'll take the bus with you."

We have fifteen minutes to wait for the next bus. A flash of red catches my eye. I focus. The American flag is waving in the gentle breeze next to the river. I realize I have not seen the American flag in a long time. A bit of sadness flutters over me.

"Let's check that out," I point.

The American flag and the Luxembourg flag—three horizontal stripes, red, white, and blue—fly on two flag poles adjacent to each other. There is a large stone with a plaque.

IN GRATITUDE
TO THE VALIANT SOLDIERS OF THE
83D, -4TH AND -5TH U.S. INF. DIVS.
WHO LIBERATED THE CITY OF ECHTERNACH,
OCT.–DEC. 1944, AND TO THE
76TH U.S. INF. DIV.
WHO CROSSED THE RIVER SAUER HERE ON
FEB.-7-1945
ENDING THE NAZI OPPRESSION OF OUR COUNTRY.
THE CITIZENS OF ECHTERNACH

I wonder how the soldiers and the townspeople communicated during those difficult years. There were interpreters, but hand gestures and body language must have helped.

CUCKOO?
(DAY 22)

We leave the Petite Suisse Luxembourgeoise behind and follow the Sauer River until it joins the Moselle and becomes the Moselle River Valley. We walk upriver because the Moselle flows north, though it is hard to tell as the river moves so slowly here. The source of the Moselle River is in the Vosges Mountains, where we will be in less than a month. Five hundred and forty-four kilometers from the source, the Moselle flows into the Rhine in Germany.

We are frustrated because there are no places to stay along this part of the route, yet Jim finds a small hotel off route in the charming city of Trier, Germany, where he bought his hiking boots, just across and down the Moselle. It's a train ride away. In the late afternoon, after walking twenty-five kilometers, we take a five-stop ride east away from the GR5. I feel tired but not exhausted.

Arriving in Trier, we shop in a bright, plasticky supermarket. Having not been in a supermarket for a long time, it feels confusing and harsh, especially with all the signs in German now. So many choices and so much packaging.

We buy lunch for the next day and prepared salads to eat in our room for dinner. We want to save money and eat more vegetables, which we are both missing. It's nice to have a change of pace, eating in our room instead of having a long dinner at a restaurant. We slip back into eating quickly, like good Americans.

Jim's snoring keeps me awake much of the night. There is no other place to sleep. Sometimes if he is snoring loudly, I sleep on a couch or make him sleep on the couch. But here in this tiny hotel room there is barely enough room to walk around the double bed. I nudge his shoulder a few times to get him to roll over, and he is quiet for a bit. But then the snoring starts again. My ears are blocked. My legs are sore. Anger, frustration, and weariness lie with me, scheming. *Is his snoring a sign that we are not right for each other? Do couples who fall in love at first sight sleep peacefully? Why does my mind go to such dark places?*

I try meditation, but the snoring keeps interrupting me. At least one of us is sleeping well. I'm trapped in the eternal night of darkness. I fantasize about putting a pillow over his face to make the snoring stop. *But then who would I walk with in the morning?* I must have slept some because I wake up, feeling drained.

We take the train back to Wasserbillig, where we left the GR5. We are not carrying full packs, just water, lunches, and raincoats. We leave most of our possessions at the hotel. It feels fabulous to walk with practically no weight on my back, though I still don't have much energy. My back and kidneys hurt. *When am I going to feel completely well? Should I take another day off and sleep? Am I pushing myself too hard?*

The first seventeen kilometers of the morning take us on a dogleg away from the Moselle River. Part of me wants to stay along the river even if it might be along trafficky roads because it is more direct. But I will trust the GR5 and support her.

After climbing up and away from the river, the trail descends into a shady wooded gully with a gurgling stream running down the middle. The burbling stream and the songbirds compete for our attention. I move leisurely today, one foot in front of the other. Then I hear the hollow echoing call of the cuckoo bird.

Coo-coo, coo-coo, coo-coo. The rise and fall of the same syllable repeated over and over. *Coo-coo, coo-coo, coo-coo.* We have heard cuckoo birds over the last few days.

"There it is again," I call up to Jim.

"Yeah, I hear it. It's as if it is following us," he says. "Sometimes I hear them answering each other."

"Are we cuckoo to be doing this walk?" I ask again. We have been joking each day we hear the bird. But today I feel more serious about the question.

"Maybe we are crazy," says Jim.

He is silent while the cuckoo call rings through the trees again. The sound comes in sets of three. In some ways it is a mesmerizing and comforting sound. The repetition is like the beating of my pulse.

"Did you learn anything about the cuckoo from your dad?" Jim asks.

"Maybe. I think the cuckoo is one of those birds that lays its eggs in the nests of other birds." I pause thinking. "Like a parasite. I don't ever remember hearing so many of them in the States. They seem to be everywhere here. That's probably why they used the sound for the cuckoo clock."

"The cuckoo can be our mascot," Jim jokes, lightening my mood. "What do they look like? I can never see them."

"I have no idea. We will have to google it when we get to the hotel tonight. The sound is everywhere but I can't see them either."

It's as if Mother Nature is throwing uncertainty at us or echoing my skepticism about this adventure. Every morning I wake with a jolt of excitement to forge ahead because each day is something new and different. At the same time, the questions float around my being: *Can I do this? Can I walk day after day after day?*

Now we are out of the woods, walking between apple trees that have just finished blossoming. When I look closely at the branches, I see tiny green apples the size of my pinky nail. They are young and vibrant, not exactly the way I'm feeling today. It's an effort to lift each leg and place it on the buttercup-lined trail. Words float into my head: *It's okay to ask for what you want and need.*

Finally, we end up back at the river in the next town further south. We walked seventeen kilometers, but we are only five kilometers from where we started. The GR5 is cuckoo. I'm not sure what we were supposed to be seeing. I read through a blog that has been guiding us by Carroll Dorgan, an American living in France who had walked the GR5 with his wife, Mary, three years before. The next year Carroll walked the northern section again and wrote a guidebook for the northern part of the GR5, though it will not be published until six months after we finish the trail. It turns out Carroll and Mary skipped the dogleg and took a bus down to the next part.

We encounter a range of walkers on the GR5 and in the books we read. The pure walker does exactly every part of the trail. Wherever they left off the day before, they go back the next morning. They do not miss an inch of the trail. At the other end of the range is the relaxed walker, like our friends, Carroll and Mary, who wrote the blog. I call them our friends even though I have never met them, but I feel I know them after reading their blog every day. They will take a bus if the trail does not work for them. We are somewhere in the middle of this range. Jim tried to be the pure walker but eventually relaxed. And of course, we have already broken a walking "rule" by biking the beginning. My view is as long as at least one of us is walking, it does not matter if we are on the GR5 or some other trail.

As we eat our lunch on a bench in the shade of the church in Grevenmacher, I decide to listen to my body. "I'm going to take the bus and train back to Trier so I can sleep during the afternoon. I'll see you later."

"All right. It's about ten kilometers down to Ahn. Then I'll take the bus and train back to Trier." We are both comfortable with this new way of adventuring.

The next day, I decide to skip the morning part of the walk and rest again. I'll take advantage of the fact that there is public transportation that can move me from town to town. The map tells me I will only be missing more vineyard walking. I need and want to care for my body.

Before leaving Trier, I stop at the bank and the supermarket to buy lunch. I stock up on vegetables for lunches for the next two days—cherry tomatoes, cucumbers, and carrots. But I'm careful not to overdo it, as we must carry what I buy. I select one basket of fresh local strawberries and eat them all on the train to Nennig, Germany.

It's lovely sitting on the train and watching the scenery. Vineyard after vineyard flashes by. We have crossed the invisible line into wine country. Train travel is the way most tourists see Europe. For a minute, I fantasize about taking the train all the way to Nice. It would be a luxury to travel by train, and in my fantasy, I would go first class, dining in the wood-paneled dining car. But in truth, if someone offered to pay me to take the train I would refuse. Throughout my life, when I've been on trains looking out at the landscape, I've wished to be out walking—to become a part of the landscape. I love our walking. In three stops, I'm where I'm supposed to be. I walk across the bridge over the Moselle River into Remich, Luxembourg.

Between the river and the hotel where we are staying tonight is a playful statue of Bacchus, the god of wine. He is sitting on a wine cask, riding it like a horse. In one hand, he raises a goblet to the sky, and in the other, he holds a wine bottle. His hair is bunches of grapes. He is having a raucous time next to the Moselle River. Ironically, we are in famous wine country, but

I've skipped the wine, as I worry it will compromise my immune system. But after two half days of resting, I'm feeling lively like Bacchus.

After I check in early at Hotel de l'Esplanade, a three-star hotel, and deposit my belongings in the small room, Jim shows up just as the noon bells toll. I love the deep sound of the bells. Most days at noon we are close enough to a village to hear the dozen bongs. It's become a comforting sound, part of the landscape.

"I had a great morning. It was a vineyard after vineyard. I'm amazed at how much work goes into keeping a vineyard: hand pruning suckers, tilling, fertilizing, and cutting the grass. How are you feeling?" Jim asks.

"Well rested. Let's eat lunch with Bacchus by the River."

After lunch, our path is laid out in front of us, rolling across the vineyards. Again, we walk with superlight packs this afternoon. The plan is to walk twelve kilometers to Remerschen then take the bus back to the hotel. Today the GR5 keeps the river in sight. We climb up the vineyard hillsides and down from village to village.

Skirting along the edge of the vineyards and the woods, we encounter black locust trees in full bloom. From a distance, the white cluster of flowers make the trees look like they're covered in snow. When I get close, the intense sugary fragrance similar to orange blooms dances in my nose, and I know it is not winter. In some places, black locusts are considered weed trees because they proliferate, especially in disturbed areas. But I've always loved the flower because of its heavenly scent. I pick a cluster, bring it to my nose and breathe deeply. I examine the creamy white flowers of the legume family, similar in shape to the snap dragon.

I pull a bloom off and drop it on the trail, one by one, until the stem is bare, leaving a trail like Gretel out of the woods and into the open view of the vineyards yet again.

We are astonished at the steepness of the vineyards. *How do they drive the tractors up these steep hillsides?* And just then, we see that they can. A small red tractor the width of a grape row comes charging along, spraying a cloud of chemicals. The driver, covered head to toe in white protective clothing, wears a respirator. He is ten rows away from us, paralleling us. But on his next turn, he veers away from us and heads to a different part of the vineyard. *Thank goodness.* We can smell the acrid chemicals as they blow our way. We move faster along the farm road, racing the chemical cloud. Even with the polluted air, the view across the valley of patchworked vineyards and the silver-blue river winding onward flows into my heart.

That evening we dine on the hotel porch overlooking our friends, Bacchus and the Moselle. White tablecloths speak of a bygone era. In the last few days, we walked by hotels that have gone out of business. Maybe Airbnb or the barges on the river have taken over. I read about biking and barging trips on the Moselle.

Two short days of walking have helped me heal. My ears are finally clear. Jim and I order a glass of local white wine, but we pick an organic one.

For dessert, we feast on fresh local strawberries layered with Chantilly cream in elegant tall glasses. Tubular packets of sugar lie next to the tall spoon so that we can use just the right amount.

Looking back, I see that these two days were a final transition time for my body. Jim took the helm and walked all the kilometers for us, while I walked half days. We had walked through a gate and become mega-walkers, people who have the endurance to walk day after day after day. No, Mrs. Cuckoo bird, we are not crazy. I can do this.

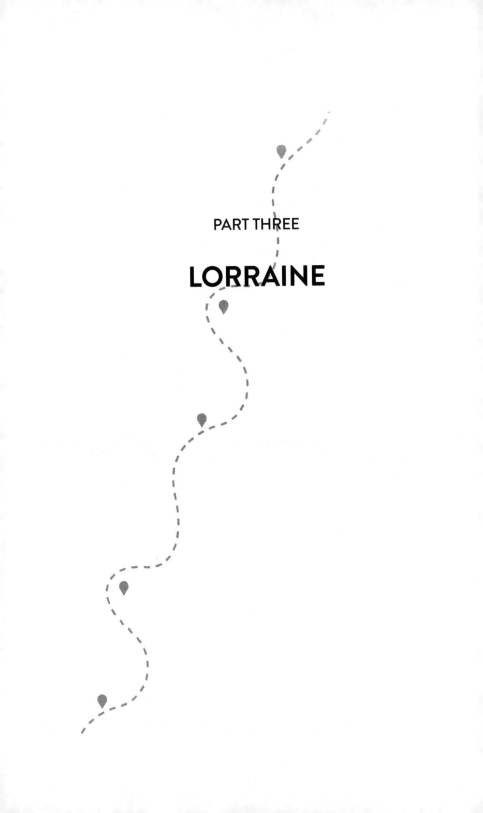

PART THREE

LORRAINE

TO WALK IT IS TO SEE IT
(DAY 24)

We walk out of Luxembourg and into France. It's a satisfying feeling to step out of one country and into another. Now that these countries are all part of the EU, there is no ritual anymore of showing our passports to walk across a border. We just traverse a bridge over the Moselle River. But of course, it is a little more complicated; the GR5 crosses into Germany for a few minutes, and then heads into France. Here along the Moselle the three countries come together at the town of Schengen, Luxembourg. In 1985 the Schengen Agreement was signed by Luxembourg, Belgium, France, the Netherlands, and Germany. The town symbolizes the freedom of movement of people and goods.

We walked the whole length of Luxembourg in ten days. It's a cute little country, long like a finger, but I never got a feel for the people who lived there. The waiters and people working in the hotels and campgrounds were all very polite, but they did not share much of themselves. Except for the school children on the field trip, we did not talk to a local.

The next eleven or twelve weeks will all be in France: two weeks walking through Lorraine, two weeks in the Vosges Mountains, two weeks in the Jura, and finally, to mix it up, five or six weeks in the mighty Alps. It's a bit strange to not know how long it is going to take, but that's what makes it an adventure and not a vacation. There is no exact end date.

Within ten minutes of being in France, I notice the land is not nearly as well tended and taken care of as it was in Luxembourg. We stride along a bike path with invading blackberry canes leaning over it like spectators leaning over police tape, cheering on marathon runners. In Luxembourg, the canes would have been trimmed to the edge of the pavement. "Keep everything in its place" seemed to be Luxembourg's motto.

The path narrows with the leaning blackberry canes, and Jim and I walk side by side in the ten o'clock sunshine. An older couple walks towards us. As they pass, I move closer to the blackberry canes to give them room. I feel a gentle prick of a thorn on my right ankle.

"*Bonjour*," I say. They return the salutation and continue walking. Then the tall and broad-shouldered man who sports a dark gray fedora stops, turns, and inquires in French, "*Où marches-tu?*"

I answer in English, "We are walking the GR5 to Nice."

He answers back in English with a sage, deep French accent, "Oh, I have walked parts of the GR5 in the Alps. It is magnificent."

I smile and hop from one foot to the other. "Yes, we are looking forward to the Alps."

"Where are you from?" he asks.

"We are from the United States. We started the GR5 in Hoek van Holland," I say.

Jim interjects, "We are from the state of Vermont." The man squints and looks a little puzzled. Jim goes on, "Near Canada and north of Boston." Jim is proud to be from Vermont, even though we have only lived in Vermont for five months.

The neatly dressed woman looks like she wants to take her husband's hand and keep him walking. But the man keeps talking. "You have good packs and travel light," he says, eyeing our packs with a discerning gaze.

This compliment, coming from a French walker, makes me feel proud and I gently pull back my shoulders and stand taller.

He continues, "I have walked in Germany and many parts of Switzerland. Walking is the best way to see a country! To walk it is to see it," he says with delight.

"Yes, to walk it is to see it." I repeat the poetic words more to myself than anyone else. The words roll around my tongue and taste divine. Like when I heard "Grande Randonnée Cinque" for the first time, I get an electric charge up my neck, signaling that these words are essential. The simplicity of the words flows directly to my intuition and falls into place.

The woman continues walking. He watches her go. It looks like he would like to stay and talk with us longer, but he knows it is time to go. "*Bonne journée, bonne route,*" he says, turning to follow her.

"*Merci, bonne journée,*" we reply in unison and continue on our way.

"Well, that was fun," I say with a hop in my step. "Our first ten minutes in France, and we run into someone to talk to. Luxembourg was beautiful but it felt empty to me. And I love, 'To walk it is to see it.' That is so true." My mind is animated with thoughts.

The simple words embody a deep essence, like "small is beautiful."

When I attempted to write in high school before spell check, because I struggled with spelling, I spent long hours puzzling with simple words to get my point across. My English teachers would comment, "You have the essence here. Can you explore deeper?" I wanted to write back to them, "No, I'm exhausted." I appreciate simplicity and sparse writing.

When I slow down and walk through a country, I not only see the place, but I also notice, observe, and witness the landscape and the inhabitants and come to know the whole of it. My mind takes the word *see* and turns it to *be*. To walk it is to be it.

Will the GR5 support us to be it?

"If I ever get a tattoo, that's what the tattoo will say, 'To walk it is to see it.' I'll get that on my arm," I say. "And 'powered by pastries' will be tattooed on my tummy."

We have never eaten so many pastries as we have in the last few months. Every hotel breakfast offers croissants and chocolate croissants. When we enter the local bakery to buy bread for our lunch, we also buy an éclair, almond brioche, or some new pastry we have never experienced. *By eating the jewels of the country, will we become the country?* Pastry eating with gusto will only continue as the GR5 leads us on.

Jim laughs, "Yes, powered by pastries." We both rub our bellies. He knows I will never get a tattoo. We both know I'm too scared of the pain, and I don't want to mark up my body.

A few minutes later, I muse, "Maybe I'll have a T-shirt made up that says, 'To walk it is to see it' on the front, up top, and 'powered by pastries' down low over my stomach. And on the back, the other saying I love: 'I'll follow the GR5 anywhere.'"

I continue, "I think T-shirts with slogans are for people like me who are too afraid to get tattooed." Jim listens to me talk on and on. We slowly drift into silence. And walk on.

Maybe I should be walking with the French man? He and I could keep talking and talking. Jim is happy to talk for a bit, and then he has had enough. Though, maybe in each couple there is a talker and quieter one.

Another saying we have used throughout the whole trip, including Italy, is, "Don't pass powder for powder." This maxim comes from the skiing community. Jim and his buddies use it when they are heading out of bounds trying to find the best powder snow. In other words, ski the first powder you find because you never know when you will find more.

When we were in Italy, we changed it to "Don't pass gelato for gelato." Don't pass a bathroom for a bathroom. Don't pass an ATM for an ATM. Don't pass a patisserie for a patisserie. What I like most about this aphorism is that it keeps us from arguing. We take the first one that we see. Some couples walk from restaurant to restaurant looking at the menus and peeking in, trying to decide. Now with Google and Yelp, if you have done your research beforehand, it is easier to make a choice. For us, though, if we stick with "Don't pass powder for powder" as our motto while trying to find bakeries, cheese shops, and restaurants every day, we may miss the best restaurant, but we save our relationship by not arguing.

An hour after meeting with the French walker, we come to the town of Sierck-les-Bains. Since entering France, the GR5 has changed clothes and is back to wearing white-and-red rectangular waymarks. She leaves the bike trail along the Moselle and turns east up into the town. We follow her, and she leads us to the doorstep of Patisserie Peter in the central square. We enter a world of colors and aromas. The brown scents of yeast, chocolate, coffee, almond, and flour mix with the air's oxygen, becoming new essential elements. The display case offers intricate patterns, feathered chocolate icing, overlapping toasted slivered almonds, and cake layers topped with raspberry spirals. Clusters of fresh ruby-colored currants, sliced strawberries with the green leaves, or a ground-cherry with its dried husk opened, revealing a golden orb, crown the cakes and tarts. All are fairy dusted with powdered sugar. After fondly perusing the offerings, we order two individual raspberry tarts.

I carefully place the tarts into my pack, and we walk further up through town looking for a place to picnic. At the top of the town is the Duke of Lorraine's castle, with a picnic table out front. I scarf down my lunch so I can slowly enjoy the delicate tart. My front teeth slice through the jeweled berries into the rich custard and then the tender shortbread crust. The best part of

European pastries, and French pastries in particular, is that they are not overly sweet. I taste the bright juicy berry with a hint of sun, the pristine cream custard, and the bold brown-buttery crust not contaminated with sugar. The pastries in the United States are encrusted in that flavor-stealing substance. French bakers are brave and confident that their ingredients will shine through. US bakers hide behind frostings, icings, and the power of sugar.

I take a meditative breath before eating the last bite, willing myself to slow down even more and to be with the tart. To eat it is to be it.

It has been a notable first day in France.

CHURCH SERVICE IN THE WOODS (DAY 26)

Up ahead, I hear children's voices, high, shrill, and bubbly all at the same time. On our third day of walking in France, we are on a muddy woods path paralleling a road. To skip the mud, I contemplate cutting through the woods to the pavement. But in a few minutes, we come face to face with the children. *"Bonjour,"* I say, flashing a smile.

"Bonjour," they all say. There are four of them, aged about eight to ten. They step over to the side of the path, respectfully, to let us pass. We pick our way around a puddle and continue down the footpath. The kids' frothy voices fade behind us.

And all I hear again are the birds of spring, their chorus strong this sunny morning.

The bird songs sound familiar to me, but I struggle to name the birds. My father was an amateur ornithologist. As a teenager, I was awakened on Sunday mornings to Roger Tory Peterson's voice coming from a record player saying, "And that's a red-eyed vireo." The names were stored somewhere in my brain forty years ago, but I can't access them in this moment.

Maybe the birds are singing in French? Perhaps they have a slightly different accent than American songbirds, and that is why I can't come up with a name. I do hear the ethereal, flutelike song of the thrush, but it is probably a French thrush; it sounds slightly different. I remember struggling to know the difference between a hermit thrush and a wood thrush.

Maybe it is my dad speaking to me through the bird songs? He traveled for a few weeks every year in either Brazil or Belize banding birds for Manomet Bird Observatory. He never took off big chunks of time from his stockbroker job to travel and explore, but he did create his own adventures. On a weekend, when there was a bird-a-thon for the Massachusetts Audubon Society, instead of driving all over the state to count birds like the other birders, he decided to bike and bird. His goal was to bike one hundred miles and see one hundred bird species. People sponsored him for the number of birds and the number of miles. He raised thousands of dollars for MAS. It was devastating to our family when he suffered a stroke at age sixty-six and could not bike, bird, or work any longer. He learned to walk, drive, and live on his own again, but he was never the same physically or emotionally.

I would not be on this adventure if I hadn't learned from my father that I can make an adventure my own and do it my way. I learned from him that I don't always need to follow the rules or societal norms.

Now I hear songs, but not bird songs. *What is that?*

Humans singing. A quiver runs through my body. The GR5 turns right, as if she is saying, *Come look what I have to show you.* There below, across the country road, is the back of a small stucco chapel. As we walk around to the front, we see a congregation sitting outside the chapel. It's an outdoor Mass. More people sit on wooden chairs lined in orderly rows than could fit in the tiny chapel, like an outdoor graduation.

The singing stops. A priest stands by the front door of the chapel. Next to him a large table is covered with a white cloth and a flower arrangement—nothing fancy, a simple collection of yellow and white meadow flowers. The table acts as an altar. From where we stand, it looks like the priest is reading or speaking.

We tiptoe around the edge of the congregation to the back. Part of me wants to sit and join them. But we have miles to go before we sleep. We are walking thirty-seven kilometers to Metz; our longest day yet.

Jim is not religious; he is uncomfortable with religion. His mother was Jewish but grew up in a family that was trying to assimilate, thus she turned to nature. His father was Jewish and wanted to practice the rituals. This conflict was handed down to Jim as discomfort. Like his mother, his spiritual source is nature and the outdoors. I'm not religious either, but I enjoy observing different religious services like an anthropologist. We pause and watch from the back.

A man with slick black hair with a hint of gray wearing a white starched shirt and flannel dress pants approaches us.

"Are you pilgrims?" he whispers in English with a friendly smile and his head slightly tilted.

"No, we are walking to Nice on the GR5," Jim whispers back.

"Where are you from?" he asks, looking first in Jim's eyes and then in mine.

"The United States," I answer in a soft voice.

"We will pray for you. The congregation will pray for you," he says quietly.

We thank him. *"Merci, merci." What do you say when someone offers to pray for you?*

He glides back to his seat.

I smile, feeling like a flowing river that goes on and on. My heart surges. We have a whole congregation praying for us.

I don't think I've ever had anyone pray for me—what a lovely sentiment. I've been lucky that I have not needed anyone to pray for me. When my father was dying, I prayed to a higher power that he would not suffer. And I remember as a young girl praying to a white bearded man to do well on spelling tests. The bearded white man did not come through, so I let his image fade away.

Jim moves on up the road. I reluctantly follow. Up ahead is a long open shed where people used to park their horses and carriages when they were in church. Tables are laid out with immaculate white cloths. Women sit in chairs facing the May sun, chatting. It looks like they are waiting for the Mass to be over, and then there will be a large communal feast.

I wonder if they are content not to be part of the Mass. Did they choose to set up and serve so they did not have to listen to the Mass? Are they happier socializing? Or do they miss being part of the service? I will never know the answers. I realize the children we saw off walking in the woods were probably kids from this congregation. *Did they sneak off or were they let out to explore?*

As the GR5 turns to the left, she re-enters the woods and begins to climb, and the singing commences again. The song of the congregation reverberates off the valley walls and rises and expands like whorls of smoke from a chimney. The sound continues to fill my center, which powers my legs, and I keep walking with renewed energy.

Hymns are powerful. I grew up going to church six to eight times a year until I was about twelve. Then in high school at Milton Academy, we sang one hymn every morning in assembly. I didn't connect with the words of the hymns. Some of the words made me angry. At fifteen, it bothered me that god was male and not female, but I loved the feeling of singing in a community. All the voices flowed together, like wires coming together with a twist to form a guitar string. The music is greater than the sum of the parts. I also love chanting "om" at the end of a yoga class. I feel the vibrations in my lips and trace them down to the bottom of my belly, the source. From my lips the invisible vibrations, like a laser beam, converge with the vibrations of the others in the yoga class and the vibrations become visible with my eyes closed. Community singing bonds the singers.

Maybe the women sitting in the May sunshine apart from the

Mass are choosing connection and turning away from patriarchal words?

I strain to listen as I move farther up the ridge. I think I can still hear the song, but what is real and what is memory? Slowly the birds have taken over the human chorus, and I continue walking with the vibrations held in my center.

I pull out my phone and record a video telling the story of the church service in the woods. Then I push a bit to catch up to Jim, and we chat about what we just saw. We are both grateful that the congregation is praying for us.

Jim jokes, "We are heathens because we are walking to the beach in Nice, not to Santiago de Compostela."

"Yes, we are heathens; I love the beach," I exclaim. *I worship the beach. Maybe I'm on a pilgrimage across a continent and through the mountains to the beach?*

The world needs heathens and rebels just as much as it needs the believers.

The GR5 now overlaps with the pilgrimage to Santiago de Compostela. Two days ago, we met two women who were walking down to Spain on a pilgrimage. They were walking for two years. I was impressed. Now when we see the familiar white-and-red rectangles of our waymark, we also see the yellow scalloped shape on a blue background, which is the waymark for Santiago de Compostela. The lines on the shell represent the different pilgrimage routes coming down to Spain to form the Santiago de Compostela.

Even though I have a congregation praying for me, I need to keep walking. Through woods, down muddy paths lined with yellow buttercups and downed logs, along an empty country road, across a highway, out over expansive wheat fields and rapeseed fields, we walk and walk.

We stop and eat our meager, pilfered food. This morning at the hotel restaurant we asked if we could take and pay for some extra food for our lunch, but the manager said they had a big group coming for breakfast and they needed all the bread and cheese. He said it was a holiday, Whit Monday. It is another name for Pentecost Monday, and in the Catholic Church it is the Memorial of the Blessed Virgin Mary, Mother of the Church.

We were the only ones in the restaurant at 7:00 a.m., eating kiwi, yogurt, and croissants. I devoured three kiwis and slipped one into my coat pocket. I felt a little guilty. We both also swiped a few packages of the French version of Laughing Cow cheese. Again, I felt guilty, but not guilty enough not to do it. After breakfast, I wandered around town prowling for pastries and lunch food while Jim finished packing. The two bakeries in town were both closed. Maybe because of the holiday?

Now, we walk through two empty villages with no open cafés; the third one has a bar open. We enter the empty dark tavern and ask if they serve any food. They say they can make us sandwiches. We ask for two, and an Orangina and a Perrier. We slide into a booth in the dark bar instead of eating outside in the afternoon heat.

We are served a baguette slathered in butter with sliced cheese. It tastes divine, maybe because someone else has prepared it for us. Even though we have eaten bread and cheese for lunch every day of this adventure, this tastes the best. It could also be that we are so hungry that any food would taste divine. The baguette dissolves in my mouth. The butter and cheese compete with my taste buds to be the queen of dairy.

Shouldering our packs, we still have fifteen kilometers to go.

The afternoon is warmer and warmer. Out in the open I'm happy to have my dorky sun hat. My feet hurt. Jim's feet hurt, even though his new boots feel much better than the old ones. Because we were in the dark bar for lunch, we did not get a chance to air out our feet and socks. We find the shade of a lone oak tree in an expansive hayfield. We sit on the edge of the trail and take off our shoes and socks, then place our socks in the sun. It's three forty-five in the afternoon. Usually, by this time of day, we have arrived and are relaxing in our hotel. But not today. Though the sun is still high in the sky, we have about an hour and a half to go, which is not long but *is* so long.

An hour later, we see the steeple of a cathedral in Metz, which makes me think about why people might become religious and worship the church. A steeple, when seen from afar, represents food, water, and shelter. We also see a high-rise apartment building on the outskirts of the city. We have not seen any high-rise buildings on this whole walk. The field and trail we walk on come right up to the edge of the complex. It turns out there are two high-rises. They are maybe ten floors high.

The GR5 runs on the sidewalk leading into the city, down toward the river. My feet are burning and sore walking on the pavement. The trail takes us through a fort that used to protect the city. I have no energy to read the plaque; I just want to get to our Airbnb.

I text our host and tell him we should be there in fifteen minutes. We walk alongside our old friend the Moselle River again. Definitive gray clouds gather in the west, their reflection on the river peaceful. I do have the energy to pull out my camera and take a few pictures.

Finally, we cut away from the river and the GR5 and head off to follow Google Maps. As we climb up through an alley, we enter a giant plaza, and in the center is the cathedral. It is massive, as long as two city blocks. I'm drawn to it, but don't have the energy or the time right now to seek its beauty. Tomorrow is our day off, and we will explore the city and the cathedral after resting.

We take a wrong turn, backtrack, and walk up a narrow cobblestone street. Halfway up the street, a petite man is sitting on a small folding chair. He stands when he sees us and waits.

"*Bonjour,* I'm Roland. You must be Kathy and Jim. This way."

He folds up the chair and opens a small door that has been cut into the gigantic door that used to let carriages in. Leaving the folding chair next to the bottom of the stairs, he leads us up three long flights and opens the door to our apartment for two nights. Thirty-seven kilometers is done. The longest day so far. We made it with the prayers and the songs of the congregation.

CHURCH, A PLACE TO MEDITATE (DAY 27)

At the end of our day off, and our last evening in Metz, we are invited for dessert and champagne at nine thirty—past our bedtime—by our Airbnb hosts, Roland and Marie. Their apartment is on the top floor of the four-story building. Roland is an architect and modernized their apartment. Its north side is a wall of glass facing the cathedral, which rises above all the other buildings in the city. While sipping champagne and nibbling on rose biscuits, we discuss the height restriction on the buildings. This restriction allows their view and all the other views of the cathedral to be retained forever. European cities are good at protecting the views of the historical buildings, at least in the old sections of the cities.

As we talk about their life in Metz, the black night quietly approaches, engulfing the city view. Then suddenly the floodlights flip on, bathing the cathedral in gold. Its beauty glows like the center of the sun out over the city. Our hosts worship it, and their words turn us to converts.

What is ironic is that the Metz Cathedral, or Cathédrale Saint-Étienne de Metz, is famous for its expanse of stained glass seen from the inside. It has the third tallest nave in France and the largest expanse of stained glass in the world. There are works from the medieval and renaissance periods all the way to modernity, represented by Chagall. Earlier in the day, I sat in a pew in the massive building, bathed in color. I couldn't help but feel the presence of a higher spirit.

But now seeing the outside of the monolith bathed in an amber glow, bedazzling the city, I'm in love. The champagne on my brain, the late hour, the glass wall, and the kindness of our hosts help amplify this feeling of love and appreciation of architectural beauty.

We have been on the trail for thirty days. In the last two days, we have walked twenty-seven kilometers then twenty kilometers, and today will walk twenty-seven again.

My lips are parched. I unzip the pocket on my backpack's hip belt and retrieve my Blistex sunscreen. The gel soothes my cracked lips and relaxes my shoulders. The intense late-May sun makes me stiff. You would think the sun would relax my muscles, but today I feel exposed and sensitive as if the sun is just too strong, so I tighten my shoulders to protect myself. This is the third day walking due south, parallel to the Moselle River, heading toward Liverdun. The GR5 then turns east, heading to the Alsace region and the Vosges Mountains, forming a backward *J* when looking at the map.

We are in open, poppy-lined wheat fields all morning. Jim sits on a boulder at an intersection and takes off his left shoe and sock. He massages his third and fourth toes. His toes have been bothering him for a few days, and he has found that massage helps. He stops three or four times a day when his toes are hurting. It worries me some, but he never complains. His allergies, exacerbated by the cultivated fields, also bother him, but again he never complains.

Walking empty farm roads, I feel lonely today. I'm a social person. I have many friends—running buddies, book groups, and women's groups. Connecting with friends is my mental health tonic. Besides Jim, I have not had a conversation with anyone in person since our cathedral lighting event.

As I walk up to a chapel at the edge of a small town I wonder, *Will this one be open?* We have already been in one church this morning. Most days, one church is enough for me, but it would be nice to get out of the heat of the sun for a bit. The Netherlands, Belgium, and Luxembourg had benches everywhere. France seems to have churches and chapels, which are good places to rest.

I try the worn wooden door, and it swings open. I turn and face Jim, who is a bit behind. I motion with my head that I'm going in, and he nods in agreement. I close the door to keep the cool air inside. There are two steps down into the chapel. It is empty of people like all of the country churches and chapels we have visited, except for the one on Whit Monday with the outdoor service.

I sit in the second-to-last pew. We have been visiting chapels, churches, and cathedrals since we started in Italy. At first, I would move around and read the plaques and pamphlets about the building and the art, but after a while, I felt like I could not absorb any more history, so I used the time to meditate.

I have a love-hate relationship with churches. I have a hard time with most of the Catholic and Protestant teachings. The history of violence and intensity to convert instead of respect for other religions turns me off. Throughout history, most religions have held women down and not allowed them to speak, and this bothers me the most.

It is the art and architecture of the entire church, both inside and out, that I love. I also appreciate the community that churches provide. I was part of a Unitarian church for many years in Harvard, and it was the community that I connected to.

Shockingly, hanging on the column in front of me is a casement of a bomb. I'm not sure if it is from WWI or WWII. This is the first time we have seen a bomb displayed in a chapel. *Is it a reminder? Was this chapel bombed and rebuilt?* Upon the wall to the right, old frescoes have been exposed, revealing its history. I notice a plaque by the door talking about the restoration, all written in French. Jim will read it.

I have no more room in my head for details and historical facts. It's enough for me to know there are people in this town who want to uncover and share the past.

I was brought up to learn more and more, to honor the scholars, to admire the academics, most of them white males. But it is too much. Too many blogs, newspapers, magazines, op-eds, books, fiction, nonfiction. There is too much information.

After taking in the pure white reflective light of this chapel, I close my eyes and keep them closed. I breathe and breathe. I follow my abiding breath in and out. I notice my feet are happy to rest. A tingling sensation runs along the bottom of my feet like the energy of kids let out to recess. My back muscles feel free and expanded with my pack off. But I still feel some tightness in my middle back from lifting my pack twenty times a day. Melancholy arises inside my body too, heavy in the bottom of my throat, putting pressure on my heart.

I hear Jim come in and quietly walk around.

What is the energy in this chapel? What is the energy of the faithful? I'm sure there is oppression, but I'm not going to focus on that. I can feel the sorrow of a woman who lost her child. There are lots of sorrows. There is also love. And there is a connection. This is a place where women came to be together. Two people talking creates connection. Connection makes us feel whole and grounded. I send compassion to my loneliness. I allow my loneliness.

I open my heart up to all the women who have gathered here. I send compassion to the ones who suffered or who are suffering. I wonder about the older women in this community now who still come every week to church. I would love to know their stories. *Do the younger women come to church? Are there any younger*

*women in this community? Have they all moved to the city? Are the
rural communities in the French countryside drying up?*

I bring my focus back to my eternal breath in and out, following, tracing, and being the breath for some unknown, incalculable
time. Meditating without a timer is freeing. I'm not waiting for
the timer to go off. I'm not controlled by external forces. I'm free
to meditate for as long as my being needs.

Slowly I creep back into my body. The physical tightness in
my middle back is still there, but the melancholy at the bottom
of my throat is gone. *Maybe I'm good company to myself?* I gently
open my eyes. The white light greets me. I sip my water and am
grateful for the cool air, a form of communion.

Jim studies the painting at the altar.

Without a word, we shoulder our packs. It's time to move on.
We walk out of the church together.

We walk out of town, not seeing a soul.

SLEEPING ON THE GR5
(DAY 31)

Two mornings later, we walk through the misty woods along the edge of a large pond and marsh. Yellow flag irises hide among the taller marsh grasses. Two white swans lazily float far across the pond in and out of the gray fog. I search carefully to see color in this muted landscape. The musky smell of rotting logs and decaying leaves reminds me of the cycle of life.

"Wow, look at this!" I exclaim. At our feet, hundreds of creatures pop up and down, like popcorn in a pan. I lean over to get a better view. A dull brown matching the dirt and the size of penny, they have tiny legs. "They're baby frogs. Don't step on them."

The wooded road looks like it's alive, undulating. *Had they hatched in the marsh and are now moving across the road to the pond?* There is no apparent direction of the frogs' movement; it's graceful chaos. I want to pick one up to get a closer look but decide to leave them be. "Look! What are they doing?" I point down the straight road that goes for more than a kilometer. A lone person in the distance stoops and stands, stoops and stands, like they are collecting seashells.

"It looks like they are collecting the baby frogs."

We pick our way down the path, careful not to injure the babies.

By the time we get up to where the forager had been, they have disappeared, like a ghost. Looking east and then west down the crossroad, we see no one.

"Where did they go?" I ask.

"I don't know. They vanished into the mist," says Jim.

"Do you think they were collecting the frogs for frogs' legs?" I ask. My stomach turns over.

"Maybe. But we have not seen any on menus."

"Maybe they collect them and raise them over the summer and then sell them to restaurants or markets," I speculate. "Have you ever eaten them?"

"No, but I hear they taste like chicken," he says with a smile.

We walk on in silence. I've come to appreciate the surprise moments of natural cycles we have witnessed on this walk. If we had walked here a week earlier or a week later, we would not have beheld hopping baby frogs.

In the late afternoon, entering the village of Vic-sur-Seille, we spot a woman in a white T-shirt and shorts sitting at a picnic table studying a map, her navy-blue backpack leaning next to her. My first thought is that she is brave to wear white. She is a large, confident woman in her early thirties from the Netherlands, and best of all, she speaks English. We sit across from her and chat. She walks two weeks each year along the GR5. She only has two more days, and then she is done for this year. We talk kilometers. She walks many more kilometers than we do each day. She likes to get up and get going in the mornings. Her name is Sabin.

"Wasn't that awful to walk over and over those downed trees just back a few kilometers in the woods?" she asks.

"We skipped that dogleg into the woods," Jim says. "We stayed on the country road because it cut off four kilometers, and the road was quiet walking."

"Well, that was smart. It was the worst logging mess I have seen."

For the last few days if there has been a shortcut, we take it.

We are both in agreement about experimenting with shortcuts. The shortcuts are small, saving us a kilometer here and there.

Today was the third one. We are never sure what we are missing, and I would hate to miss something important. But here we get a confirmation that our instincts are good.

We show her GAIA, our GPS app. "The more we use GAIA, the more we like it. I download the geographic maps. The French map has the GR5 marked with a purple line. It makes life easy," Jim says with a grin.

Then we study her map laid out on the picnic table. We complain about how hard it is to find places to stay.

"You should check out a website called Sleeping on the GR5. It's Dutch, but you can figure it out. It's a spreadsheet of all the accommodations in all the towns the GR5 passes through. I've used it every night."

"Thanks, we'll check it out," I say. "Where are you staying tonight?"

"Down at the campground on the other side of town," she answers.

"That's where we are staying too," I say. "We've rented a mobile home for the night." Part of me wants to invite her for dinner, but I hesitate. Jim and I have an underlying agreement that we will ask each other's permission before extending an invitation to someone new. I can't figure out how to pull Jim aside and ask him.

Maybe it is time to change our agreement? Jim can be a fussy old man sometimes. It's time for a change. It's time to trust each other's judgment and for me to speak up even if he isn't happy about it.

Sabin is young. *Does she even want to have dinner with old folks like us?*

Twenty minutes later, we wait in the office of the campground to register, watching wiry wet kids congregate in dripping bathing suits. The office also acts as an ice cream shop, selling popsicles and chocolate-covered ice cream on a stick. The kids finish paying for their treats. Part of me wants ice cream, but I'm thirty kilometers too tired to eat one. We finally register, and the owner of the campground, a short, slightly balding man with a black mustache, settles up with one more group of kids who have come in from the pool.

He then leads us into the campground, which is more of a trailer park. Colorful flowers cascade out of overflowing flower-boxes on most of the decks attached to the caravans and mobile homes. The narrow dirt roads are clean where they meet the manicured grass edges.

The owner guides us up the steps to a newer, nondescript gray mobile home and unlocks the door for us. It is bare and immaculate. There are two bedrooms and a living room/kitchen.

I'm excited to have two bedrooms and to sleep by myself. I used to feel bad about not wanting to sleep with Jim, but from research and talking with other women, I'm not alone. Many couples sleep better when they are not in the same bed. Traveling, we have not often had the luxury of two rooms. But tonight we have the luxury of sleeping in separate bedrooms in our mobile home, our castle for the night.

We unpack, put on our bathing suits, and head to the pool with the kids. I've been ferrying this bathing suit for a month now, and this is the first time I have needed it since Italy. I'm conflicted about carrying it. It's not an itsy-bitsy-teeny-weeny bikini. It's a one-piece that weighs six ounces. It is not one of those bathing suits for women that pulls your stomach in. I have one of those at home, but it weighed eleven ounces, so I left it behind. *Has the six ounces of extra weight been worth carrying?*

Loquacious parents lounge around the giant community pool overflowing with kids splashing around like bait being chased by a fish. Normally I would not go into a pool like this—it's just a little too crazy for me. But today it is hot, I'm tired, and the idea of floating in water sounds divine. We find a quieter corner in the deep end. I lay my head back with my ears below the waterline. All the sounds are muffled. The cool water lowers my body temperature. *What is it about water that feels so wonderful?* All day long on the trail we push forward. But here in the water, I'm cradled, held, and suspended in space. I feel every part of my body exhale and rest, even with the commotion all around. The extra six ounces is worth its weight.

I scrub some of the mud that is attached to my ankles above my sock line. It's hard to know the difference between the tan line and the dirt line.

Jim attempts to swim a few laps slowly, dodging the rambunctious kids. I climb out and dry off. I'm ready to lie down on my bed where it is quiet.

As I get to my towel on a chaise lounge, I see Sabin.

"Hi there, how is the water?" she asks.

"It is wonderful. Where are you staying?" I ask.

"I put my tent up at the end of the road next to the lake, which is more like a shallow pond. There are a few other tents there too. A few of us are eating dinner together."

I regret not inviting Sabin to join us for dinner. I make sure not to miss an opportunity again. Four days later, we have the chance to invite two other women from the Netherlands to have lunch with us. I have stayed in contact with them through Instagram over the years.

I will remember Sabin as the woman who I missed out on. I'd love to know how far she has walked each summer. *Has she finished the GR5?*

Around six thirty that evening, after a little nap, we walk back into town—one kilometer, but all uphill. The village looks out over the wide-open rolling farmland of the Seille Valley.

We find the only restaurant that is open besides a pizza place.

We sit outside in the Sunday evening sunshine next to a stone planter filled with sage, thyme, basil, and marjoram, close enough to smell the culinary potpourri. We are the only ones sitting outside. Compared to the crowded campground, the village is a ghost town. We peruse the daily menu while the waiter, who also happens to be the chef and owner, brings us two glasses of local wine. Tonight, we cherish the relaxed pace of dining.

We split an appetizer of foie gras on a bed of greens. The buttery rich earthiness sliding across my tongue contrasts brilliantly with the bitter greens. Foie gras is the quintessential luxury French food.

When I raised chickens for eggs in my back-to-the-land phase, I made chicken liver pâté from my chickens. I learned how to harvest my chickens from YouTube videos. Not wanting anything to go to waste, I made chicken liver pâté and stock from chicken feet. The pâté was okay, nothing spectacular, but what I made was not technically foie gras. I recently learned that foie gras is liver from ducks or geese that have been force-fed. It's a practice that has been going on since 2500 BCE by the Egyptians. I don't think I'll be eating foie gras again now that I know that they force-feed the geese.

The taste of the foie gras at the small brasserie, on a bed of spring greens the same color as the spring fields we have been walking through for the last month, will stay with me for the rest of my life.

The chef-owner glides over, delivering our main course with a flourish. In front of Jim, he presents a white plate with two small but thick slices of beef au jus and three new potatoes sprinkled with crispy shallots. My plate has a piece of delicate white fish with fresh peas served in a cream sauce. We nod our heads in thanks as he gracefully retreats. The flakes of fish dissolve in my mouth while the tender green peas burst with spring sweetness, offset beautifully by the velvety creaminess of the sauce.

"Oh, you have to try this," I say as I hold a fork balanced with fish, peas, and cream precariously in front of Jim. He opens his mouth. Then his lips close over my fork, taking in the gastronomic delight. He closes his eyes and smiles as the food dissolves in his mouth.

"Do you want a taste of mine?" he asks, his eyebrows raised.

We have always shared food. When we first started dating, Jim would put a little morsel of his food on his bread plate and politely pass it to me. Or he would put the food on his fork and turn the fork so that the handle was facing me like he was handing me scissors. He did not like it when I put a fork full of food in front of his face. Then, I thought his way of sharing food was stuffy and boring. But he has relaxed and become more playful over the years.

"No, thanks. I can see how it tastes," I say, refilling my fork with peas and fish.

We cannot communicate well with the chef-owner, but with hand gestures we show him it was the best meal we have eaten on our trip so far. I want to ask him about frogs' legs and how the frogs are harvested, but my French skills fail me.

We share a perfect crème brûlée for dessert. *How can eggs, cream, and sugar taste so good?* Simple, fresh, local ingredients made into soft creamy clouds contrast with shards of caramel sugar. With our taste buds satisfied, we skip back down to the campground on the edge of town. The pool is flat now, mirroring the calm lake behind. I wonder what all the kids are up to.

I sit out on the deck, watching the sky beginning to blush. Two carloads of people say good-bye to each other across our little "street." I don't understand what they are saying exactly, but I figure out quickly they are leaving for the week and will be back next weekend. The two moms hug each other while laughing. The two dads give each other air kisses on each cheek the way the French do. Most of these families come every weekend. They are not transient like us. There is another car with a family saying good-bye to the grandparents. It looks like the grandparents live here in the summer and the family comes on the weekends. This is a real summer community.

I miss my summer community: three families that come together for two weeks every year on an island off the coast of Massachusetts. Our kids have known each other since they were babies. The dads have known each other since they were kids. I love the way I can talk to the other moms when I first see them every year and it feels like we were chatting just the day before. I'll miss connecting to my women friends this year. But knowing and trusting that they will be there every year is a comfort.

The two cars drive out of the campground, arms waving out the windows at the neighbors. Ten minutes later, the grandparents stand at the end of their ten-foot-long driveway, waving while their children and grandchildren drive back to the city. A tear flows down my cheek.

It's a quiet evening as I walk into our temporary mobile home, kiss Jim goodnight, slip into my silk sleeping sheet in my bedroom, and sink into a deep slumber.

TREATS ALONG THE WAY (DAY 33)

I bite into golden custard studded with ham nuggets and supported by feathery crust. Quiche Lorraine in Lorraine. The salt, butter, and tang of cheese nourish my craving for salt. I'm back in town procuring breakfast and snacks for the day. Today we will go through a town that has a grocery store, and we will stock up on lunch supplies. Sitting outside of the town bakery, my mouth waters and I cannot wait for Jim to join me, so I eat one of the six coaster-sized quiches. On the second bite, I see Jim across the central square and give a wave. He joins me to drink coffee and enjoy our special breakfast before we are off under a cloudy sky to walk across the rolling hills of Lorraine to the *pays des étangs*, large ponds that were built in the Middle Ages to drain marshes and provide fish.

In the afternoon we watch white storks as we walk through a stork refuge where the birds have built large stick nests on platforms. Their prehistoric shape—long red legs, red dagger-like beak—and white-and-black plumage make an indelible print on my brain. I keep an eye out for babies being carried in their beaks the way Hans Christian Andersen storied about them. But we only see them feeding in marshy meadows on our way to Château d'Alteville, an eighteenth-century château owned by the same family since 1906, so very different from the mobile home of last night.

LORRAINE

After twenty-four kilometers, we walk between stone pillars onto a manicured gravel driveway ringed by a formal garden of peonies, lavender, and roses. The château is stucco with large windows framed with white shutters and wisteria vines climbing the walls. David and Annette serve a four-course dinner with three different wines under a sparkling crystal chandelier. We even have a brass chandelier hanging from an ornate ceiling medallion in our bedroom. We don't get to enjoy the gardens, as it rains all evening and into the next morning. After a leisurely breakfast, it's difficult to push ourselves out the door, but as soon as we start walking the rain stops.

At lunch we sit on a wooden bench in front of the church in the center of a small village called Fribourg. "Look what I have for you," Jim says, his eyes wide with excitement. He bends down and pulls out a pair of small glass jars filled with chocolate mousse. "A surprise treat," he says.

As if the bell tower is excited about the mousse, the bells chime twelve on cue.

"Where did you get these?" I ask, bending closer to him. My heart and stomach are delighted. Food is love.

"When we stopped at that grocery store yesterday in Dieuze. I bought them and hid them in my pack. I put them out on the ledge of the window last night to keep them cold."

"Sneaky of you," I say as I carefully peel the foil off the rim of the jar. I search in the top of my pack for a stashed spork. The chocolate creaminess plays in my mouth. After our regular picnic of cheese, bread, carrots, and apples, it's nice to have sweet ending to lunch. This is not Jell-O pudding in plastic cups. It is pure eggs, cream, and Belgian chocolate. And the glass jars bring French civility to our picnic. Quiche and mousse are not the only treats of Lorraine.

Three days ago in Liverdun, I had bought a jar of mirabelles, tiny golden plums. That same evening, I carefully opened the jar, extracted one soft drippy plum, and placed it in my mouth. The flesh melted away in plummy goodness, revealing a small pit the size of an olive pit but flatter. I offered Jim one, placing the plum on his tongue as my syrupy fingers grazed his lips. He loved the gesture but was not smitten with the fruit. So, I consumed the rest of the jar, as there was no way I was going to carry it in my pack.

We first learned about the tiny golden plums when we were in Metz talking with Roland, the Airbnb host. He spoke with reverence, "Oh, oh, oh, you will be walking through mirabelle country. Keep a lookout for small plums growing in backyard orchards. They are famous in this area. They are a delicacy, but they won't be ripe until August when they turn a deep golden color. You will have to come back to try them!"

Once I started looking for mirabelles, I spotted them everywhere. In almost every backyard we walked behind as the GR5 cut across the countryside, we found small dark green plums growing on fruit trees. I wondered, *Can I grow mirabelles in Vermont?*

After our sweet chocolate dessert, we continue on our way.

Later, in the afternoon, we walk along the Canal des Houillères de la Sarre next to a lake, surprised to have a canal and a lake next to each other. The channel offers up reflections of puffy white clouds bursting in a deep blue sky. A small blue workboat puttering along sends ripples through the reflected clouds.

On the grassy bank separating lake and canal, wild strawberries flourish, like little red jewels. Our pace slows as we stop to graze. A blast of intense sweetness explodes in my mouth with each handful.

"These are amazing. Here's a big patch of ripe ones," says Jim, stooping over intently.

I smile. Jim has never been a fan of picking berries. Over the years I've cajoled him into picking blueberries or raspberries with me. But here on the trail he transforms into a passionate picker.

Two women with packs catch up to us.

"*Bonjour*," I say.

"Hello," they say. They have big backpacks, and one has a green tent strapped on top.

"You speak English," I say.

"Yes, we are from the Netherlands. You are from the United States."

I'm surprised by their statement. *Have we met them before?*

"We walked with Sabin a few days ago, and she said she had met you," says the one with gray walking shorts.

"Yes, how far are you walking?" I ask.

"We walk about two weeks each year. We have three more days and then we are done for this year," one of the women says.

"Her daughter is expecting her first child, so we have to get back," the other woman says, pointing to her friend.

"You have a tent. Do you camp every night?" I ask.

"Yes, most nights. Do you remember all the rain last night? While we were walking into town looking for a place to set up camp, it started drizzling and a woman stopped and offered to let us set up our tent in her side yard. In the evening it started pouring. She made us come in and sleep on her couch. It was nice not to be out in the downpour."

I love hearing stories of human kindness, and I speculate about how our trip would be if we carried a tent and cooking equipment. Then I remember last night we stayed at the château, and I'm glad we are walking our walk.

"We'd better be getting on," one of them says. "We will see you on the trail."

That night we sleep in Le Love Shack, a round shack that looks like a hobbit built it. When entering, I duck my head. One twin bed sits on each side of the small room, which seems contrary to the idea of a love shack. As I drift off to sleep, the B-52s play loudly in my head.

The next morning when we walk over a rise, an expansive landscape paints the scene in front of us. Reverence hovers in the view. The winding road in the foreground curves through rolling green hills. In the near distance, the Vosges Mountains' enthusiastic blue peaks are silhouetted against the tranquil sky. We are leaving the Lorraine. Good-bye to baby frogs, nesting storks, quiche, mousse, and the mirabelles. Good-bye to poppy-edged wheat fields.

The GR5 enthralls me with her diversity and offers us treats along the way, like a grandmother spoiling her grandchildren.

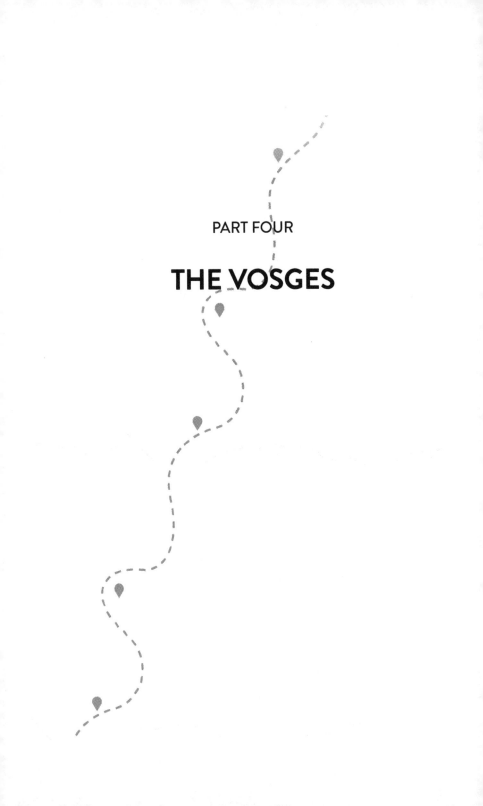

PART FOUR

THE VOSGES

SAVORING
(DAY 40)

The ferns can't be any greener as the filtered sunlight ignites their fronds across the forest floor. My legs brush by the ferns, releasing an ancient scent that mingles with the humus below my feet. After our first hour of walking, aches and stiffness give way to a footstep rhythm and flow. In this magical second hour, my body wakes up and finds its groove. The still air kisses my cheeks as I walk through the awesome beauty of the morning.

We are on the third day in the Vosges Mountains. The curvaceous GR5 meanders gradually uphill through conifer woods.

My heel lands on the soft pine needles, and my foot rolls gracefully forward onto its ball. Just like breathing, my footsteps are automatic now. But this morning, I choose to focus on the feelings in my feet, and the repetitive motion, like a metronome, lulls me into a state of being. I'm not thinking about what happened last night or ten years ago or where we might eat dinner tonight. I'm here in my body, every cell alive and alert—not alert for danger; alert for joy and grandeur.

I step from left foot to right foot over and over; my body is a pendulum, swinging ever so slightly back and forth to the rhythm of my breathing. I am one with my moving body. Like the ferns, I can't be any more present. I'm here.

The path through the ferns is really the absence of ferns. Ferns are ancient plants. They have been on Earth for over one hundred million years. I trust ferns. The trail and the ferns cross a quiet road and head into the woods. Gradually gaining height, the path widens to three feet across. To my right, I see a stone wall ten feet high in places. It's nothing like our gray New England stone walls. I stop and examine. The reddish oval stones, one foot tall and two or three feet long, are mostly covered with moss and blue-green lichen.

"Here's the Pagan Wall," I call to Jim, who is just catching up. We read about it last night in the guidebook. Now that we have entered the Vosges, we have a guidebook, as if the GR5 now has a partner to share information. The Mur Païen is ten kilometers long and was built in the seventh century. Archeologists argue whether it was built for religious reasons or defensive reasons—a mystery only the ferns know the answer to.

"I'm going to go explore it for a bit," Jim says.

"Okay, I'm going to hang here." I sit on one of the fallen stones and look closely at the sandstone. The conglomerate stones are made up of white, black, and brown pebbles varying in size from cherry pit to peach pit. Red sand is the matrix holding them together. Lichen tends to grow on the sand, not the clast, and dark green moss tends to grow on the top layer of stone or the few protruding stones. The beauty of the wall comes from looking at the spaces between stones. No mortar here—just irregular empty space created centuries ago but altered minutely here and there every year by the erosion of water and frost, the work of humans to build up and the work of nature to slowly reclaim.

Jim returns. "It does go on into the woods for a long way."

"Let's keep going. The convent is supposed to be up here somewhere soon," I say, gathering my pack. Ten more minutes of walking, and we hear motor buses and people chattering. Through the trees, we spy a parking lot filled with tour buses and cars.

I take a deep breath and ready myself for people. So many

different feelings gather inside of me. I'm grateful to the GR5 for taking us by all these historical and cultural sights. I feel shocked by all the people after my quiet time in the woods. And I feel proud and maybe a little cocky that we walked here using only our own energy and did not take a tour bus.

We march through an arched tunnel to an inner courtyard ringed with pink sandstone buildings, the same color as the Pagan Wall. This is the convent of Mont Sainte-Odile. I'd read the story from the eighth century: Odile was born blind, then she miraculously could see again. Her father tried to marry her off, but she ran away and started the convent to help others. Blind people still come to visit her sarcophagus in the twelfth-century chapel.

We enter one of the smaller chapels. The ceiling is a mosaic of scenes from the Bible. I recognize the birth of Jesus and the crucifixion. The ceramic tiles are the size of my pinky fingernail. The intricate detail and kaleidoscopic range of colors make it one of the most beautiful ceilings I have ever seen. The blue glaze matches the outside blue sky perfectly. Built into the ceiling's center is a smoky glass square that allows natural light to illuminate the images. There are two signs in the chapel asking people not to talk, but a cluster of people in the corner are chatting away in their native tongue. I hold my finger up to my lips and point to the sign. They are quieter for thirty seconds and then begin to chat again. I'm irritated. This is a sacred place, as sacred as the fern forest. I don't like that they are being disrespectful, and on top of that, I cannot communicate effectively with them. Rage rolling through me, I exit out into the sunshine.

After calming myself by taking in the panoramic view of the Rhine Valley from the formal gardens, we head downhill through woods, vineyards, and villages of the Alsace. The GR5 did her part in sharing cultural and historical sights today. All the while the walking in the woods was delicious.

Later that evening, we finish dinner outside in the town square of Andlau. I love the way the restaurants sprawl out into the center squares with umbrella tables. The sun is so low at eight thirty that the umbrella is useless, but I don't mind, as the evening sun on my tired shoulders has the touch of a masseuse. The central fountain lulls me into a deeper state of relaxation. I order dessert, as I've always wanted to try a chocolate *liégeois* and this is the first time I have noticed it on a menu. Jim orders one too. We don't feel like sharing tonight. Just saying the name *liégeois* is sexy and yummy.

"*Voilà,*" the waiter says. He places a tall frosty glass on a small plate with a long spoon in front of me and one in front of Jim. *Liégeois* is part sundae and a part milkshake. In slow motion, I pick up the spoon and scoop out a bit of chocolate ice cream and a smidge of milk. Chocolate ice cream and frozen bits of butterfat from the milk flow over my tongue. In moments to come, the butterfat will melt, multiplying the ecstasy. I'm relishing a chocolate *liégeois*. Eating with relaxed pleasure has not always been my way.

In middle school and high school, I was incapable of enjoying cookies and sweets because I scarfed them down so fast. I did enjoy the first three bites of chocolate and sugar, but then I would drop into the fog of overeating. I was trying to fill a void and numb the angst and shame I felt related to my struggles with dyslexia.

My paternal grandmother was an alcoholic, which caused my family shame and hurt. She was a lovely and warm grandmother, but her dark sadness hid inside the folds of her skirt. I had always been cautious around alcohol. Food became my obsession to numb the hurt.

In college, just before midnight, when the IGA closed, I would saunter in looking for ice cream or Freihofer's cookies. I would buy carrots along with them to camouflage the shame I felt for buying the "bad food." I never made eye contact with the cashier under the bright fluorescent light. Out in the empty parking lot, concealed in my Chevy Chevette, I would stuff the cookies in my mouth, not tasting a thing. The sugar and the chocolate calmed my nerves. The treats became the love and comfort I craved. It was an attempt to fill the loneliness and the shame from struggling in college.

When I went away to college, I mistakenly believed that I had outgrown dyslexia. I figured if I could graduate from a so-called prestigious high school, I could handle what lay ahead. I was done with dyslexia, but it was not done with me. Dyslexia followed me to college. Not having my mother there to read aloud my textbooks the way she had in high school and not having the extra help from teachers, I tumbled and floundered. After hours and hours in the library alone struggling to get through chapters and more chapters, I turned to food. I struggled with overeating on and off for decades.

In my early fifties, I became an Eating Psychology Coach and started my own business, intending to heal myself and others who struggled with food. Working on my final project to become certified, I read one of Brené Brown's books and learned that shame cannot last if it is brought out into the light. Even though I had come to terms with my dyslexia, I still hid it from the world, pretending to be normal. I had never brought up dyslexia when I talked with friends. My best friends had no idea I had dyslexia.

Brené Brown also wrote about self-compassion as the antidote to shame and referenced Kristin Neff as the expert. Fireworks went off in my head. That night I signed up for Kristin Neff's Mindful Self-Compassion (MSC) training. My complex story fell into place. The shame from dyslexia was a deep wound. When I felt not good enough—for example, when I sat down to write—it would trigger old deep feelings. I would reach for food to soothe uncomfortable feelings.

After taking the MSC class, practicing for a year, completing the teacher training, and finally teaching MSC, I became competent in self-compassion. I could recognize uncomfortable feelings that we all have—shame, loneliness, fear. I could give myself compassion and self-kindness instead of eating the cookies to numb my emotions.

I have befriended the dragon of overeating, seeing the desire to overeat as a message from my body that emotions need to be dealt with. Don't get me wrong. Sometimes when I'm not embodied, I still numb out with my drug of choice, cookies. I have had absolutely no desire to overeat while on this walking adventure. None.

The final component of healing overeating is learning to relish the food. I learned this slowly over the years. The crescendo of my learning was when we were on our preamble in Sicily. I watched an eighty-year-old woman who sat next to us at an outdoor café. She sat with her face to the sinking sun, her black leather purse carefully placed on the small empty café chair. Her stylish wool coat over her even more elegant gray wool dress kept her warm on the cool April day.

She ordered an espresso and a slice of almond chocolate torte. She seemed to know the tall, lean waiter. They bantered back and forth in Italian. *Did she come here every day at four?*

When her espresso and cake were presented, she sipped her espresso first. Then she slowly began to eat her cake. She was enjoying her cake, but she was not fixated on it. She watched the crowds shuffle by. She was relaxed and present. Her exquisitely made-up face was calm. No stress marks deepened her scattered wrinkles.

After relishing the last bite of torte, she carefully used the tiny spoon to scrape out every last drop of the espresso. I watched her go inside to pay her bill and then disappear into the crowd. I silently wished her well. *Thank you, wise woman, for showing me the way.*

Walking across Europe has given me the time to practice savoring all the delights. I'm an expert now. I use the tall, slender spoon to scrape out every last drop of chocolate *liégeois*. I'm full and content in infinite ways.

My hunger for walking, pure food, beauty, connection with my partner, and alone time is satiated. The GR5 becomes the wise woman showing me the way.

We walk back to the hotel, and I savor the evening light, when even pebbles have long shadows.

FEELING STRONG
(DAY 41)

After six weeks of walking on rolling hills, I'm finally feeling strong. I enjoy going uphill, especially in the morning. We are in a rhythm now. We climb out of a village, into the mountains, and then walk along ridges or up and down smaller mountains. In the later afternoon, we walk downhill for two or three hours into the next village.

Jim and I have found our pattern of the day. Most days, we walk apart from each other for about two or three hours. We talk if we need to figure out which way to go, but we are quiet other than that. Either he is ahead, or I'm ahead. We are usually in sight of each other, but we both enjoy a quiet time. We have been together for three months 24/7, not to mention the last twenty-seven years. *Really what more can we talk about?*

Our routine of walking separately started on the third day of walking. That morning, we had set off late from the village of Commanster, Belgium, as we had been making reservations for the days ahead. This had taken longer than we anticipated. Right away, Jim stopped to take a picture and then a video of an anthill. I kept going, not being interested in the anthill that day. Mostly I was annoyed that we had started so late. I walked about half a kilometer ahead of Jim for the next hour through wide-open farmland on a narrow country road that divided the landscape; yellow dandelions lined the pasture on one side, young green wheat on the other. Not one car passed us. Eventually, I came into a tiny village with an intersection. I set my backpack down on a picnic table in the shade and gulped water. Jim showed up five minutes later. We did not plan this; it just happened. Ever since that day, we walk separately together for the mornings, then hang together in the afternoons.

I love our rhythm of walking, and Jim does too. The time alone gives me space to walk the interior landscape of my mind and heart.

Later, back home in Vermont, I look back at the marriage vows we wrote decades ago and find a quote from the poet, Rainer Maria Rilke:

> A marriage is not a matter of creating a quick community of spirit by tearing down and destroying all boundaries, but rather a good marriage is that in which each appoints the other guardian of his [or her] solitude. . . . Once the realization is accepted that even between the closest human beings infinite distances continue to exist, a wonderful living side by side can grow up, if they succeed in loving the distance between them.

I have succeeded in "loving the distance between" us because it was born of trust and respect. The GR5 has shown this to be true.

This morning Jim is up ahead. When there is an intersection, he waits until I have seen which way he is going. We have another system too. The person out front checks the GPS and looks for waymarks, and the person behind just follows. Again, it just happened.

Once in a while I double-check that we are going the right way when he is in the lead. He would say that I don't trust him, and sometimes I don't. I'm a better observer. I distinguish details better than he does—at least in nature, maybe not in house projects. Picking blueberries with my mother gave me practice discerning the shades of blue to know the true ripe ones, and birdwatching with my father helped me to become an astute observer. Jim is more in his head, more intellectual. Sometimes he misses waymarks, and we get on the wrong track. Then, I get a feeling that something is not right, my internal GPS says that we are not on the right path, and I check the external GPS. Most often we need to go back and find the correct turn.

Around here it is tricky. There are forest logging roads throughout these woods. The GR5 follows them some of the time, but she also forks off onto a single track. If we are not paying attention, we can easily miss the turn. The GR5 is sly. She tests our observation skills. She seems to say, *Honey, can you keep up? Trust me, and I'll take you on a walk of a lifetime.*

This morning we climb Mount Ungersberg, 901 meters (2,960 feet). The next intersection has a sign saying how much time it will take to get to the top: "1 hr., 15 min." In the United States, the signs tell you how many miles to a specific place. In Europe, the signs show distance in kilometers and often time in hours and minutes. The times on the signs are there more when there is a big elevation change. We will see more and more of these signs.

We also have the distance on our GAIA app. Now that our feet are broken in and I feel completely healed from my sickness, we know our pace. We walk fifteen minutes per kilometer on average. It makes life easy, because in one hour we can cover four kilometers, including small stops.

It is eleven in the morning. If my pace is the same as the sign, I will get to the top at twelve fifteen. My body starts buzzing as my competitiveness opens up. I pick up my pace. Stretching out my stride uses my muscles in a different way, and I feel zippy. The temperature is rising. Luckily, we are in the shade of a beech forest. But even so, sweat drips down my face.

I look ahead; Jim has picked up his pace too. He is three switchbacks in front of me. The trail is steeper, and I feel good. The birds sing loudly, filling me with energy, as if their songs were Gatorade. I pass by big patches of purple foxglove growing where the soil has been disturbed. I think about the foxgloves that grew in my garden in Harvard. I miss my garden, but I don't miss the work it took to keep it beautiful. I'd much rather walk and experience the purple foxgloves without having to do a thing for them to grow.

I take my pack off and pull out my purple headband, the color of the foxgloves. I put it on to keep the sweat from dripping into my eyes. Since I have my backpack off, I drink from my water bottle. Checking GAIA, I see that there are no more intersections until we get to the top. The trail just zigzags up, and so must I.

I have not felt this full of energy in ages. I feel like I did in my thirties. My sense of physical power fuels my emotional power, and the two glide me up the mountain. Even as the trail gets steeper, I pick up my pace again. My body pulses with energy as I ascend. I'm in the flow today. I feel like Wonder Woman. High on life. High on walking. High on a mountain. High on endorphins.

It occurs to me that I'm finally through the transition of menopause, at fifty-seven. For eight years, I've been working on supporting the transition as smoothly as possible. It's a wild hormonal transition from a fertile body to a not-fertile body.

I remember at two in the morning on a rainy night six years ago, I lay in my bed experiencing the traditional night sweats and sleeplessness. Sweat formed on the back of my neck and dripped onto my pillow, creating a damp spot on the soft cotton. I felt each drop form and fall away from me. *Drip, drip, drip.* Outside, it poured rain. Inside, my body poured sweat, heat pouring out of me until none was left. I felt lost, empty, and out of control. I remember thinking, *Maybe this is the old me pouring out, and the new me waits to be filled in or filled up. I will allow it to happen.*

The great thing about menopause is I get to choose what I fill myself back up with. I can fill up with regret, heaviness, and old feelings, or I can fill up on kindness, compassion, wisdom, and acceptance. I intentionally choose the latter.

I've worked on my emotional health by learning and practicing self-compassion. I've worked on my spiritual health by meditating, reading, and writing. One of the books that I read, by Susun Weed, an herbalist, talked about not exercising too much during the transition. I learned from her to listen to my body. I stopped running. Now I have come through the other side. I have energy. I am powerful. Listening to my body has worked. My body is grateful for my listening and rewards me with her power.

I pull out my phone while I walk and record a short video about how great I'm feeling. I call myself Breathless Kathy because I huff and puff while talking into my phone. I feel energized making the video. It inspires, and maybe one day I will put these videos together as a film about the trip.

I look up the hillside and see the trees thinning out four switchbacks ahead. I'm almost there. Anticipation fuels my fire.

I need to remember that we still have fourteen kilometers of walking this afternoon. *Should I back off the pace? Naaah, keep going. This is fun.*

Breathing hard. Sweat dripping off my nose. The trail swings around to the left and rises straight up to a flat area. There is no more up. I feel triumphant, like I'm standing on air. Jim is there sitting on a downed tree. I glance at my phone. Eleven forty-five. Really? I look again. Yes, eleven forty-five. I beat the time on the sign. And not by just a little. I flew up the mountain. My body is humming. I'm over being sick and more importantly I'm strong, not a youthful strong but a wise strong. The English language needs more words for *strong*, just the way the Eskimos have so many words for snow.

I look around. There is no view. Disappointment drags me down a bit. Jim points to an old fire tower platform twenty feet high. "Let's eat up there," he suggests. Even on top of the platform, there is no view, as the trees have grown up.

We free our feet from socks and shoes. Pulling out the insoles, we lay them in the sun to dry. The sunshine on my pale, tender feet feels therapeutic.

Jim pulls the muenster cheese from the plastic bag. Its strong scent accosts my nose. I'm not sure which smells stronger, our sweaty socks or the cheese. But this local muenster tastes delicious with the salami and bread that we bought this morning at the bakery and *fromagerie*. I lie back and stretch like a cat in the sunshine.

We have three to four hours of solid walking this afternoon. We ramble down the other side of the mountain, cross roads, and start climbing again. Eventually, two hours later, we come to a castle ruin, Château du Bernstein, a thirteenth-century castle. The roof is off like a doll house, but the walls and round towers built of massive stone still stand.

We put our packs down on a picnic table next to one of the towers. I take my shoes off again to rest my feet. Jim goes off to explore the abandoned castle. I lie down on my back, facing the sky and raising my feet in the air. My feet stand on the blue floor of the sky. My calf muscles relax as the blood flows out of my strong legs.

I decide to check out the castle and slip on my Allbirds so I can give my feet a few more minutes of rest out of my walking shoes. I shuffle into the main room and look up. Jim is four floors up, gazing out of the tower.

"Come on up," he yells. "The view is spectacular, looking out over the red-roofed villages."

I'm tired, and I just can't walk up four flights of stairs when I should rest, but there is finally a view. *Do I listen to my body, which says no, don't do it? Do I listen to my critical self, which says you are here; you should do it?* I climb one flight of stairs, and I have a partial view of the valley below. Sitting on the top of this staircase, I take a few pictures. My body says, *Don't go up any higher.* I listen to her. I call up to Jim, "Take some pictures for me. I can't go any further."

We walk for another hour and come to a second abandoned castle. In the guidebook, it says to be careful if you go walking around this castle, as parts of it may crumble. That's enough for me to find some shade and sit down. Jim goes off to explore. I'm annoyed he has so much energy. Maybe I used up too much climbing the mountain earlier. My euphoria from this morning has vanished.

I open the top of my pack and reach inside, looking for my knife. My hand touches a cellophane bag. *What's that?* I pull it out. A cellophane bag filled with melted chocolate. I forgot we bought these this morning. In the bakery where we bought the bread, they also sold fancy chocolates. We bought six: two filled with liquor, two nut ones, and two raspberry ones. The liquor has separated and is pooled at the bottom of the bag. I stick my finger in and scoop up some liquid chocolate. It tastes divine. I hold the bag up to my mouth and pour a little of the liquor into my mouth. *Whoo.* The liquor burns going down my throat.

How did we forget about the chocolates? It's not like us to forget about chocolate. I must have been consumed by thoughts of strength and power.

Fifteen minutes later, Jim returns, and I present the chocolate to him. He flashes me a smile and consumes. We shoulder our packs once again and are on our way into town for the last four kilometers of a twenty-five-kilometer day.

As we approach the valley floor, I turn to look back towards the mountains. The two castles are silhouetted against the blue sky—castles in the air. When you climb, or hike, or walk, i.e., do the work, the castles are no longer in the air; you are on the ground level with them. For most of my life I had extravagant hopes to experience an epic adventure, but I never thought it would be possible. Now I'm doing it. I've brought the castles in the air down to earth. I've made an extravagant and preposterous dream come true. This knowing brings me joy and possibility. What other castles in the air can I make come true?

Turning to look ahead, I see a few steeples of the town we are heading for. *But look at this! Right now we are entering a cherry orchard.* Not old or abandoned, but active. The trees drip with dazzling cherries! Each tree tries to outdo her sister by showing off her ruby jewelry. I smile and look at Jim.

"Look what I grew for you!" he says with a grin and a flourish of his hand outstretched to the trees.

"Wow, you are amazing," I answer with love in my voice.

I look to see if anyone is around. I hear a tractor engine rumble at the far end of the field. *I don't mind picking from wild or abandoned cherry trees, but is picking from an active orchard stealing? Yes, probably. But I'm going to do it anyway.* I reach out and fill my hand with cherries and yank. I walk on, examining my treasures. Each one is shaped like a heart and the color of the traditional valentine heart, deep blood red.

I place one in my mouth. My teeth squish through the meaty flesh just shy of the pit, as the tart sweetness explodes in my mouth. Walking, eating, replenishing my system, I notice Jim is not eating any. *He is a good boy,* I think to myself sarcastically. He respects the people who own the orchard. We come to the end of the orchard. I want to fill my backpack with the jewels, but that would be stealing. I tell myself that what I'm doing is grazing or gleaning.

As we leave the orchard, we enter the edge of Châtenois, which is a large town. The route now is a sidewalk along a busy road with cars whizzing by. I look at GAIA; our hotel is on the other side of town. My feet hurt. My legs hurt. My whole body is worn out. My energy level is almost in the negative. Those cherries fueled me for a kilometer, but I still have two more to go.

I fantasize about calling a taxi. I could try to figure out the bus system. I could put out my thumb, but my French being so limited makes me think hitchhiking is a bad idea. I keep walking.

We are in the Alsace region of France now. Cobblestone streets are lined with stucco timber-framed houses elaborately decorated with overstuffed, multicolored window boxes. Each house is like the cherry trees, trying to outshine his neighbor. The second floor of buildings on the main street jut out over the sidewalk. We learn that they built them this way to avoid taxes because they were taxed on the footprint of the building.

We arrive at our hotel, which is an ancient-looking building from the sixteenth century. At the entrance to the attached rustic dining room, a dark-haired, wiry young man checks us in at a small desk. Black beams that could be five hundred years old hold up the low ceilings. Cool and dark, the room smells musty, but I can also smell onions—the beginnings of dinner cooking in the back kitchen.

"Dinner starts at seven. Here is the Wi-Fi password. Your room is on the third floor," he says in very clear English. We learn later that he attended hotel school in Switzerland last year and plans to take over the hotel when his grandfather cannot run it any longer. It warms my heart to know that the hotel will stay in the family.

We thank him and shoulder our packs for the final time. I amble up the carpeted wooden steps. The first and second flights are wide and grand. The last flight is up a narrow back staircase that twists and turns. There are only three rooms up here. I fit the old skeleton key in the lock and open the door to a hot, stuffy, small room with a double bed in the center.

Jim opens both windows to let the light breeze crawl through. Without unpacking or washing my socks, I lie down on the bed; every muscle I own aches. The unknown bed embraces my body, easing my weariness.

There are four stages to becoming a super-walker. The first is being able to walk for a whole day. I worked up to that in Vermont and Italy. Second is being able to walk day after day, and third is being able to walk week after week, a mega-walker. The final stage is feeling strong enough to walk up mountains every day. I'm still working on the pacing of this, but I know my wise and powerful body will get there if I keep listening to her, respecting her, and feeding her cheese, chocolate, and cherries.

TAKING SHELTER IN A SHRINE (DAY 43)

All night, I hear rain pounding on the windowpanes as I walk in and out of dreams. In the morning, a rosy mist greets us as we climb out of the Alsace village of Ribeauvillé on a trail running diagonally up the side of a forested valley. Within fifteen minutes, we come to an open area where the trail vanishes. An ashen mudslide has covered the path entirely for about forty feet. The landslide must have happened last night or early this morning. From the absence of footprints, it looks like we are the first ones to try to cross it. Jim is in the lead. He tests the waters—or should I say mud—with a tall, fat stick to see how deep it is. On the edge, it is five inches deep. He picks his way across the sludgy debris, placing his feet on rocks and sticks when he can.

I follow more tentatively, pulling out my walking poles to help support me across the mucky river of detritus.

In the middle, I put my foot down, and it keeps going. The mud oozes over the top of my walking shoes and clings to my socks like a child to her mother. The next step is luckily onto a rock. But pulling the right foot from its resting place deep down under takes all the strength I have. Finally, my shoe releases from the mud with a *shloop*.

I step onto solid ground and exhale my nervousness. The mud in the middle was not the two feet deep that I had feared.

Looking back, I see that what shook me up was the worry

before crossing. *How deep will it be? Is it dangerous?* Later, in the Alps, we will pass over an avalanche slide, and I will have the same feelings before crossing. In life I've had many bridges to cross, and it is the apprehension that brings me down, not the actual crossing. The practice of getting across to the other side unscathed has given me confidence. I'm hopeful that when I come to new potential bridge crossings, I will keep my worry in perspective. My intention is to observe my uneasy feelings and check to see that I can be present with them and not ruled by them.

Jim is bent over with his pack on. He diligently but futilely scrapes the cement-like mud off his shoes and socks with a flat rock. Ten minutes later, we come to big puddles on the forest road. We wade into the pools just far enough to wash the rest of the mud off our shoes, but not so deep that water seeps over the tops of our shoes. I scrub with a pine branch. The mud does not want to let go. My shoes kept the water out; the Gore-Tex has done its job. My socks are damp, but not soaked.

The trail continues to climb for another two hours through the deep conifer woods. As we climb higher and higher, the mist floats above us in stripes but also below us deep in the valley. The monoculture forest of pine trees is more crop than ecosystem, the tall trunks all growing straight and all the same diameter, like spindles on a Shaker railing. When I look out, the wet black trunks look like the warp of a loom and the tendrils of mist snake in and out of the trunks like the weft, creating a black and white weaving. The neon lichen and moss-covered boulders on the sides of the path hold a miniature world for ants and spiders. Young ferns grow out of cracks and depressions in the eroding rocks.

I'm awed by the eerie feeling of this spirit world and grateful to be part of the tapestry of the forest.

Up ahead, Jim stops and takes off his pack at the top of a ridge. There is no more up, at least right now, but we are still in the pine woods. I climb the outcrop of rocks that serves as a summit. The rocks form a semicircle, like a chair for sitting. A big chunk of rock has been plucked away centuries ago by a glacier. Over time it has been smoothly eroded into a curved backrest.

"It's the King's Throne," says Jim as he sits with his hands on his knees looking over his kingdom.

"That's right. I remember reading about it last night."

"But it is wet," he says, standing and reaching for his pack.

I nod.

"Pastry time." Jim carefully opens the zipper to the top pocket of his pack and slides out a large cheese Danish in the shape of a heart. The cream cheese glistens and glows under a glaze of syrup against the backdrop of wet tree trunks and gray rock. It's as if Jim holds the moon in his hands.

"Your turn to cut, my turn to pick," I say, fishing in my pack for my knife.

We sound like children, but this our little game. The act of walking and being free from normal adult expectations has loosened our souls and allowed us to be children again—stomping in puddles, sitting in thrones, and demanding fairness in food.

Jim and I are both the oldest in our families. This has brought friction over the years of our marriage, but we also understand each other. The competition of wanting to be first or best resides in both of us. Over the years we have discovered that one way of noticing it and toning it down is by using humor and turning it into a game.

Silently we enjoy our pastry in this magical pine forest kingdom.

For the next hour, the trail leads us down and up along the ridge, like a roller coaster. We eventually come into the small village of Thannenkirch, the highest village in the Vosges Mountains. We move on, out of town, heading south, although it is hard to tell as the dark clouds seem to be getting lower and lower and there is no sign of the sun anywhere today.

Back on a forest road we walk side by side, talking here and there. Drops of rain begin to fall. In less than a minute, it is raining—not misting or drizzling. We put on our pack covers for only the second time of the trip. My pack changes from purple to bright green. Jim's transforms from sky blue to gray. I'm trying to decide if I should put on my raincoat. My wool T-shirt keeps me warm, and I think it will be too hot if I have my raincoat on. I tell myself, *The rain will stop shortly like it has every other day we have walked. And we will dry out like we have every other day that it has rained.*

An hour later, the rain has not stopped. I feel the raindrops rolling down my forearms, navigating around each hair and goose bump, then dropping away off my fingers. I finally dig out my raincoat, and it warms me up a bit.

We pick up our pace to stay warm. We walk gradually uphill as the temperature goes down. Is it the change in elevation or the storm bringing in colder air?

My socks are soaking now. At least the mud has washed off my shoes. My shorts are wet. My wool T-shirt is damp. I'm hungry. The motion of walking is not enough to keep me warm anymore.

I pull out my phone to see how much further we must walk today. But my phone will not read my fingertips on the passcode. It is supposed to be water-resistant. I wipe it and my fingers off with the driest part of my wool T-shirt, but it still doesn't work.

"I can't get my phone to work," I call up to Jim.

He slows down and tries his. He has kept his in a plastic bag, but he cannot read the map through the heavy plastic. We both lean over his phone to create a little shelter from the fat drops. He takes the phone out of the plastic bag, wipes his fingerprints carefully, and tries his passcode. It doesn't work. He tries again. This time it works. We still have nine more kilometers to walk. We look for shelter anywhere on the map but do not see any until we get into town.

The raindrops are finding ways to get to the phone. He places the phone back in the plastic. And we keep going.

The rain is relentless. I'm a bit worried about getting hypothermia.

We stop under a dense spruce tree, hoping it will give us a little shelter. I pull out the salami and cheese. Jim pulls out his knife and cuts a few slices of each. By the time I take a bite, both are slimy and soggy. "This is not going to work. Let's keep going," I say.

Quickly we put the food away. We get one more slice of each into our hollowed stomachs. We keep walking as we chew the wet cheese and salami. I will remember in the future, *Slice up the salami when it looks like it might be a rainy day.*

Around a corner there is a closed-up refuge that has seen better days. We look for a place to get under cover, but there is no over-hang on the building. There is a shed out back, but it is locked.

Discouraged, we continue walking. The forest road now cuts into the bank of the hillside as it contours around the ridge. Sometimes we are in the forest, and sometimes we are out in the open. If it were not raining, we would have beautiful views of valleys and mountains to the south.

I'm in the lead. The narrow road, made up of sharp gravel, curves around to the left. I look left at the wall of exposed gray bedrock. Just up ahead is an opening. As I get closer, I see that it is a shrine built into the rock outcropping. I slip into the narrow three-walled alcove with a roof and no door.

"Look at this. This will work as a place to shelter," I yell over my shoulder to Jim.

"Wow, this is cool," he says as he enters.

It is tight, about the size of a phone booth or a confessional booth—just enough room for us to both stand and bring our packs in out of the rain. On the back wall is a three-foot statue of Mary with her arms stretched out. She is welcoming us, adorned in her majestic blue-and-gold robes. If we were her size, there would be plenty of room.

I extract my warm wool shirt, buried at the bottom of my pack, peel off my soaking bra and T-shirt, and don the cozy long-sleeved layer. I could put on my puffy jacket, but it is not that cold and I don't want it to get wet, as I may need it later. My wool hat replaces my wet purple headband. My transformation is complete.

Feeling warmer now, we pull out cheese and bread to eat. I long to sit down to rest my legs, but there is no place to sit. It seems disrespectful to lean my butt on the shelf where Mary, mother to all, is delicately shining. Also, I might knock her over and I want to honor the artist who worked diligently to carve and paint her. *Who created this shrine? How many others have found shelter here?*

This is a part of Catholicism that I can't wrap my head around—a religion that worships Mary but does not allow women to be priests? Catholicism has been around since the Middle Ages, even before France was France. But maybe it is time to shift and change. *If Mary is powerful, why not let today's women use that power for the good of the church and the good of humanity?*

The walls of rock are straight, and as I look up, I see that water is dripping down on us. It is not a completely dry shelter, but it is better than being out in the deluge.

I try my phone again. It still does not work. Even though it is water-resistant, it does not read my fingerprints, so it is useless. I will have to keep it in a plastic bag from now on. Forty-three days on the trail and we are still learning. Our phones have been indispensable, holding our GPS and guidebooks, but if they don't work in the rain, they are useless. I see why other walkers still rely on paper maps.

Jim tries his phone again. It works. We have walked twenty-three kilometers already today, and we have four kilometers to go, mostly downhill.

An icy tingle jumps from one shoulder blade to the other as I begin to shiver. My blood is around my stomach, trying to digest the food, not helping to keep me warm. It's time to get moving, as the drips from the rock ceiling are coming down faster and faster.

"Let's get going," I say, tapping my foot up and down. "Thanks for sheltering us," I turn and say to Mary in a reverent tone as I hoist my pack and step out into the storm.

We have seen many shrines of Mary in Luxembourg and France, some with lit candles and fresh flowers out in the middle of the countryside. The Catholic religion is embedded in the fabric of the country. I'm growing to appreciate and venerate these shrines of Mary. My mind and spirit absorb the faithful French devotional energy.

Twenty minutes later we come to a rolling misty meadow that looks out over the valley. The clouds dissolve and the rain slows, revealing layers of gray and green. The deep green of the field is at its peak of intensity, and the green of the trees in the distance is a light but glowing green like the lichen earlier today. The earth is rebirthing.

Down, down, we loop along the sides of the valley, through cow pastures and along hayfields, like marbles rolling down a maze. We see the steeple of the church before we see anything else from the town. If I ever do this walk again, I will keep track of how many churches, cathedrals, chapels, and shrines we encounter. But now, as we walk by the church, we don't even think about going inside. We just want to get to the hotel.

The main street has two restaurants, one other hotel, and a bakery. We plan to stop there in the morning to replace our soggy bread.

From the outside, our hotel looks like a traditional village hotel. We check in. They tell us our room is in the new building out back. We walk across a manicured lawn to a modern wood and black metal structure with massive triple-glazed windows. The room has clean lines with white walls and shiny wood floors. A large balcony allows us to hang our dripping clothes in the sun that has just come out. The sun always comes again.

FORMAL RECEPTION
(DAY 49)

Six days later we are climbing Ballon d'Alsace, the highest point in the southern Vosges. The GR5 rises and falls along the ridge like the graph of a sine wave, and so do we. Off to the left and down below is a cold and lonely lake, Lac des Perches. The banks of the lake rise sharply up to the ridge. Only the very rugged would take a detour and bushwhack down to it. Maybe the lake enjoys the solitude. Only visited by the local animals, it stays protected and pristine. I'm happy to keep my distance and to admire it from above.

Because we are already on the ridge, we do not have many meters to climb up. I read in the guidebook that, for part of the time today, we will be walking along the divide between the North Sea watershed and the Mediterranean watershed. *Once we cross over the divide, does that mean there is no going back?*

If I were a drop of water and rolled down the south side of the divide, I would flow into the Rhône River and eventually flow to the Mediterranean. That drop of water has gravity pulling it. *What is pulling me? The challenge? The love of walking? The thirst for new experiences? All of the above.*

I look forward to immersing myself in the warm Mediterranean Sea in Nice. My brain smiles with the phrase, "Nice will be nice." But I seldom let myself think ahead to the end, Nice. I stay focused on where we are and where we need to get to today. If I think ahead to two weeks in the Jura and six weeks in the Alps, I get discouraged and question my fortitude and endurance. I've discovered that staying focused on today eases the pressure I place on myself, and I don't find it too hard to stay in the present moment. All my life, I've heard the saying, "One day at a time." Now is my chance to play and practice it. *One day at a time, one day at a time*, I repeat over and over as I walk—a footstep for each word. The beat of my footsteps on the drum of the earth transforms the words into a mantra.

The trail is rockier and steeper than other days. We climb up. We climb down. Over and over. Jim is up ahead. As I'm coming down, he is already climbing up the next spine. We have seen no one on the trail this morning. It's another cloudy day, which I do not mind, as it's a pleasant temperature for walking. To the south, showers fall from darker clouds. Overhead, petite patches of blue sky are the exception, and they never coincide with the sun to allow it to shine on us. Streamlets born from yesterday's rain flow across the trail, prattling at me.

Another hour passes. Now we are no longer going down. We are only walking up, meter after meter.

I can't see Jim any longer, but that is okay. We have less than a kilometer to the summit, and he likes to push himself as he gets to the top. I like to push myself too, but not today. I'm content moving at this pace—not too fast and not too slow. With faith, I follow my body. She takes me up, up, up. I trust her wholly now.

The higher I go, the larger the boulders and the shorter the trees. Up ahead, a couple climbs slowly. They look to be about the same age as me, maybe a little older. I come up behind them. *"Bonjour. Bonjour."* They step to the side of the trail, breathing hard. They smile and say something in French like, "You are moving faster. Enjoy your walk. See you at the top." But I'm not sure exactly what they have said. I say, *"Oui, bonne journée. Merci beaucoup."* As I step past them, I don't make eye contact. I'm embarrassed I don't understand what they've said. I'm clouded in a shadow of shame.

This is one of those mountains that is very steep just before the top. I need to climb up a lip to reach the peak. When you get over the lip of some mountains, it turns out to be a false summit. I hope that is not the case with this one.

I hear voices and excited chattering above me, but I can't see anyone. Looking down so as not to trip on the boulders surrounding my feet, I step gingerly up stone steps formed into the trail. The trees are gone now. I'm out in the open, exposed to a multitude of shades of gray that make up the sky, though I still can't see the top. Four more giant steps up, and I'm over the lip.

People are cheering like at a parade. I look up. Directly in front of me is an arch made of hiking poles. Five people on each side of the trail thrust their hiking poles into the air, like a wedding or a military procession. I pace through the arch smiling the biggest smile of this adventure. I put my hand out to high five them as I walk through but realize they can't high five because they use their hands to hold the poles up. I drop my hand and continue walking through the arch. They continue to cheer. I say, *"Merci, merci, merci!"* as I come out the end, and they gather around me like I'm a famous movie actress.

One of them speaks English well. He says, "Your husband told us that you are walking the whole GR5. We are impressed. We don't see many Americans walking. We are a local hiking club out for a few days of walking. Did you see our friends down below?"

"Yes, they are a few minutes behind me. Thank you again for the welcome. That was the best greeting I have ever had. You made my day!" I say with the smile still imprinted on my face.

He smiles and translates to the others.

"Bonne route," they all say.

"Merci beaucoup. Merci beaucoup. Bonne route," I say, placing

my hand over my heart and tipping my head with a gentle nod of gratitude.

I look around the flat mountain summit, like a giant football field. I see Jim over by the viewpoint indicator a hundred meters away.

"Did you see my welcome?" I ask with a little hop in my step.

"Yes, you are Queen of the Mountain. You got a royal welcome. They offered me dried fruit. Nice hiking club," he says with a sparkle in his eye. He goes back to studying the viewpoint indicator.

"No view today," I say. The clouds sink lower and the view dissolves into a blur.

"Yep, the view indicator points out Donon to the north, where we started the Vosges Mountains," he says. "I can't believe it was almost two weeks ago." He shakes his head.

The raw wind gives me a shudder. "I'm starved. Let's eat," I say. We look for picnic tables or shelter but see none, so we continue to the other side of the giant plateau to a statue of Joan of Arc. It's an animated statue. Her horse is rising on her hind hooves. Joan is in complete control of the horse and holds a flag high in the air, similar to how the hiking club held up their trekking poles.

I stand in front of the statue and raise my hiking pole, parallel to Joan's flag. "Take a picture of Joan and me," I say.

We have seen quite a few statues of Joan. It's gratifying to see statues of women. Mary and Joan are cloned and celebrated all over France. Mary represents purity and the bond between mother and child. Joan represents bravery, martyrdom, determination, and power. Joan helps me feel more powerful.

In the United States we have so few statues of women, I feel angry and sad.

This statue of Joan of Arc was erected in 1909, when Alsace was still part of Germany. The mountain was right on the border of France and Germany at the time. The statue represented the love that France still held for the lands of Alsace.

Jim and I each sit on a cement post, the only seating we can find, and eat our cheese and bread. It begins to drizzle. The cold bread and cheese do not warm my insides. I put on an extra layer and my wool beanie. Just then, we hear cheering from far across the field. The couple from the hiking group has arrived on top. I smile again. My center is warm, even if my legs are cold.

The formal reception of walking under the hiking-pole arch was my initiation into the walking community. Part of me wishes I had whipped out my phone and recorded myself walking through the archway. But I did not think fast enough. And maybe that is okay. Perhaps I will remember more because I experienced it firsthand, not through the lens. I will savor the glow in my heart and the cheers in my ears for a long time. I'm a proud walker.

Ceremonies to celebrate transitions are important in my life. I remember all the birthday, graduation, anniversary, and retirement parties I have created and executed over my lifetime, usually for other people. Women in our society tend to be the planners and the doers of holidays, traditions, and ceremonies.

When I went through menopause, I had a strong longing to create a ceremony for myself. I searched for information about ceremonies but only found a few articles, and none of them made my heart sing. I did more research about archetypes, especially the Crone, the Wise Woman. I stumbled on the book *The Queen of Myself* by Donna Henes. Henes outlines the traditional stages of womanhood—young Maiden, fertile Mother, Crone—and she argues these stages need to shift. She asserts that because women are living long and stronger, the idea of becoming a Crone at the middle age of fifty does not apply anymore. She suggests we slip a fourth archetype, Queen, between fertile Mother and aged Crone. Henes's definition of Queen—someone who knows what she wants and steps into her power with grace and wisdom—resonated with me.

At first, I struggled with creating my Queening Ceremony. I couldn't figure out whom I should invite or how many I should invite. I also had this nagging feeling that the whole Queening Ceremony was a little selfish and egotistical. I felt lost and frustrated, though at the same time there was a powerful desire deep inside me to have a ceremony. Eventually, I realized the inspiration had to come from me, not from books. It must come from my inner wisdom.

Now that I look back on it, this realization is the moment when I became a Queen. I had to tap into my inner wisdom and find out what was right for me. While writing about how frustrated I felt, a glimmer of wisdom popped into my head. *Follow your heart.* I asked my heart what was important about this ceremony and ritual. My heart quickly answered, *Intentions, mentors, and doing what you love.*

On a June evening at the age of fifty-three, five women who had supported or inspired me during my transformation joined me in my backyard. They brought nourishing food and blossoms from their gardens. We fashioned crowns from the flowers and wrote our intentions for the next fifty years, leaving big blank spaces for the intentions that didn't yet have words. We listed the mentors who helped us become the women we are. Finally, we listed people we mentor or will mentor; again, leaving blank space for the unknown people we'll mentor in the future.

As the sun paused on the western horizon, the vibrant June light amplified the confident spring colors—magenta, crimson, and chartreuse. A crown of pink rhododendron and lilac blossoms on my head, I walked under an arch formed by two crab apple trees reaching out and kissing each other. I walked from Motherhood to Queendom. It only took a few seconds to cross over. The four seconds of ritual symbolized four years of transformation to becoming a Queen.

The seven seconds of walking under the trekking-pole arch symbolized the seven weeks of transformation to become a walker. Without the queening ceremony, I would not have had the determination to walk the GR5.

It's a quick lunch—no resting in these clouds. The GR5 begins to wind gradually down the slope to the south. We see day visitors in sneakers. We enter a car park with a restaurant on the far side. As I open the glass front door, hot air hugs me. This is the best part of walking in Europe—coming across a restaurant in the mountains.

I order waffles with chocolate sauce to celebrate my initiation as a walker. Jim orders coffee and a *tarte aux myrtilles*, blueberry pie. Clouds of whipped cream encase his pie. We have not seen ripe blueberries yet on the sides of the trail, though we have picked an abundance of wild strawberries and cherries.

We are warm inside and out. But we must go back out and walk another sixteen kilometers down into the village of Giromagny.

Reluctantly I open the glass door, and a chill air greets me; but I step into it with renewed morale. We walk along the sidewalk back to the GR5. A cheer rises from across the car park. The hiking group is just coming down to the parking lot. We all wave at each other. We shout, *"Bonne route, bonne route."*

They shout, *"Bon courage."*

THREE PHONE CALLS (DAY 49)

Later that afternoon, in a modern hotel in Giromagny, France, I lie on a pearl-colored comforter that feels like puffy clouds. I long to stay still, to sink into the comfort, and to dream. Jim is lying next to me with his iPad on his chest. He is looking into reservations in Lake Geneva, where we will take two days off before beginning the Alps.

I gather my energy and shuffle down the hall to the front desk with a small piece of paper in my hand, seeking help with a difficult accommodation. The paper has my name, phone number, the date we want reserved, and the phone number of the *gîte*.

A *gîte* is a simple accommodation made up of some configuration of small dorm rooms and private rooms. They are usually part of someone's house or a barn that has been converted into sleeping rooms for the family to make extra money. Communal dinners and breakfasts are served. When we get to the mountains, we will stay in mountain refuges, which are like *gîtes* but are larger and located in the mountains not in villages. An auberge is a small hotel with private rooms and usually has a restaurant.

A young woman with a short sharp haircut and cherry red lipstick stands behind the polished chrome and white desk, smiling in a welcoming manner.

"Would you do me a favor and call this *gîte* and make a reservation for my husband and me for June fifteenth, please?" I ask.

She happily agrees and dials the number on her cell phone. I understand her "*bonjour*," but after that, not much. The talk goes back and forth. Finally, she writes something down and says good-bye.

"Their *gîte* is full for that night, but he gave me the name of an auberge in the same village. I'll call that one for you," she says.

"Thank you so much," I say, leaning on the desk to ease some of my weight off my tender feet.

More conversation I do not understand. Again, she writes something down.

"The auberge is also full that night. But she gave me the number of another place to call. I'll try this one too."

"Wow, thank you so much. You're so helpful," I say with a big smile of gratitude, trying to stand a little taller.

I watch, feeling useless. For the third time, she dials a number. She holds the phone up to her ear for a long time before talking. She leaves a message. "No one answered. I'll try again later."

"You have been so helpful. Thank you."

I amble back to our room while a mint dissolves in my mouth.

"No luck yet," I say to Jim as I join him on the soft comforter. "The woman at the desk called three places. I'm going to check and see if we can walk off trail and take a train to Montbéliard. It's a bigger town that has a bunch of hotels. The trains are not running often because of the train strike, but I'll check again to see if I can make it work. How are you coming?"

"It looks like it is going to work out. I used the website Sabin told us about again." He pauses. "Finding accommodation is the hardest part of this trip. Walking is the easy part," he says.

We have another system that has emerged in how we make reservations. I look a week or two or three ahead and plan out how far we will walk each day—the broad view. I brought a notebook with me, but once we started walking, I did not want to carry the weight, so I ripped out six sheets of paper and tossed the rest. I use the lined paper and a pencil to plan out the dates, locations, and number of kilometers to travel. I tried doing this on my iPad, but I prefer seeing it written out. Visually on the paper I can see us walking from blue line to blue line.

Then we take turns picking a date and making a reservation. Once the reservation is made, we add it to our calendars on our phones with the address. Jim tends to pick cheaper lodging and I tend to pick nicer hotels, so we end up with a balance.

Jim also does the detailed work of plotting out the route on GAIA and uploading the maps we need. These systems we have worked out help us keep our power struggle in check.

Ten minutes later, there is a knock on the door. Pulling myself up to a standing position, I open the door, and the nice young woman tells me we have a place to stay. It is at someone's house, a friend of the auberge owner. She gives me the address and a phone number. As she turns to leave, she adds, "Try to be there by four in the afternoon because they are going out at seven."

I don't understand this cryptic message. *Who are these people who are putting us up? Will they serve us dinner?* But at this point, I'm so happy to have found a place to stay that I don't ask the woman any more questions. She has done enough. We'll figure it out when we get there. Persistence has paid off.

MUD IN THE WOODS
(DAY 50)

"I'm going to take a few pictures of this veggie garden. You go ahead," I say as we maneuver through the back alleys of Giromagny on our way out of town the next morning.

The GR5 leads through back alleys between rows of houses to avoid the main road. Wooden picket fences—not painted white—frame meticulous vegetable gardens showcasing flowering potato plants and pea tendrils growing up three wooden stakes forming a teepee. The rows of green and red lettuces are bold like the Italian flag. Black currants grow on the edge of the garden. A cherry tree dripping with cherries leans over the alley about eye level, just begging to be picked. I eat a perfect breakfast dessert.

Two hours of walking lead us along plain farm tracks to the outskirts of a nondescript village and up towards a squat mountain. We read that it has a fort on top, Fort du Salbert, one of the twelve forts built in 1875 ringing the city of Belfort.

"Do you think this is the right way? The waymarks go east, but there is a trail going to the top of the mountain right here," Jim asks. He holds his phone up close to his tanned face.

"It does not make sense to be heading east and then back north up the mountain," I say with a sigh. "But I think we should stick with the waymarks. They are usually right."

Jim agrees. We walk for twenty-five minutes halfway around

the base of the mountain. I gaze up to the mountain on my right and know we would have been on top by now if we had taken that other trail. I feel like the GR5 is playing tricks on us. Up ahead, a tall sign indicates an intersection. "This is where a variant of the GR5 came from the city of Belfort," I say. Many people walking the GR5 in sections start or end at Belfort because it has a train station. The trail now heads north, finally climbing the short mountain. "Where is the fort?" I ask, searching the uninviting flat summit. "Two benches. At least we don't have to sit in this overgrown grass and worry about ticks."

"There's Ballon d'Alsace," Jim says. He rests his pack on one of the cracked benches. "The guidebook said we should be able to see the Alps. But not today with this haze." He sighs. "Bummer. I really want to see the Alps."

We eat our undistinguished lunch, looking out over the mucky sky with the weeds at our feet.

I pack up and start down the slope, eager to move on, nothing to see here. Surprisingly, there is a crumbling grand staircase leading down to an expansive plateau thirty feet below.

On the plateau, the fort is built into the side of the mountain. It features three big entrances. I shout up, "The fort is down here."

He takes his time packing up, which annoys me today because I just want to keep going. I not only feel annoyed, but I also feel despondent. I don't know why.

I walk along the bridge of the first entrance, crossing over a dried-up moat. A giant gate is locked with a chain and padlock. Black-and-orange graffiti decorates the walls. It looks like the gate opens into the mountain. I feel like I'm at the Temple of Doom from the Indiana Jones movie.

I lean over the stone bridge, waiting for Jim, and scan the moat, which is empty of water, but filled with wildflowers. I search for new species I have not seen before but see none.

"Not much of a fort," he says. "It looks like they have not bothered to restore it."

I nod without a word and start down the trail back into the woods.

Two hours later, we are still in the woods, walking along muddy trails. The waymarks keep taking us off the main path and into the woods. These offshoots are trying to avoid the big puddles of water created by logging machinery. We have to step up and over downed trees. I look down so as not to get my feet completely submerged, but I'm afraid to miss a waymark heading east. It's slow going, looking up, looking down. Looking up, looking down.

How many more hours of woods walking do we have? The forest road winds out of the chaotic logging area, but we are still in the hot, pine-scented woods. The imprint of a recent tractor tire tread digs deep into the black soil and water fills the impressions, creating a pattern of angular puddles. The mud is slick, and I fear falling.

I stretch out my tired leg to miss a puddle, but my right foot falls short of the dirt landing and slides uncontrollably into the muddy pool. I feel the black water ooze over the top of my shoe and soak into my sock like a sponge. *Bummer, I had been doing so well.* The black water sinks into my spirit, dragging me down deeper.

The energy from lunch has burned up. I have almonds and banana chips in my hip pocket, but I'm sick of them. They taste like salty rotten wood and sweet stale cardboard, respectively. I look at GAIA; we have seven more kilometers of walking to get to the hotel—at least an hour and a half. The kilometers get longer in the later afternoon, not something I learned in math class. I need a break, but there is nowhere to sit. I keep walking. *How am I going to make it out of these woods with this empty body, empty spirit?*

I pull out my phone again and start making a video. I whine and complain about the day. *I've proved myself, and maybe I should just stop. Maybe this whole trip is done. Perhaps we should go home? We still have the Jura and the Alps. I can't do it.*

Jim and I have always said if we don't like this adventure, we have a plan B. Plan B is murky and not well defined, but something like biking from Germany to Hungary. So far, we have each had bad days, but we have not had a day where both of us have wanted to quit. This has been my worst day except when I was sick, and even then, I was enjoying the adventure.

I finish the video and say to myself, *I'll never post that whining one. No one will want to see me complaining.* Then I softly recall self-compassion, like a faraway mourning dove whispering a gift. *When life is not going well, give yourself compassion.*

I gingerly slide my hand into the top of my sun shirt and place my palm over my heart. I feel the pressure of my hand on my beating heart and the warmth of my fingers. A bit of oxytocin releases in my bloodstream. I take a conscious breath, filling my lungs with wonder.

In a tender voice, I say out loud, "This is hard, Kathy. You're frustrated and tired. You've been on the trail for close to fifty days. It's okay to have a bad day. Not every day is going to be good. It is frustrating to have to walk off the trail to find lodging. Aww, sweetie you are having a bad day. Other people in the world are having a bad day too. You are not alone."

I speak in a gentle, affectionate voice. Using a soft, tender voice with myself has taken years to learn. It's not easy to pull out a soft, tender voice, especially when my mind is in the mud.

Ten minutes later, we come out of the woods onto the edge of an expansive sunlit hayfield with two small villages in the distance. The twin steeples are beacons of hope.

My energy has shifted. I pull out my phone and record part two. I share how I used self-compassion to comfort myself. How the act of recording, giving voice to my feelings and then giving myself compassion allowed the emotions to be felt and then let go. Instead of finding energy from nuts and banana chips, I receive energy from self-kindness. The work of practicing and teaching self-compassion works. I get a bonus jolt of energy from that knowing.

Jim hears me recording the second video. He jokingly says, "Good; now you never need a therapist. You can just talk to your phone. Look at how much money you will save."

In his sassy way, he is right. Talking into my phone and sharing my feelings with my phone has helped. It brought me out of the funk I was in. It brought me out of the quagmire.

Over the years, I've gone to a therapist to help me through complex parts of life. Jim has gone at times also, and we have always learned and grown. Having an outside person hear our struggles and mirror them back to us has helped us put our differences in perspective and understand and communicate with each other.

We walk between fields of ripe hay waiting to be harvested. The first farmhouse we come to has a large picnic table out front near the barn. No one is around. We sit in the shade at the table and nourish our bodies with the rind of the cheese and stale bread. But it tastes delicious to me now that my spirit has been fed with self-kindness.

Later that night I edit the two parts of the video into one video and post it on my YouTube channel. This video ends up getting the most likes and comments. People like to hear the hard parts of the trip and how I got through them. A few people comment about the metaphor of coming out of the woods and into the open as part of the shift.

The woods can be deep and dark as compared to the open meadows and farmlands. But the woods are also protective during storms. I need both dark enclosure and light expansiveness.

My father always told me there are more bird species on the border between the woods and meadows than there are in either the woods or the meadows. If I were always out in the expansive field, it would get boring. Learning to appreciate and be with the dark shadows of life like struggles with reading, overeating, and general dark moods has made my life more diverse. The feeling of coming out of the woods and into the open expansiveness is powerful and glorious.

ZESTFUL AGING
(DAY 51)

Two days later, we walk through an abandoned cherry orchard, picking and eating in the late afternoon sunshine. The GR5 was mellow today. She was canal towpaths and rural farm roads winding from village to the village. We have left the Vosges Mountains and are in the lowlands before entering the Jura Mountains—the between lands.

We have tried to pace the day so that we arrive in this village at about four. All day, in the back of my mind, I've been a little nervous about showing up and staying at someone's house when we have no idea who they are. I'm happy to stay at *gîtes*, auberges, and Airbnbs, but just someone's random house is a little concerning to me, mainly because our French is so bad. *How will we communicate?* We have brought extra bread and cheese in case they don't serve us dinner. I've checked; there are no restaurants in the village of Vandercourt.

We walk out of the orchard and onto a narrow farm road heading down into the village. A small, battered red car pulls up to us and rolls down the window. "Kathy and Jim?" an older balding man with a bushy gray mustache questions us in perfect English.

"Yes!" we answer with astonishment.

He introduces himself as Joseph. Marie, his wife, is driving. "We are hosting you tonight. We have been driving around for a while looking for you because we were afraid you were lost and did not have our address."

Right away, I feel bad that I did not call them and try to tell them when we would arrive. Next time, I will reach out and call, even if I'm scared and they don't understand me. "Oh, I'm sorry, we were told to get to you about four o'clock."

They don't offer us a ride, which is a good thing because the car is so small. I do not think we would fit in the back with our packs. Instead, they give us exact directions to their house, which is only a few blocks away, and then fly off, raising dust into the blue air. My worry and concern float away with the dust.

We wander into the village and out one road a few blocks to a three-story Victorian house the color of tomato soup. The whimsical house with contrasting dark green shutters sits looking out over the gently rolling hills. We open the wrought-iron garden gate, and it squeaks its welcome. The overgrown plantings lean over the garden path, which leads to a large wooden front door that has been left open. We step into the foyer, where the cool air greets us.

"Hello," Jim calls out hesitantly.

"In here," a high voice calls back.

We walk around the corner and into the kitchen, which looks more like a living room with a stove and refrigerator added in recent times. There is a wall of overflowing bookshelves, a small wooden table, and two comfortable chairs framing a west window. In the middle of the room with a table next to it, the stove acts as a kitchen island. The sink and the brown refrigerator are on the back wall with a few handmade cabinets connecting them. So many books living in a kitchen. *My two loves brought together. I could stay here forever.*

Marie stands at the stove. She is short with just a hint of gray hair amongst her thin brown hair. She chats and cooks with efficient motions.

"Welcome, welcome to our home; we are so happy you are here. We are going out to a concert tonight, but I'm making dinner for you. Joseph has gone to a neighbor to pick some cherries. I hope you like cherries," Marie asks without wanting an answer. "I'll get you some beer. Go sit on the deck," she demands. "You relax. You must be hot and tired!"

We offer to help with dinner, but Marie hands us two short, cold bottles of German beer and shoos us out to the porch. We sit on a battered couch and put our feet up on the faded plastic coffee table. The sun is still high in the sky, and I feel drops of sweat roll down my side. Jim figures out how to lower the awning so that we can see the view but not look into the sun.

I raise my brown beer bottle to Jim's. "Here's to life and going with the flow. It all worked out. Someday I won't worry so much."

We clink beer bottles, then bring the bottles to our lips and sip the clean, cool fizzy liquid. Jim leans in, and I follow; our lips meet in a kiss of gratitude with a side of salty sweat.

"Hey, do you like cherries?" Jim asks with sarcastic love and a wink.

"Cherries are Mother Earth's rubies. Of course, I love them," I say.

After getting settled into our room upstairs and taking a shower, we return to the kitchen. We chat with Marie and Joseph as they work. They will not let us help.

"We used to run the auberge in town, and now when the auberge is full, we take in people occasionally. But you are the first this year. That's how you found us," Marie says.

"Why is your English so good? You speak perfect English," I say.

"We lived in Acton, Massachusetts, in the 1970s for three years," Joseph says.

"Acton?" Jim says, as our eyes widen.

"We lived in Harvard, Massachusetts, and I had an office in Acton!" I excitedly spit out.

Marie stops what she is doing. We all look at each other. I'm sure we are all thinking, *What a small world this is.* We all enjoy the mystery and the magic for a silent moment.

"I worked at Honeywell, and our kids went to the Acton public school," Joseph says.

"What was the name of that school?" Jim asks looking at Marie.

"Merriam," she answers. "Do you know it?" she asks, looking at Jim and me.

"Yes, I know where Merriam is," I say.

"It was a great school for our children. They loved it," Marie says as she continues to stir a steaming sauce on the stove.

"What did you do for Honeywell?" Jim asks.

"I wrote computer programs to change measurements from English to metric."

While Joseph is talking, I'm calculating their ages. If their kids were in elementary school in the 1970s, then their kids are just a bit younger than we are. That must mean Joseph and Marie are in their late seventies or eighties. They look and act so much younger.

"I remember when the United States was going to go metric." Jim says. We laugh that it never happened. Now that I have been immersed in kilometers and centigrade for the last three months, I find the metric system so much easier, and I wish we had changed to it back in the 1970s.

"Dinner is ready. Now go sit in the dining room, and we will serve you. Then we need to get going to our concert," Marie says.

A bright red-and-orange damask tablecloth covers a large oval dining room table that is set for two. The table is a picture of abundance: a round loaf of bread on a wooden cutting board, a plate of paper-thin slices of ham folded accordion style with crumbly white cheese, all decorated by bright blue borage flowers and orange calendula petals. A bowl of just-sliced cabbage with cumin seeds also graces the table. I suspect Marie gathered all these herbs and flowers from their garden surrounding the house. And to top it all off, a basket overflowing with dark red and yellow blush cherries, just picked with the leaves attached, rests at the end of the table that faces the window. Our hosts have created a vision that looks like it is waiting to be painted by Charlotte Vignon or Henriette Tirman.

Joseph pours a deep Burgundy into our goblets, then presents an open casserole dish with thick-cut pork chops covered in braised vegetables in a cream sauce.

"Enjoy your dinner. We will see you in the morning," they giddily explain as they rush off to the Russian piano concert.

I feel like a kid when my parents had gone off to a party and we got to eat alone, except this dinner is so much better than the TV dinners we were left with. At the same time, it feels odd that the couple in their eighties is going out for the evening, and the younger couple is staying in and going to bed early.

We drink most of the bottle of wine while slowly devouring most of the food on the table.

At eight thirty, it is still light out. We clean up the dining room and wash the dishes in the kitchen. I feel a little awkward figuring out how to store the leftovers. I see no Tupperware or glass storage containers. But we get the job done.

They have given us the password to the Wi-Fi, and we sit in the living room reading about tomorrow's walk. I edit the exercise videos we made at lunchtime, when we ate in a park that had ten different pieces of exercise equipment. Jim figures out how to upload the music from the movie *Rocky* into the video. We laugh hysterically as the *Rocky* theme song plays, and we watch ourselves run around the park trying the different exercise machines with our backpacks on.

We send the video to Margo and Todd, our friends who will meet us in the Alps in two weeks. We explain to them that we are training extra hard to keep up with them.

At nine thirty, the sun finally sinks behind the horizon, filling the rooms with golden light. I climb the dark wooden staircase to our room and hoist myself into one of the twin beds. The springs squeal at the weight of my body compressing them.

The next morning, we all sit around the dining room table with coffee and croissants.

"It was the best concert we have been to in a long time," Joseph says. "Wait, I bought a CD last night. I'll play it for you." He jumps up to retrieve the CD and put it in the stereo. Russian piano music vigorously swims around the large Victorian rooms. We stop talking and soak up the music for a meditative moment. Then, slowly, we begin to share stories about our children. Marie is sad that three of her four children live so far away in Paris. I think about my children living two thousand miles away from us, and I'm sad too. I miss my kids.

Finally, it is time to say our good-byes. But before we leave, I ask to take a selfie of the group. We take a picture out on their porch. We feel like we are saying good-bye to longtime friends. We promise to send them a picture when we get to Nice. We walk out of their garden and close the garden gate behind us. We are ready to begin another day of walking in the June sunshine in France. We walk into the village to find our loyal friend, the GR5, right where we left her.

I look at the selfie we took. We are all genuinely happy. Marie and Joseph look twenty years younger than they are. They have fewer wrinkles than Jim and I do. I so admire how Marie and Joseph live an adventurous life by having lived abroad. How they grow a bountiful garden, attend concerts of foreign musicians, fill their kitchen with books, ran an auberge in their seventies, and now welcome people into their home in their eighties, and it makes me wonder how all of these elements contribute to the way they're growing old with energy, grace, and ease. I want to be like them.

Sometimes, when I look back over our entire journey, it's only then that I see how much we were in flow. Magic happenings transpired again and again. I feel that we were looked after by a higher power, and I did not realize the scope of it at the time. Mother Earth held us in her arms, and the GR5 led us to inspiring humans.

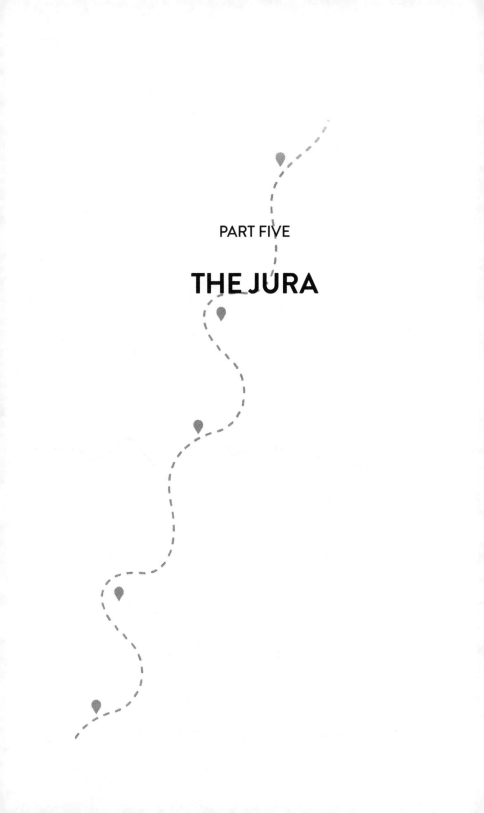

PART FIVE

THE JURA

EXTERNAL IMAGE (DAY 54)

It's another spectacular morning for walking, our fifty-fourth day on the GR5. The mist from the River Doubs rises to meet the sunbeams. The dew sparkles on the long marsh grass blades. We walk along the river for eleven kilometers against the current. This is the river where Jim skinny-dipped and I forest bathed yesterday.

Slowly the limestone walls of the valley grow taller and move in closer. At this point, the GR5 guides us up, up, up out of the deep river gorge and onto a high bluff. The GR5 used to stay along the river, but the limestone outcroppings have eroded and fallen in places, so it is too dangerous to walk along the river in this section.

I'm happy clambering up out of the river valley. The uphill exertion releases more endorphins, and as I climb, my mind churns faster, ideas rising and taking form. I've noticed I usually have more ideas as I go up. I don't know if it is from the endorphins or from more oxygen to my brain. I pull out my iPhone and record a Breathless Kathy video. I talk about how strong I feel. Then I watch a bit of it while I walk.

I gasp when I see myself in the video. So, I record another video, talking about what just happened when saw I my external image. Internally I feel strong. But, when I look at the frame of myself, it does not match the picture in my head of a young thin woman. The picture on the phone, like a mirror, is of a woman starting to turn gray with a rounded belly. I have not seen myself in a mirror much this trip, except my face in the bathroom mirror. In fact, I can't remember the last time I looked in a full-length mirror.

Looking back, I see that not looking in a full-length mirror was a blessing, a gift to myself.

Our culture brainwashes us, to the extent that when I think of "strong," I automatically think, "thin and young."

Strong can be older, wiser, and rounder. Both my character and body are proof of that.

I know it intellectually, but I just got triggered by my photo. *I thought I had completely accepted my body. Standing in the river yesterday when I was forest bathing, I felt one with my body. I loved my belly. How can an external image crack the internal image so quickly?* Body image acceptance continues to be a long road.

Because I overate cookies and sweets through middle school, high school, and college and I have a big-boned body, I was always the big girl. I was never super fat because I did sports and stayed active. But I was different from the stick-thin bird girls in my competitive private schools.

How do we help change society's views of older, rounder women, when I can't even change my own beliefs? That picture of me is me.

My body has changed some. I've shed a little here and a little there from all the walking. I don't use the word *lost* because *lost* implies that I want it back. Though in truth, I know it will wander back to me when I get home.

Still recording, I talk about my fears of going home at the end of the walk. Will I unshed a little here, a little there? Once home, there is no way I will be able to keep up with walking six or seven hours a day, nor do I want to. What will my new norm be? Why, at the age of fifty-seven, do I even care what I look like on the outside? Maybe I care more about the inside. Wouldn't it be healthier for everyone if we didn't judge others for their size? No one knows what is going on inside another. I have had thin female clients that endlessly worry that they will gain a pound. They are so wrapped up in their body image that they can barely participate in their lives. I send compassion for all the women and men who worry about their size. As a culture we need to get over this. We need acceptance. I will keep working on accepting my body—my lovely body.

I stop recording.

Jim loves my body and always has. In the first ten to fifteen years of our marriage he would make disparaging comments about a heavy person out running. Those fat-shaming comments hurt me. But he never said overt words about my body. As I learned to love my belly, I also learned to speak up for people who were big. When he would make a remark I would say, "At least they are out there moving, and please don't comment on people's bodies. You don't know what they have been through in life." He eventually stopped.

What I do know is this: I can walk day after day. I breathe, walk, and absorb this feeling into my bones. That picture of a rounded woman who can walk all day across mountains is strong.

She is me.

Up on top of the bluff, it is easy walking along empty farm roads and then forest tracts. The views are spectacular across the valley and into the Swiss farmland, and I wonder, *Do the French and Swiss farmers hang out and socialize, or do they stick to their borders? Are the Swiss women farmers comfortable in their bodies?*

We stop for lunch in the cool shade of the pine woods. We climb up on a large boulder covered in spongy moss with two trees abutting it. The trunks are perfect backrests. The boulder is an erratic. It reminds me of an erratic boulder on my grandparents' property in Massachusetts. That erratic was a giant piece of rounded granite, ten feet tall and eight feet wide. It was the only boulder around in a sea of white oaks. I was always drawn to it. One side angled up like a ramp, which allowed me to climb up the lichen-covered rock and perch. While growing up, it was my private lookout tower, my special place in the woods.

My father explained to me the erratic had been picked up by a glacier thousands of years ago, traveled south as the ice sheet moved, and then was deposited there when the glacier melted. It was far from home.

I learned recently that the Latin word *errare* means to wander. It's funny to think that a giant bolder is a wanderer. It wandered once but will not move until the next ice age, while the trees around it will move through hundreds of generations of time.

I often felt like an erratic. Out of place. Different. Bigger than the others around me. Not quite fitting in. Dyslexia and my rounder body caused these feelings.

Now I see the erratic makes the landscape story more compelling and complex. I've accepted my differentness and erraticness (a new word I invented), which bolsters my belief in myself. I am part of the composite landscape.

Our world going forward needs older, wiser, stronger, more powerful, big women to shape the fabric of the landscape.

DISOBEYING SIGNS
(DAY 54)

In the afternoon, the trail leads us up to an empty car park. The guidebook says to walk across the car park to the fence and enter a steep staircase down to the river, a dam, and a river walk. This is a popular walking area.

The opening at the fence is closed off. A bright orange construction sign with lots of French words is a warning. Jim translates, "They are doing construction on the dam starting Monday, June eighteenth. The trail is closed. Go back and follow the reroute. It is dangerous to walk on the stairs and the dam when the helicopters are in action."

"I think today is June nineteenth. But I don't hear helicopters. Do you? Let's go back and look for the reroute," I say. It's true that in many situations I like to break the rules, or at least make my own rules. But if doing so would endanger us, then I'm happy to follow the rules.

"It's funny that we didn't see a reroute sign on the trail," says Jim walking back across the car park to where the trail entered it. I follow as I run the options through my head.

"You would think they would have a sign here telling people where to go back to. Let's check GAIA," I say as I pull out my phone and bring up the map. Jim looks over my shoulder as I scroll back along the trail looking for a road or trail that will take us to the river a different way. "I don't see another route."

We wander back to the padlocked fence and listen for helicopters.

Jim follows the chain link fence for six meters. "Look, you can see where people have walked around the fence and started walking down the stairs. Let's do it."

"Are you sure about this?" I ask Jim, but I am also voicing the question to myself. My heartbeat increases a bit, but I'm not getting a feeling of dread. I take that as a nod. I scan the car park one more time. No one is around.

"I don't know what else to do," says Jim.

We descend quickly down the five flights of slick metal stairs to the edge of the river. I tread lightly so as not to make noise on the metal stairs, which is impossible, as the sound of our footsteps echoes off the limestone cliff.

No one is at the bottom. I look up. No one is following us. We move quickly along the trail to the dam, like spies in a thriller. We climb two flights of stairs up the side of the dam. We see three workers across the river on the Swiss side. They see us but do not say anything.

"We will plead innocent and say we could not read the sign if anyone comes up to us," says Jim. I'm a little surprised he is so nervous about this. He usually likes taking risks. Maybe being in a foreign country has him on edge.

We descend the other side of the dam to the river-locked lake. It is pretty, but dammed up rivers always make me sad.

We see no one on this side and no helicopters. Two bulldozers and an excavator sit silently waiting for action. Maybe the plan had been to start on June 18, but like so many government projects, it got delayed. I hope that is the case.

We have gotten away with breaking the rules.

The trail leads us out of the dam area and along the lake. A few kilometers along, we see a dirt road come in from the right.

"I wonder if that is where we would have come from if we had backtracked and taken the reroute," I say.

"Yeah, I bet you're right."

A collection of small, weathered cabins lines the lake. They are empty on this Tuesday afternoon in June. I'm sure in August this is the place to be. The rowboats that are pulled up on the shore would be out on the water with frolicking families or men fishing.

I look down at the next cabin. *Wait, what's that?* A man with no shirt is sitting on a wooden picnic table on a deck. Someone is around. Then I see his backpack; he's a visitor. I look closer at him. He looks at us. We say, *"Bonjour."* It's the solitary Frenchman from the hotel last night.

Yesterday evening we sat near a lone Frenchman who ignored us until he heard us tell some other guests that we were walking the whole GR5. Suddenly he could speak English, and he told us that he too was walking the entire GR5. This morning on the way to breakfast I spied him out the window, heading to the trail an hour before us.

Now he calls out, "You walked fast!" He's incredulous. "You caught up with me."

I answer back, "We weren't walking any faster than normal." I smile proudly. To myself I think, *I walk as fast or faster than an arrogant French male walker.*

We say, *"Bonne journée.* See you later." And walk on.

As we walk, we chat. We realize he probably did obey the sign and went up and around. Who knows how many more kilometers he walked than we did? We might not be faster than him; we just don't obey the law. But he does not need to know this. I like that he thinks we are faster than he is. And maybe we are? We will never know.

An hour later, we sit at a little tourist café near a giant waterfall, drinking Orangina and resting. I knew from the guidebook that there were cafés near the waterfall. Jim and I have been speculating all day if they would be open for the season or not. Sometimes the silly things that keep our minds occupied while we walk make all the difference and keep us sane. Plus, the possibility of an Orangina is tantalizing, like a carrot on a stick.

The lone man walks by us. We wave and give a big smile. He says hi but does not stop.

I wonder if he is going to take the boat. This is another dilemma I have been pondering all day. We can take a boat from the nearby dock that will take us seven kilometers into the town of Villers-le-Lac, where we have a reservation for tonight. One of the bloggers I read took the boat and said it was beautiful.

A part of me wants to take the boat, but the other part of me feels we should walk. Tomorrow we are taking a day off, so we should walk to deserve the break. That is my father's voice in my head.

Jim does not care.

We are not sure if the boat is even running yet. It could be too early in the season.

With renewed energy from our drinks, we begin walking again.

As we get closer, we see the tourist boat at the dock. If we take a left and walk down the path, we can catch it. But we don't. "Let's walk," I say. We walk the seven kilometers into town and relax for the next thirty-six hours.

This is a decision I regret. We should have taken the boat and enjoyed the ride. When I analyze it now, I see I overrode my intuition and did what the inner critic or the inner good girl said I should do: walk. Maybe, because I broke the rules at the dam, I wanted to be a good girl and not break the walking rules in the afternoon. Maybe one would make up for the other? Did I feel guilty about not obeying the sign?

I want to wash out all the sludge of being a good girl. I want to question and separate the inner good girl and signals from my intuition. I also realize that, because Jim did not care, the decision was mine to make. Looking at our marriage I see how often I have waited to see what he wanted. If I agreed, I would go along with it. If I did not, I would argue against it. I was reactive to his decisions. When they are my decisions to make, sometimes I freeze. *Who knew walking on a path could bring up so much sludge?* The GR5 nudges and prods me to look at intersections with renewed awareness.

UNDER A TRAMPOLINE (DAY 56)

I lie in the young grass under a trampoline, trying to escape the intense three o'clock sun. Jim is on the grass but not under the trampoline. This is our first day of walking after our day off, and, as usual, walking after a rest day is harder than other days. It does not make sense, but it is the truth.

The patch of grass with a trampoline and ping-pong table makes up the side yard of a dusty horse farm in the countryside. Further down the driveway is a row of low barns and sheds with paddocks attached. We wait for the *gîte* owner to arrive and let us into the farmhouse. Many of the *gîtes* are run by people who have other jobs, and they don't open up until they get home. This one is only open in the summer for walkers and in the winter for cross-country skiers.

An hour ago, as we walked up the farm track, I saw a woman in a large tractor cutting hay in a massive field. My guess is she is the owner of the *gîte*.

I pull out my phone and look up the email the owner sent us. At the bottom, in fine print, it says it opens at 5:00 p.m. I lean over to Jim and show him. "I guess we need to pay better attention." He nods.

Surprisingly, I am not alone under the trampoline; three others seek the shade. A Brit with a strong accent chats with a young couple, Julie and Davey. We met along the trail today. We first passed them while they were eating nuts and talking intimately. They are in their late twenties. When they talk to each other, they look each other in the eye, and they actively listen to each other. They are French but speak some English.

Even though the Brit is speaking English, I strain to understand what he is saying. He jabbers on and on about the different treks he has done in the Himalayas. This week he is walking in the Jura to get in shape for his trip to Nepal later in the month. It's ironic that the one person who speaks English I don't want to listen to.

"Let's play ping-pong," I say to Jim, who is listening in on the conversation about the Himalayas. I point to the table. I love the way, in Europe, they have their ping-pong tables outside. I've seen them at campgrounds and at a few *gîtes*. We usually can't find the paddles, or we have been too tired. But today I'm bored, and from my position on the ground I see the paddles in a holder under the table.

We rally back and forth, filling the air with gentle pings and pongs. I miss the ball. It arcs behind me, landing in the grass. I lean down to pick it up as my hamstrings scream. I groan and push into the stretch. Jim has a quieter groan on his quest for the ball, but I can see in his movements that he is feeling all the walking. We continue our volleying while half my attention is on the other walkers.

Two French couples in their early sixties join our waiting group. They sit on the back staircase.

A car comes careening up the hill, and a woman in her seventies with a backpack jumps out. The car zooms off. She speaks in French to the others. I try to follow along, but I'm lost. She sits down in the grass and chats with the two French couples. Her name is Celeste.

We tire of ping-pong. I lie in the grass and close my eyes. I'm jealous of the people chatting and wish I spoke French. Jim is chatting with the Brit. I miss my female friends, and I'm too tired to try to speak to this group of people who might not speak English.

Finally, the owner—the tractor driver—shows up. Tall and tan, her biceps bulging under her faded blue T-shirt, her sun-washed hair beginning to escape from her ponytail, she stands on the back steps, welcoming us and telling us what is going to happen, like a camp counselor. I only understand a bit of what she is saying.

She shows us to our room. Jim and I are the lucky ones because we made the reservations a week ago; we get the king-size bed in the loft. The two French couples are in a small bunk room below. The young French lovers are with the older couple and the Brit in a back bunk room.

Celeste's husband, Martin, eventually shows up. Martin has graying hair and is slight in frame, not handsome but distinguished. It turns out Celeste was tired and did not want to walk the whole way, so she hitched a ride. I admire her spunk to hitchhike.

We wait for our turn for the two shower stalls. The owner carries in a round tray with eleven cold bottles of beer. She deftly sets it on the white dining table in the central room that also has a couch and TV. We learn the next day that this beer is not free; it gets added on to our tab.

Most of the men and Celeste are gathered around the TV, watching France play Peru in the World Cup. There is much cheering and chatting in French. I'm enjoying the refreshing beer, and I'm acting the part of a local. But I'd prefer to be outside on the porch chatting with two of the women. I'm learning it is hard to join a conversation when you don't know what people are saying. I'm not the most outgoing person, but I've learned to join a discussion—however, not when it is in French. I sit on the couch listening to the World Cup commentary and sipping my beer. The beer cools my throat and relaxes me.

The owner says dinner will be served at seven thirty. At eight, she carries in a tall stack of plates, and everyone begins setting the table for eleven people—I can help with this. We settle into our places. Red wine is poured—this is also added to our bill.

The owner's teenage son, who just got home from *le football* practice, places a large *tarte flambée* (a thin-crusted pizza with no sauce) cut into twelve slices and a large wooden bowl of greens in the center of all of us. The *tarte flambée* is delicious. There is one piece left; who is going to get it? The Brit takes it. I take a second helping of the greens. The sharp vinegar dressing satisfies my taste buds. *But I'm still hungry. Will this be it?*

I remember a *gîte* we stayed in ten days ago, where the owner kept bringing out one *tarte flambée* after the other. There were eight walkers that night, and I lost count, but I think they brought out ten or twelve tarts—all with different cheeses, *jambon*, and mushrooms.

Looking back, I see how lost we were. At each *gîte*, we learned more about the systems.

This time, no more tarts come out. I turn to Celeste on my right, the older woman who jumped out of the car. She has short, dyed-black hair. I try asking her a few questions, and she answers me in French. I think she said that she and her husband walk part of the GR5 every year. But I'm not sure. She asks me something in French, but I do not understand her. I apologize to her that I don't speak French very well. She looks at me with a blank face. I get the feeling she thinks it is crazy that we are walking in the Jura and we do not speak French. She is right. We are crazy, but we are also brave.

What I've noticed is that language proficiency seems to be generational; while most of the young women we've met speak English the older women don't. Their blank faces and lack of reply come off as rude, but maybe through compassionate eyes, they're just embarrassed. Many of the older men speak some

English either from work or travel. So maybe Celeste is not rude, just feeling frustrated. Then again, we are in France and perhaps she feels we are the ones who should be speaking French. She is right to feel irritated.

Her husband, Martin, is chatting with Jim across the table. He seems to speak English pretty well. He traveled across the United States on a Greyhound bus back in the 1960s. His animated voice tells of his visits to the national parks, Las Vegas, San Francisco, and of course, NYC. I'm always amazed at people who say they visited the States and went to Las Vegas. I've never been, and I don't think I ever will. If visitors believe Las Vegas represents the United States, then they don't know my life. It's just an example of how we can't judge people and countries by a short visit. I've visited Paris twice before this trip, but I'm learning so much more about the people of France by walking in the countryside.

Earlier today at noon, I was ahead of Jim. I walked out of one field through a hedgerow to a freshly cut hayfield. I was surprised to see a small sedan parked on the edge of the field with its trunk opened. Looking closer I saw a mom and two young kids setting up a picnic with a green-and-white checkered cloth. The dad jumped down from a large tractor with a mower attached and walked towards his family. It was not a fancy picnic. I saw crackers on plastic plates. They looked up at me as I got closer. "*Bon appétit*," I called to them as I continued on the trail. I felt like I was interrupting an intimate family moment, but at the same time I felt blessed to witness it. I was proud of myself for remembering to say *bon appétit*, words I have heard wished to me at almost every meal. Now I could hand the words back with homage. "Enjoy your meal."

Questions poured out of me as I continued walking. *Do they do this every day at lunch? Or was this a special occasion? Do all farmers in the Jura gather together for lunch as a family during the mowing season?* I do not know the answers, but I did peek through a window of the people of the Jura's life.

I glance at my phone—nine o'clock. The sun is low in the sky and still bright, though I'm fading. I'm ready to go to bed hungry. I just want to lie down. The owner bursts back into the room, hoisting a heavy casserole dish, showing off her biceps. She places it on a trivet in the center of the table. *"Bon appétit."*

Celeste begins to fill everyone's plate with the potato-cheese mixture with a large sausage on top like a cherry on a sundae.

The potatoes melt in my mouth. The cheese is sharp in flavor and soft in texture. My stomach is smiling; soon I'm full. There is plenty of potato and cheese for anyone who wants seconds, which is most everyone. It's interesting how my moods can change depending on food scarcity vs. food abundance.

Then a fruit and a cheese plate is passed around. I've had enough cheese for today. I fill my plate with cherries and an apricot. It's the first apricot I've had this trip, and the flavor is bright earth, rounding off the meal perfectly.

We all clear the table and set it for breakfast. Celeste again takes charge of assigning people tasks. I like helping, being part of the group. My heart warms to these walkers. They know the ropes. Over the evening, we have shifted from observers to participants.

It is the longest day of the year today, June 21. At nine forty-five, the sun has set. I climb onto the big bed made up with crisp white sheets and look at the mauve dusk out the window. These days I wear my sunglasses from morning to bedtime. I don't ever put on my regular glasses because I'm never awake when it is dark. I'm so happy to be here, spending an evening with people who love to walk, even though I cannot talk with them as much as I would like. I hear the rustle of the other couples settling into their beds. I snuggle up next to Jim and whisper, "I want to call out 'Good night, John Boy,' to the other walkers down below, but I don't think they would get the reference." He smiles. "And tomorrow we get to walk again. We are so lucky."

We turn, our lips meet in a quiet kiss. Then we slip apart to our own sides of the bed. My lids fall closed, but I open them one more time to look out the window at the solstice light. From this angle I see across the farm road to a bank covered with a profusion of daisies and red clover. The once bold colors of yellow, red, and green are now iridescent. I close my eyes for the final time of the evening.

BOOKENDS
(DAY 60)

The abundant beauty of the Jura reminds me of a song by the Grift, a local band in Vermont, which includes the lyrics, "I'm drowning in the beauty all around, all around." But instead of drowning, I'm buoyed by the beauty all around, all around. Instead of walking, I'm floating through the Jura in June sunshine.

While we walked through the Vosges in the first half of June, we had light rain on and off with some sunny days. For the last eight days in the Jura, we have had sun—glorious sun.

Today we walk up the side of a ski area that in the summer is transformed into a downhill mountain biking park. The guidebook complains about the ski industry and their chairlifts scarring the mountain landscape. But for me, they give a little diversity to the day. We hike under a quad chairlift that carries hikers and mountain bikers up to the top. The mountain bikes hang off the chairlift like dead carcasses on a conveyor belt. As we ascend, we crisscross biking trails coming down. A bright yellow triangle sign says in French, "*Danger, Cohabitation Velo/Pietons*." I think it means watch out for bikers if you are walking and vice versa. I like the word *cohabitation*, living together in harmony. Can bikers and hikers live together in harmony? Jim thinks of himself as more of a biker, and I'm more of a walker. As long as we respect each other, then there is harmony.

Jim stops to watch the mountain bikers launch off a high jump above us. The padding they wear is called armor and looks like combat gear. Dressed head to toe in black with full face masks and helmets, they look like alien hornets. They jump over our heads as the GR5 is under the jump, like an overpass with no pavement. I can't look and hurry on with my head down. If any of the bikers missed the landing, even with armor, there would be carnage. I don't want to see lifeless hornets. I don't understand male desire for risk. Even Jim, who loves to watch, does not partake in the jumps of downhill mountain biking.

As we walk under the chairlift again, I look up, searching for Martin and Celeste. We saw them last night at a small restaurant. Martin told us that they were going to take the chairlift and save some energy. He asked us if we would too. We answered no. I surprised myself at how quickly I dismissed taking the chairlift. Maybe when we are in our seventies. I see now it's nice to know there is a different way to walk. We don't always have to climb high and exert energy; we can take a chairlift and enjoy the ride, like the boat ride I skipped five days ago. I'm going to want this before Jim, I suspect. But I'm learning that when I'm ready to take the chairlift, I will. And I'll enjoy the view while I wait for Jim to walk up. There are unlimited ways to climb a mountain.

Since we met at the trampoline *gîte*, we have been parallel walking with Celeste and Martin and the young couple, Julie and Davey. We are the middle couple in our fifties.

We don't actually walk together although we start at the *gîte* together. Celeste and Martin start early because they need more time to cover the distances. Davey and Julie are the last to leave as they sleep in like many young couples.

Davey and Julie are not married but cohabitate. When they walk, they talk to each other the whole time. Like new love, they are discovering more about each other.

We have not seen Celeste and Martin in the act of walking.

I don't know if they talk and walk the whole day. We pass them when they are resting. Sitting in the shade, she looks exhausted, her dyed-black hair plastered against her skin from the sweat. Martin tenderly passes her a water bottle to make sure she is getting enough to drink. But late every afternoon they wander into town. They are the last ones in, first ones out.

These two couples are the bookends of our walking life. We look to the young couple and are reminded of hiking before we had kids, when we were excited and not just exploring the outdoors but exploring each other.

We look at the elder couple and peek into our tomorrow: still walking ambitiously in our seventies, maybe taking a little longer and enjoying a full day of walking, possibly taking the chairlift up or a lift in a car on a humid afternoon.

At the top of the ski area, we leave the bikers behind and walk further up to the summit of Le Mont d'Or, where we lunch with distant views to the south. Finally, we can see the Alps. It is said that three hundred peaks are visible—an ocean of rickrack peaks. The sight of the massive mountains unnerves me. We will be there next week. *Will I be able to climb those mountains?* The white jagged peaks are harsh compared to the quaint farmed high plateaus stretched out in the foreground. A sheer cliff of limestone drops off to the east creating uninterrupted views looking into the Swiss Jura. The beauty is astounding.

Then I zoom in on all the comforting wildflowers surrounding our picnic; daisies, Queen Anne's lace, Indian paintbrush, and buttercups are the ones I recognize. New to me, a low-growing lavender soothes my soul, releasing a tranquil scent when I brush my hand over it.

Three hours of walking down the other side through cow pastures and beech woods leads us to the village of Mouthe, the source of the River Doubs.

Later that evening, we meet up with our entourage, snuggled

around a wooden table tucked into an alcove of a *gîte* in Mouthe: Davey and Julie, Martin and Celeste, and another couple we have not met before. The owner, a slight woman with wispy hair, pours us each a petite glass of green black-walnut liqueur made by her husband. She calls it *Brou de Noix*. She tells us in French about how her husband collects the unripe black walnuts and how he must be very careful not to stain his hands or clothes. Davey and Julie translate the highlights of the story for us.

As the liqueur slides over my tongue, my brain says, *Yes, the perfect name*. The green tastes like fresh grass, the walnut nutty, and the black is a pinch of tar, which sounds bad but subdues the green taste.

I eventually learn that historians believe the liqueur was first made in Britain. There was a pagan ritual of picking the green walnuts on June 24. Later, when Christianity took over, it was associated with St. John the Baptist, who was born near the summer solstice. Later it was made in parts of Italy, where it is called *nocino*, and in parts of France where it is called *Brou de Noix*. Many stories and legends explain the making of the liqueur. One mentions barefoot virgins picking the walnuts on June 24. Another mentions witches trying to steal the nuts on June 24 and the farmers lighting fires to keep the witches away. The night that we are drinking the green black-walnut liqueur happens to be . . . June 24. Either serving us the liqueur today was deliberate and that part of the story was lost in translation, or the synchronicity is staggering. We were meant to be with these people in these mountains at this time in our lives.

"Passer moi le pain, s'il vous plaît," says Martin, enunciating each word. Jim repeats the words back. *"Passer moi le beurre, s'il vous plaît; passer moi la salade."* Martin becomes our tutor. He feels it is vital that we speak French. Jim picks up the phrases quickly and uses them with confidence.

My dyslexic brain just does not process the phonological aspects as quickly. After repeating the phrase quietly to myself five or six times, I feel confident enough to try it out. "*Passer moi le pain, s'il vous plaît.*"

"Please pass the bread" is the essential phrase for this dinner, as we are feasting on fondue. The husband owner of the *gîte* made the fondue using the local Comté cheese and the local wine. The melted cheese and the softness of the wine coat the crusty squares of bread in a layer of lust, and my tongue is grateful that it struggled through the language to get to this pleasure. "*Passer moi le pain, s'il vous plaît,*" my tongue says again with more confidence. This is the way to learn a language: struggle, then a quick reward. I've never been good with delayed gratification.

The owner delivers two more baskets of bread squares. The aroma of the freshly cut bread mingles with the wine fumes bubbling through the cheese, intensifying the atmosphere of the room as if we were the bread chunks in the cheese sauce. Sharing the communal meal of fondue glues me to the walking community.

At the end of the evening, we are served gentian liqueur. Again, this is homemade from the root of the gentian plant, which is different than the little blue flower gentian I'm used to. It's a tall stalk with yellow flowers covering it and broad leaves at the base, like a yucca plant. We have walked by it for the last two weeks. It can grow as high as five feet in a cow pasture. It's toxic to the cows, and they leave it alone. The root is grated and then steeped in alcohol for months, then strained and drunk. When I put the glass to my lips, the smell of the alcohol assaults my nose before the liquid touches my lips. I pull back the glass just to get a smidge on my lips and feel the burn run down my throat. This liquid is harsh compared to the green black-walnut liqueur. I pass my glass to Jim.

Our tutor, Martin, looks out for us in other ways. The next afternoon in the town of Chapelle des Bois, Jim and I stay in the only hotel in town. I assumed our walking buddies would stay here too. We settle into our room and wash our socks. The sound of familiar voices rises from the front terrace. I skip down to see who is there. Our bookends, Julie and Davey and Martin and Celeste, drink beer in the late afternoon sunshine.

"Join us," says Julie, reaching over to pull another chair to the small round table. "We can't get into the *gîte* until four thirty."

"Where are you staying?" asks Martin.

"Here." I point up to the open windows of our room.

"Oh, save your money. I make you a reservation at the municipal *gîte*," says Martin.

"That is so nice of you. But we are all unpacked and settled. *Merci.*"

"Next time you let me help you make reservations. I save you money." He is so sweet to worry about us. From what I have picked up from watching and listening, the French walkers are a breed of hearty, frugal beings. They love walking, they love the countryside, they love the food, and they feel it is their birthright to walk and stay in lodging that is priced for anyone to enjoy. I want to bottle up their passion and righteousness for walking, ferment it, and share it back in the United States.

The next day we see Celeste and Martin for the last time. They are resting in the shade a few kilometers from Les Rousses, the last village before arriving at Lake Geneva (Lac Léman). We assume we will see them in Les Rousses, but it's a big town full of tourists, and we never do.

We meet Davey and Julie in Les Rousses for one last drink at an outdoor café. Julie introduces me to beer rouge, a beer with blueberry syrup. It looks like liquid rubies in the glass when the late June sun shines through. The bar has it on tap. I taste a hint of sweetness and bubbliness of berry flavor but not artificial berry flavor. I'm sure those berries were picked in the woods we walked through this afternoon; they taste so true. Julie explains that mostly women order it. Feminine beer rouge is now my favorite beverage. Just saying the word *rouge* is sexy as it rolls out of my mouth.

Julie and Davey are jealous that we get to continue walking through the Alps, as they have to go back to work. They invite us to stay with them in Lyon if we are ever in France again. We invite them to come to visit us in Vermont. We stand up to go, with hugs all around.

This past week of communing with people not our age has been uplifting. I intend to make a point of hanging out with people of different ages when I get home. The young and the old make life much more vibrant; like the sour and the sweet, we need both ends of the spectrum to bring out the full flavor of life.

REST
(DAY 63)

"**W**ake up, sweetie We need to get going," I say, leaning over to Jim in his adjacent twin bed, shaking his bare shoulder gently. The room is inky black except for a thin glow edging the shades like a frame. We need to walk out of town before breakfast is served to arrive in Nyon, Switzerland, for a one o'clock ferry. Our goal is to cross Lac Léman to the quaint town Yvoire, France, and then take a bus to Thonon-les-Bains, where we will rest for two and half days before beginning the Alps. Some walkers rest for a whole week before beginning the Alps. Jim and I could not rest for a full week; we would be too antsy. And most people who walk the Grand Traverse across the Alps begin at Lac Léman.

Today we are fitting a full day of walking—twenty-six kilometers—into a half day, though most of it is downhill out of the Jura to Lac Léman.

We emerge from the hotel into the crisp dawn light. We stride through the stilled streets past white petunias planted in a long metal gutter welded onto four milk cans. I smile at the ingenious use of discarded milk cans to create a flower planter that is either cultural or kitschy, depending on your mood. A lone shopkeeper in a red apron sweeps the sidewalk near her entrance and smiles at us. We pass the bar where I sipped beer rouge with Davey and Julie last night. The tables and chairs are stacked, waiting to be dispersed and arranged for the next set of walkers and tourists.

"Where is this place?" asks Jim, searching the street, as we are almost out of town.

"Right up here," I point. "Google said it would be open at 7:00 a.m., and it is seven right now," I say, checking my phone for the third time since leaving the hotel. I'm nervous about not having food for the long morning. We do have two apples and some leftover Comté cheese. A white van is parked in front of the bakery with its back doors wide open like butterfly wings. A young man with curly blond hair loads the van with crates of baguettes and trays of pastries.

Leaving my backpack with Jim, I follow the baker into the small shop heavily scented with morning yeast. "*Bonjour,*" I say.

"What can I help you with?" he says in English with a smile playing on his face. His blue eyes twinkle, and if I were thirty years younger, I might hang out here all morning. I scan the case. "I'll have four croissants and a loaf of your wheat bread, *s'il te plaît.*"

We walk through the yellow morning light eating our croissants and passing rolls of hay that cast long morning shadows. We don't usually walk and eat, but today is a different day. We need to keep moving. And we are nervous about walking into Switzerland.

Our worry has persisted about the French visa and staying over our limit. We are not sure how to interpret the agreement because it was written before the EU was formed. The agreement says we can be in Schengen countries for ninety days, and then we can be in France for an additional ninety days. We had been in Italy, the Netherlands, Belgium, and Luxembourg, all Schengen countries, for sixty-four days before we entered France on May 19, so not over the ninety days. Did that mean if we crossed over into another country once we had entered France, we could count it against the first ninety days? Or once we entered France must we remain there? This was one of the questions we had tried to ask the French Consulate in Washington, DC, but they had not answered our question.

After an hour of walking, we see the Swiss border ahead. Cars are being checked by gun-carrying customs patrollers in gray uniforms. Two of them inspect the trunk of a green sedan.

"There's the sidewalk. Let's go that way," says Jim. Switzerland is not part of the EU. We are fearful that they will ask for our passports and stamp them, and then what would we do when we tried to get back into France after taking the ferry across the Lac Léman?

My heart is racing as we slink along the sidewalk past the guns and patrollers. But no one stops us. We keep walking, not looking back. The GR5 ducks into the woods, and so do we. If we had done more research, we would have learned that Switzerland does not conduct passport control at its borders with the EU, just customs control.

Thirty minutes later, my heartbeat is back to normal as we cajole some Swiss cows away from the entrance to their muddy pasture, which the GR5 leads straight down the middle of. I'll take mud over uniformed officials.

We drop down 620 meters, following a Roman road that once led to Paris from Lac Léman. I think about the Romans who built the cobblestone road. Then I remember it was not the Romans who built it but their slaves. I wonder about the slaves' lives. Did they camp out in these woods? Their history is lost in the dust between the stones.

From the Roman road, we see hazy views of Lac Léman with the snow-covered Alps in the distance. The lake, almost ninety-five kilometers long, is shaped like a crescent, with Switzerland on the north side and France on the south side. It is the biggest body of water we have seen since leaving the North Sea more than two months ago.

After walking through hot, dry cornfields and vineyards, we enter Nyon's outskirts, then the city center, and finally emerge at the edge of the deep blue lake where the water laps.

I'm always flabbergasted by giant lakes. I grew up near the ocean. Massive lakes act like the ocean with waves and wind and deep blue color, but they are freshwater. They turn my thoughts inside out. The lake in front of us has little waves, a refreshing breeze, and no salt smell.

"We have forty-five minutes before the ferry comes. Let's eat lunch here," I say, pointing to the cafés along the lake.

"No, let's wait until we get across. I'm still worried about having a Swiss transaction on our credit card. Also, I don't think we have enough time," says Jim.

I could argue with him that we have cash and we don't need to use the credit card, but he is right; forty-five minutes might not be enough time, so we sit on a bench looking out at the view and share the last apple.

A restored steam ferry approaches the truncated dock edged with pylons. With the engine running, the gate slides open, and we efficiently move onboard. The gate closes, and the ferry moves on. No dillydallying.

Forty-five minutes later, we disembark onto a quay surrounded by restaurants adorned with overflowing flowerboxes.

"Let's eat there with a view of the lake," I say, waving my hand to the roof of a restaurant that has outdoor dining.

"Let's walk around and see what other restaurants are around first," says Jim, surveying the area. His eyes follow the road leading up to town.

"No, let's eat here. I'm hungry, verging on hangry, and it's a great view," I say, looking toward the restaurant and feeling like I want to stamp my foot. I see empty tables with white tablecloths on the edge of the upper deck.

"I really think we should walk around and find one that is not so expensive."

"No, we are eating here," I say as I march toward the restaurant, not looking to see if he is following. I think to myself, *This is supposed to be a celebration. We have made it to Lac Léman. Yes, we have eaten out almost every night since we started walking, but this is a special day. We deserve a nice lunch with a view.*

By the time the Hungarian waiter delivers the appetizer, the view has softened Jim enough so that he enjoys our overpriced lunch. I want to say to him, "Can't we just be tourists and enjoy the view?" But I don't. I can sense feelings that have been suppressed beginning to escape.

Looking back, I see that for two months we had adventured supporting each other in a united purpose, a union. Now, as we were beginning a two-and-a-half-day rest, our unruly individual selves were speaking up.

After being tourists for four hours, we ride the bus to Thonon-les-Bains. We trudge up the stairs to our second-floor apartment and open the door to a clean kitchen, small living room, and dark bedroom. There is an obscure view of the Alps from a southern window but none of the lake. The best part of the apartment is the washing machine. We have been hand-washing our clothes for two months. We can finally wash them in a machine.

Two evenings later, after washing our clothes twice, getting a haircut for Jim, buying microspikes and short gaiters for the Alps, but most importantly dozing, lounging, and reclining our tired bodies, we argue again.

Jim scrubs the pots from the pasta dinner I cooked. I sit on the couch across the apartment reading about what the trail is going to be like tomorrow. "Oh, I forgot to tell you," I say, "I finally found a salon that will cut my hair tomorrow just before the bus leaves."

"But I thought we had planned to take the funicular down to the lake after we clean up the apartment."

"It's the only time I could get the appointment," I say.

"Well, if you hadn't waited so long to look for an appointment, you might have gotten one today." I can hear the scratch, scratch of the steel wool speeding up and getting louder, as if he wants to hurt the pot.

He is right about my procrastination. I questioned if I wanted to get my hair cut. I had ventured into a few salons yesterday, but none of them had appointments. Today I found one that looked appealing and had an appointment. Most important, they spoke a bit of English, which put me at ease. Having my hair cut when I can't communicate clearly is a bit scary for my vanity.

He can go to the funicular himself. I don't have the energy to argue or discuss. It seems so petty to argue about the timing of my haircut. He's so selfish. He got HIS haircut! Frustration rises inside of me, like black bubbles escaping from tar. I don't want to deal with him. I want to escape.

"I'm going out to take pictures," I say, grabbing my camera and slamming the door behind me. I need to get away. Everything Jim has done or said has bothered me since we got to the apartment.

I walk three blocks to a dramatic view looking out over the lake sixty meters below. The orange sun shimmers across the placid lake before dipping below the mountains of Switzerland. I snap photo after photo, hoping the beauty will soothe me. Ironically, part of me wishes Jim were here to see this. Beauty is intensified when it is shared. Another part of me is content to be alone in the orange light.

What am I really worried about? I ask myself. A flash of uncertainty enters my consciousness. *What am I going to do when I get home? What is next? Will I make it through the Alps? I'm strong, but those are big mountains.*

I walk back into the apartment, and I sit down next to Jim on the couch. "Can we talk?" I ask, leaning my shoulder into his.

"Sure. Can I just say I'm sorry about earlier. I get frustrated by you not telling me what you have planned."

"Yes, I know. I'm sorry. We haven't had to deal with day-to-day shit in a while. I think we, or maybe just I, have forgotten how to communicate my intentions." Silence weaves in and out of the dusk. I bite my inner lip. "I also realize I'm uncertain about what is going to happen when we get home. I thought I would be thinking about the future as we walked, but it was not until we got here that I started focusing on what comes next. I get this feeling that I don't have the energy to rebuild my coaching business in Vermont. I feel stuck and lost. What is the rest of my life going to look like?" My shoulders slump.

"I haven't thought about the future at all either. I thought I would have my new life all planned out by now. What have we been thinking about while we walk? All I know is that it has not been the future." He puts his arm around my shoulder, and we ease out of a state of stress and into one of repose.

A fear of the unknown is agitating both of us.

Lac Léman is supposed to be a deep rest for us, the way the lake is deep. We rest our bodies, but we agitate our connection. Waves of emotion rise up from the depths and rock our relationship—little waves that feel big in the moment. We have argued so little while walking. Maybe we're sick of each other. Maybe we need friends to join us in the Alps.

PART SIX

THE NORTHERN ALPS

LONG APPROACH
(DAY 66)

The Alps, like all things that are magnificent, have a long approach. In many ways we have been approaching them for two months. Here, in Saint-Gingolph on the border of Switzerland and France, it's a day-and-a-half walk to enter the Alps proper. We have a new guidebook for the Alps. It's like having a new companion. When the author says, "The path is steep and rugged," what does he mean exactly? We will find out.

Jim and I stand at the lakeshore, watching passengers disembark from the ferry and searching for Margo and Todd.

"I don't see them," I say.

"Me either. Maybe they missed the ferry."

A boatman closes one gate and opens the gate to allow the new passengers on. We turn and head up into Saint-Gingolph to look for a café that has internet to try to reach them.

"Kathy! Jim!" Our names ring through the clear afternoon air. "We made it. The ferry makes quick stops. We almost missed the dock," Margo says as she and Todd strut up the hill with their backpacks swaying.

We hug and chatter greetings. Jim and Todd go in search of lunch food for tomorrow. Margo and I sit on a bench next to an open-air market. Margo pulls out the walking shoes I ordered and shipped to her house. I slip them on and put my old ones in my pack. I want to make sure the new ones fit well before I discard my old shoes.

"Where do we start?" she says, her blond ponytail bouncing around.

"Just up the hill. Jim and I found the first waymark after we got off the bus. We have about two hours of walking this afternoon to get to Novel and our *gîte* for tonight. We are sharing a room that has two double beds." It feels more intimate to share a room with friends than to share a dorm room with strangers. "I hope that's okay."

"Yes, we are fine with it all. We are so excited to be here, and we can't thank you enough for planning our week of hiking," she says.

"Well, we are pretty good at planning and making reservations now," I say with a sigh and a laugh.

Margo and I walk side by side while Todd and Jim follow. Having old friends to chat with is comforting. My body sinks further into a state of relaxation as endorphins flow, and it is happy to be walking again. Two and half days of rest was just what I needed.

We walk through a beech and conifer forest with a loud cascading stream tumbling down the steep slope. Ferns, rocks, and moss cover the forest floor.

We enter an open, narrow meadow and catch glimpses of rocky crags touching the sky. Small farmhouses and barns are nestled into the landscape, welcoming us to the mountain village of Novel.

That evening I introduce Margo to beer rouge at the crowded tiny bar of the *gîte*, where families are glued to the TV watching France beat Argentina in the World Cup. We learn that the couple managing the *gîte* was hired by the municipality to encourage walkers to visit the town.

After dinner, the rose light of the setting sun shines on the crags, alluding to the beauty yet to come.

The next morning the GR5 leads us up a paved road to a dirt track and finally to a steeper single track through amazing meadows of wildflowers. Clusters of spruce, which are shorter now, dot the landscape. Patches of snow on the north-facing slope melt at the pace of the warming July sun. Looking back from where we came, we see Lac Léman twelve hundred meters below, framed by two ridges.

I'm breathing hard, chatting with Margo, and energized by the scenery. But I know my body so well now I recognize I can't keep this pace all day. I'm facing the first col, the lowest point between two mountains, with another one to climb later today. I must walk my own walk.

"You guys go ahead. I need to rest a bit. I'll see you at the top of the col. It looks like about thirty minutes of climbing." I sit on a boulder on the side of the trail.

"I'll rest too. I need to drink more water." Jim sits down next to me.

"All right we will see you at the top." Margo and Todd stride up the trail.

Margo and Todd are amazing hikers. They have participated in full triathlons, and usually they end on the podium. They love to run uphill. Our friends call them sick, but really, we are all jealous of their athletic abilities.

"It's wonderful having Margo and Todd here, but I need to walk my own pace," I say as I lean into Jim's shoulder, my way of thanking him for staying with me.

For half an hour Jim and I fall into our walking pattern of companionable silence. We climb past blue bachelor buttons, daisies, alpine roses, pinks, globeflowers, and forget-me-nots. I love my pace where breath flows between footsteps.

As we crest Col de Bise at 1,915 meters, my breath stops. To the south, snow-covered peaks stretch into the distance. Mt. Blanc's massive white face peeks out behind a closer mountain. In the foreground, sweeping green slopes slide into the valley at impossibly steep angles. The GR5 trail, like a thread on a carpet, shows us which way we are headed. The scenery looks like Julie Andrews is going to come around the corner with her guitar and start singing, "Climb Ev'ry Mountain." We have climbed the first of thirty-seven cols. Pulsating waves of excitement move through my body. We have arrived in the Alps.

FORGETTING THINGS (DAY 69)

The sun seeps through the clouds for the first time today, so I search my backpack for my sunglasses. We are on our third day of walking in the Alps and have stopped at a small farm (*alpage*) with a Swiss flag flying. The GR5 wandered into Switzerland yesterday, and we spent last night in a Swiss refuge.

Now, Margo refills her water from a stone watering trough where two metal milk cans sit in the cool spring water. I sit on a bench in the sun with Jim and Todd, looking out over the magnificent snow-capped mountains. Awe floats in the air.

In the last few days, a system has emerged. When we walk uphill, Margo and Todd go ahead at their blazing pace for forty-five minutes to an hour and then stop and wait for us at an interesting spot. Margo spends her time capturing the beauty of the wildflowers with her camera. As for Todd, I'm not sure what he does—maybe push-ups?

We match their pace on the downhill or the flat, though there is not much flat in the Alps.

Our walk this morning contoured a ridge then a gradual downhill through sprawling alpine farms. We stayed together and chatted for two hours. We spoke about our aging parents and how twenty years ago they would have loved this walk through the Alps.

Now, I begin to panic as I search for my small gray stuff sack with my prescription sunglasses inside. I pull out my light blue stuff sack, camera case, dark green stuff sack, then all the stuff sacks are scattered on the dirt. I feel a heaviness in my stomach. *Where is my small gray stuff sack with my sunglasses, earbuds, and extra credit card?* Frantically I check the very bottom pocket of my pack that holds my emergency space blanket and emergency food bars. But it's not there.

In a low voice I say to Jim, "I left a small stuff sack that held my prescription sunglasses at the refuge. I feel sick. We are about six kilometers from the refuge; it's too far to walk back."

Standing rigid, he raises his eyebrows, and his face says, *Here we go again.*

I have forgotten other items on this trip. I left my hiking poles in a hotel in the Jura, but I remembered when I was only half a kilometer away. I've lost two knives this trip. Now we just use Jim's.

Back in the Vosges, I had to backtrack two kilometers to retrieve my sun hat, which had slipped off the back of my pack. Jim has not left anything behind. He is meticulous, and I am not.

"I'll call the refuge and see if they can give it to a walker, and we will wait here," I explain calmly but with irritation for myself in my voice.

I dial the number of the refuge. *"Parlez-vous anglais?"* I ask.

"No" is the answer.

I look around. A couple from the refuge has just come along the trail. I remember talking to the woman last night. She speaks English and is French. I explain my predicament. She calls the number and speaks in French.

After hanging up, she says, "The owner is not at the refuge. She is on her way to town. Call her in ten minutes after she has talked to her husband, who is at the refuge. We will wait and I'll call her again."

She calls back. The owner says that everyone has left, and her husband, who is at the refuge, does not see the gray sack. I thank the woman, and she and her husband walk off to the south, the way we should be going.

I think back to packing up this morning, the last time I saw the stuff sack. I was sitting on a long bench in the hallway with backpacks hanging above my head. The cramped refuge slept twenty-four, and it was full. Chaotic mayhem filled the hallway as people packed. Others waited for the one indoor bathroom clutching their toothbrushes. There was another bathroom, but you had to go outside to get to it. Even with one bare light bulb on, it was hard to see. I kept knocking elbows with a man next to me. Frustrated, I decided to take my stuff outside and pack out on a picnic table, even though it was damp from the drizzle. Obviously, I left my gray stuff sack under the bench. The other refuges we have stayed at have not been full. As we head into the high season of walking, I will have to be more careful when packing in overcrowded refuges.

Now, I run through different solutions. One is taking a taxi back to the refuge in the evening. I look at my map. It is hard to tell how the roads are from one place to the next. Today we go over two cols, so it will probably be a long taxi ride. In the Alps, it is hard to get from one place to the next. Or maybe I can call the owners of the refuge tonight, and they will ship or mail the gray sack to a hotel a few days up the trail? I tell Jim, Margo, and Todd about my solution of a taxi or mail. They look dubious.

Margo says. "Why don't Todd and I walk back and get it, and you guys go ahead? We will meet you on top of the second col."

"That would be an extra twelve kilometers for you on top of the twenty-three we have today. That's too much," I say. "Also, we don't know exactly where the gray sack is. Someone could have taken it."

I look at Todd. I can't tell if he thinks this is a good idea or not. They do not have GAIA, but they do have the guidebook.

Todd nods to Margo.

Margo pipes up, "Yes, we will go. We know exactly how to get back to the refuge. The trail is well marked. It will be a good workout! You guys keep walking, and we will meet you on the way or at the second col."

"I can't thank you enough! Are you sure you want to do it?"

"Yes, yes, we want to," they say in unison.

They pack up water, energy bars, and raincoats into small string bags. They leave their backpacks with us.

"I'll ask the owner of the *alpage* if we can put your packs up on the deck under the tables so they will not get wet if it rains, even though it looks like it is completely clearing up. But you never know. Thank you. Thank you! I'll buy you dinner and drinks tonight!" I say all in a rush.

Margo and Todd head north. They move at a fast pace without the weight of their packs and with the quest of finding my gray stuff sack.

I ask the owner if we can leave our friends' packs under the picnic tables. The woman behind the counter does not understand me. I type my message into Google Translate and show her my phone. She looks at me and smiles and says, "*Oui, oui.*" She says something else, but I do not understand her. I buy one of the cheeses on the shelf behind her.

After placing Margo and Todd's packs under a picnic table, I go in search of Jim. I don't see him anywhere; he is annoyed at my forgetfulness and is showing it by his absence. Our packs remain on the bench. I spy another couple from the refuge last night, the couple we played Bananagrams with before dinner. His name is Gerard, and he always has a smile on his face. He is French but lives in London. Her name Anthea; she lives in London too. We can't completely figure out their relationship. She mentioned a husband last night—not, apparently, Gerard. She is tall and athletic. I greet them.

Gerard says, "Yes, yes, we saw your friends, and yes, the stuff sack is still at the refuge. Someone found it this morning, and we were all trying to figure out whose it was. They opened it and saw your credit card and knew it was yours."

This is bliss to my ears. Now Margo and Todd's quest is not for nothing.

I say, "Gerard, would you mind calling the refuge and telling the owner that our friends are coming back to get the stuff sack? Thank you." I'm getting better and better at asking for help.

Gerard and Anthea order a Coke and coffee and sit in the sun on the deck. Even though I never drink Coke, this morning I could drink one. I feel guilty for forgetting my stuff sack and might as well keep up the corruption and drink a Coke.

When I think logically, I know everyone forgets things or makes mistakes, but when I'm in the moment and stripped down to my essentials, missing some of the essentials becomes more of a predicament. When I mess up, shame can cloud my mind and trigger that feeling of not being good enough.

Looking back, it's obvious that Jim's irritation did nothing to help. This is my biggest frustration with him; his practical nature and meticulousness sometimes make little room for compassion.

I look around for Jim and spot him in a stone shed with a rusted metal roof. The alpine farms have long low sheds for equipment and cheese making. These are summer farms. The family will herd the cows down to lower pastures in the fall.

Inside the shed, a thin farmer and his two sons make cheese in a shiny copper vat over an open fire. The embers of the fire glow the same color as the polished copper pot, like a glowing sunset. The copper vat has an electric stirrer and swings away from the fire on an electric arm. This electric arm with stirrer is the only modern contraption in this ancient building. Rough wood lines the walls and four prized cowbells hang from a rafter—the largest the size of a cow's head. I think, *How does a cow feel with that around her neck?* A convoluted metal-and-wood whisk three feet in length hangs on the wall, no longer in use.

The farmer tastes the cheese. He grabs two metal spoons from a wooden worktable and scoops up some of the cheese and offers it to us. I bring the hot white curd to my mouth, blowing gently. The warm, soft cheese relaxes onto my tongue. The salt, creaminess, and fresh grass taste register on my taste buds. The farmer's two sons, who look about six and eight and are replicas of their father, disappear for a minute. They reappear holding out their hands and arms to their dad as if they are interns getting ready for surgery. Dad examines their arms and gives a slight nod. No latex gloves, hairnets, or other regulations like in the United States.

Using a quart-sized ladle, the older boy begins to scoop out the curds into a round plastic tub that his younger brother holds. They know their jobs. The dad joins in too. Slowly the giant copper vat empties of curds, and all that is left is the whey. We had watched cheese making in Sicily too, also with copper pots and open fires. There, the farmer fed the whey to a sheepdog and her puppies. We never find out what happens to the whey here. Watching the father share the simple ancient way of making cheese with his boys calms me, and the fiasco of leaving items behind lessens.

After twenty minutes of watching, I am antsy to move on. We say our good-byes to the cheese makers. But before moving on, we sit on the bench and eat the whole wedge of cheese I bought. By now, it is ten and our six o'clock breakfast has metabolized. The cheese melts in my mouth. Eating food right at the source is miraculous. We see and hear cows grazing up above us on the slope. We witness milk boiling over the wood fire. I taste fire, copper, sun-soaked grass, and the loving energy of the farmer and his sons. It's all there in the cheese. We consume the atmosphere of the *alpage*.

We walk south into a dazzling day. I work hard to appreciate the day and the scenery. But I feel off-balance. Something is missing—Margo and Todd. I'm worried about them getting the stuff sack and then catching up with us. As we walk, I look at the trail with new eyes. I look to see if there are waymarks at every turn so that Margo and Todd do not make a wrong turn.

We reach the first col in twenty-five minutes and enjoy the stunning views in all directions. There are peaks to the left and right. A closed-up border patrol building is the only remnant of the border. We walk back into France and down into the next valley.

On the valley floor, we enter the woods, where logging has just occurred. At an intersection, an arrow points to a hotel and refuge and another points south to Col de la Golèse. There are no white-and-red waymarks to say which way the GR5 goes. We check the guidebook and GAIA. GPS says go towards Col de la Golèse.

Margo and Todd might not know which way to go, so we make an arrow using large pine branches, laying them on the muddy track pointing left.

I try to imagine if I were coming along the trail. "Would I even see the arrow, as there were so many other branches scattered on the track?"

"Margo competed in orienteering for years. She will figure out which way to go," says Jim confidently.

As we climb toward the second col, we emerge into open meadows. Then we approach a jumble of large boulders and trees that have all fallen downhill. As we look closer at the dirt and mud, we realize it's ice and snow covered with soil. A massive avalanche must have come roaring down the side of the valley, snapping giant trees as if they were matchsticks. The trees broken off at eight to ten feet tell us the snow was that deep when the avalanche wreaked destruction.

We see peoples' footsteps through the dirty snow. Across the avalanche, on the other side, someone built a stone cairn. At least Margo and Todd will not get lost here.

As we get closer to the top of the second col, Jim moves ahead. Sweat beads on my forehead. The trail switches in and out of the ridge's shade offering some relief.

Up ahead is a guy in white shorts and a white shirt. As I approach him, I recognize him from last night. He and his friend arrived late at the refuge. His legs were bright pink from sunburn and contrasted sharply with his white shorts, like a lobster in tennis garb. We greet each other, *"Bonjour."*

Around two more switchbacks, I pass his buddy.

I wonder what he thinks about an older woman walking faster than he does. I get a spring in my step whenever I pass men walking or hiking.

I arrive on top of a wide-open plateau covered in wildflowers. The path leads around the ridge where, at an intersection, a cluster of walkers sit off to the side of the trail. As I get closer, I realize it's more people from last night's refuge. One of them asks me where our friends are. I tell them that they've gone back to the refuge to retrieve my forgotten stuff sack. One of the women translates to the others. She says to me, "You have good friends."

I say nodding vigorously, "Yes, very good friends."

I look around for Jim. He stands on the deck of a refuge tucked into the side of the col, waving his arms. I join him and we sit at a table against the wall of the building to shelter us from the light wind. I keep my sun hat on, and I want to be in the sun to stay warm. It is almost two o'clock; Margo and Todd should be here soon.

"Well, you are not the only person who made a mistake today," Jim says. "I made a big one. I made reservations to spend tonight here, but I never looked at the map. Their mailing address is in Samoëns down in the valley, where we want to go tonight. If we stay up here tonight, tomorrow's walk will be too long." He pauses. "I just talked to the owner. He was upset that I was canceling the reservation so late. I ended up forfeiting the deposit. I feel bad."

So many emotions swirl in me: anger at Jim for being sharp with me when I made a mistake this morning; worry about where we will sleep tonight; relief that Jim is also fallible. An aspect of Jim that I do not love is he makes few mistakes. He grew up in a family with high expectations, a family in which mistakes were not tolerated. He is careful and diligent, and he is smug. It has driven me crazy over the years. Now, with this development, I can remind him that he makes mistakes too, but the urge to play tit for tat makes me sad. I want us both to realize everyone makes mistakes. It is part of life, and as a couple we need to give each other compassion when one of us has messed up.

"Wow. So where are we going to stay tonight? I guess we need to be careful and check on the map where the locations of these mountain refuges are."

"Yeah, I'll be more careful. I looked on Booking.com and there are lots of rooms in a bunch of hotels in town. It's a ski town. I'll make a reservation after we order lunch."

We order salads, a relief after no vegetables last night.

The owner delivers the most beautiful salad of fresh dark greens with paper-thin slices of dried ham, and in the center is a frilly flower made of shaved cheese. He is all smiles and has gotten over the snafu with the reservation.

I tell Jim about seeing and passing the two guys from last night. We start calling them Sunburned and His Buddy. Just then, I look over to the trail and see them standing by the sign at the intersection as if undecided whether to come over here or keep going. They keep going.

A few minutes later, Anthea and Gerard show up. They sit at the table next to us and order coffee and a colonel.

"What's a colonel?" I ask.

"Lemon sorbet with vodka," Anthea says with a twinkle in her eye.

"Wow, I don't think I could walk after having one of those," I say.

"I enjoy them on holiday, and it's all downhill from here," she says.

We chat and learn that they are walking for ten days and their luggage is delivered from town to town. They are not married but are friends who got to know each other by jumping out of airplanes on a parachute-jumping team. Gerard's partner does not like to walk, and neither does Anthea's husband, so every few years, they go off on a walking trip together.

Anthea and Gerard finish their afternoon refreshments and head back to the trail to walk to town.

"It's three o'clock. Where are Margo and Todd? I'm starting to get worried. Maybe they got lost or one of them got hurt." We try to text Todd and ask them where they are but get no answer.

Jim does not understand why I'm worrying. "Margo has participated in the run up Mount Washington a few times. Todd went to the Ironman Triathlon in Hawaii. They are very accomplished athletes. Stop worrying."

I keep my eyes on the trail out by the intersection, looking for Margo's blue shirt. Todd is wearing gray today. My eyes are tired from looking west. The sun is intense, reflecting off the young green grass.

Finally, I see them. I wave my hands in the air and call out, "Over here, Margo and Todd. Over here."

They see us waving and take the fork to the refuge. Todd pulls out the gray stuff sack and hands it to me.

"Thank you, thank you! How am I ever going to thank you enough? Thank you. Thank you!" I sound like a broken record, but I'm sincere.

I look in the gray stuff sack for my prescription sunglasses. I put them on, and my eyes relax. My head lamp is there too. Inside a little zip pouch are my earbuds, my extra credit card, and some cash: three hundred euros. I had forgotten there was so much in there. I had stashed the money away for an emergency back in March when we were in Sicily. Luckily, we have not needed it. This is the most significant emergency that we have encountered. Fortunately it happened when Margo and Todd were with us because I'm not sure what I would have done otherwise. Twelve extra kilometers is a long way.

"We had a great day," says Margo, beaming a smile. "We got to the refuge in a little over ninety minutes. It was more uphill than we remembered. The owner had the gray stuff sack for us. She refilled our water, and I practiced my French with her. We had an energy bar, then turned around and walked back."

"Did you have any trouble finding the trail?" I ask.

"No, we saw the waymarks the whole time. We did stop for lunch at the top of the first col. Wow, that was beautiful. And it was interesting to see the border patrol building. And the wildflowers were beautiful again today."

"Do you want anything to eat? We had yummy salads," I offer.

"Yes, let's split one, and I'll get ice cream, too," says Margo.

Half an hour later, we are on our way. My sunglasses shade the late afternoon sun.

After ten kilometers all downhill to the town of Samoëns, I will buy Margo and Todd a drink and a well-deserved dinner. Thank goodness for friends, especially fit friends.

TURN BACK
(DAY 71)

Two days later in the clouds, Margo, Todd, Jim, and I climb with microspikes up the snow-covered flank of Le Brévent. The guidebook states, "Climbing the Brévent should be avoided if a storm is imminent or if there is snow or ice on the steep, rocky slopes." These words float about in my brain, agitating my nervous system. We explicitly left the refuge early to get up and over Brévent before the rain was supposed to get bad.

Up on the col, at 2,440 meters, the GR5 overlaps with the famous Tour du Mont Blanc, a ten-day walk around Mont Blanc through Italy, Switzerland, and France. We watch a guide and a group of South Koreans clamber up a boulder slope. We see no waymark on the col. And because there is no visibility, we can't tell exactly which way the summit is. We discuss our options. We can walk back down part of the snowfield we just climbed and look for tracks heading in the right direction. We can follow the guide and the South Koreans, or we can walk down the trail into Chamonix, which the guidebook suggests during bad weather. I have a dark feeling in my gut. I want to walk down to Chamonix. Jim wants to follow the guide. None of us wants to go back down the snowfield and look for the trail. If we slip, we might land on jagged rocks.

Margo and Todd defer to us. I give in and say, "Okay, let's follow the guide and the group." But I don't want to.

As we follow the South Koreans and their guide, bad feelings slow me down. Jim, Margo, and Todd are up ahead scrambling faster over the boulders. The rock is dead cold under my gloved hands. The wind gusts blow my voice and courage away. I move in slow motion, not because my body is frozen, but because my intuition is telling me to get off this fucking mountain. At the same time, the adventurous part of me wearing the tough-woman skin says, *Move slowly, you can do it. Always keep moving forward.* Crashing and colliding, my wise intuition and my tough-woman skin rage inside of me, creating a stronger storm than the one outside.

How do I thaw my voice? How do I melt the words, "We need to turn back," so that they flow out of my mouth like a raging river?

Then a call rings through the clouds. I hear the guide yell, "Turn back. The ladders have too much snow on them. It's not safe."

The minute we turn around, the dread in my bones vanishes, though it is still difficult maneuvering over the boulder field.

Back on the col the clouds split open for a minute, and we get a peek down to the famous mountaineering town Chamonix. "Let's go that way," I say, pointing to the closing window of clouds. "We can check out Chamonix." They all agree.

We plunge down a ski slope just as the rain begins to tumble. A first-aid building with a large porch comes into view, and we race towards it. We wait out the rain and hail while eating our lunch on the porch. Eventually, soaking wet, we enter Chamonix, which is crawling with tourists. We decide to skip Chamonix and take the bus to Les Houches.

That evening we enjoy a farewell dinner with Margo and Todd. Together we experienced dozens of cascading waterfalls, views of Mont Blanc, unsuccessful searches for edelweiss, a refuge with four double mattresses on one long bunk with the same above, and staggering views of snow-capped mountains connected by meadows of wildflowers.

THE BEAUTY OF THE WORLD (DAY 73)

"This is phenomenal!" cries Jim over his shoulder. Two days later we balance on Crête des Gittes, a ridgeline with earth falling steeply away on both sides. The ridge is shaped like a shark's fin. The trail follows the knife-edge ridge for a kilometer then switches to the east flank and then back again to the west flank. Both sides have carpets of wildflowers flowing down, down, down.

The guidebook warns about not walking on this section if the weather is bad because of the exposure. But today is a beautiful white-puffy-cloud, blue-sky day—a beauty I could not have imagined. My heart sings as we walk along the ridge looking off both sides, trying to decide which view is prettier. It's a kind of ecstasy to walk on top of the world. We dawdle as we walk; we don't want the two kilometers to end.

"Did you see this waymark?" I call up to Jim.

He returns to see it. The white-and-red brush marks form an optical illusion as the folded rock transforms my favorite rectangles into waves. The pressure it took to mold these rocks is the same pressure it took to make the mountains. I'm awed by the power and energy of landmasses pushing into each other to create uplift. The Alps are relatively new mountains in geologic terms, having emerged a mere sixty-five million years ago.

Turning around to take pictures of where we came from, I

see Anthea and Gerard as specks in the distance. For the last two days we have walked on and off with them.

"Let's wait for them," I call up to Jim. We wait at the base of the pyramid peak that marks the end of the ridge.

"Isn't this spectacular?" Gerard calls to us. They both wear big smiles on their faces and big floppy sun hats shading their eyes. His red. Hers blue.

"It is so nice to be away from the Tour du Mont Blancers. It's just us and the mountains," says Anthea with a flourish of her arms. At lunch today, on Col du Bonhomme, the GR5 and the TMB had gone their separate ways.

After enjoying the vista we make our way off the ridge for a long, steep descent in an alpine meadow. Anthea is a landscape designer in London. She identifies flowers by both their Latin and common names in England, which are not always the same as in the United States. The Latin rolls off her tongue like satin ribbon. She has the aura of a wise professor mingled with a young botany enchantress as she gets down to eye level with a yellow flower, counting and pointing out pistils, petals, stigma, style, and anther.

At the end of the trail for the day is Refuge du Plan de la Lai, a refuge run by the Fédération Française des Clubs Alpins et de Montagne (FFCAM). On the deck, we share a slice of chocolate tart that is so deliciously intense, like our walk on the ridge, that we order another slice to share. Then beers all around except for Anthea, who orders another colonel to celebrate their last evening on the trail. They are heading back to family and jobs.

Later while we wait for dinner to be served to the group of twenty sitting around two long wooden tables, who should walk in but Sunburned and His Buddy. They register, drop their packs off by the stairs, and then stop to chat.

We attempt to ask them how they are. His Buddy shows us the back of his calf, which has a nine-inch white bandage. With

Gerard translating, they explain that His Buddy slipped on the snowy slope of Mt. Brévent and landed on a rock pile. He got twenty-two stitches, Sunburned mimes sewing in the air to us. We nod our heads and say that we did not go to the top because of the weather. We ask if it still hurts. He says a little. They go off and sit with other French-speaking walkers.

"See, I'm so glad we turned back and escaped down to Chamonix," I say to Jim. Jim realizes we ended up making the right decision.

"How did you guys go over Brévent?" I ask Anthea and Gerard.

Anthea says, "We stayed on the snow below the col and went right just below the rock outcropping, but it was scary, and when we got to the top, we took the *téléphérique* down to Chamonix. Then a bus to Les Houches. How about you?"

"We followed a guide and group from South Korea, but they turned back because the ladders were full of snow. So, we walked down to Chamonix from the col in the pouring rain and took the bus like you." I continue, "I wonder what climbing Brévent would be like if it were a day like today? And what today would have been like in the rain and wind? The weather makes all the difference."

Gerard leans in and says, "Yes. Maybe in ten years we meet and walk the GR5 again." We all smile knowing it will never happen, but dreaming is more possible the higher on a mountain you are.

We slide into our farewell dinner with Anthea and Gerard. Jim and I will be on our own again. I will miss having people to walk with, but I'm content to walk with beauty.

The next morning Jim and I are greeted by the sound of cowbells echoing off the steep mountain walls. We contour on a magnificent cirque. Jim is up ahead. The trail is easy walking; white crumbled rock cuts through meadows of wildflowers. As I cross over a stream, five velvet brown cows move toward me. One has a giant bell on her neck. With every footstep the bell clangs. *Clang, clang, clang.* It's a steady persistent sound. Two calves, looking like replicas of their mothers, trot along. The muscles in their rumps are well defined from walking these awesome mountains in their short lives.

I place my hand on my thigh and feel my muscles contract and release with each footstep.

The cowbells fade behind, and trickling water takes their place. The morning sounds shift my consciousness like a hypnotist. The mountain air quivers in the celestial sunlight. Drifts of wildflowers express every color imaginable. I fall into an ethereal pace. As if I'm broken into pieces, I become the air and the landscape.

Life is not about me. It's about the beauty of the world. This truth is what I have longed for but did not know. *What does beauty feel like? What does beauty taste like?*

Maybe an hour goes by as I float through moving meditation. I slowly emerge from the mystical feeling of beauty.

I catch up to Jim, who is dealing with his sore toes. He ties his shoe and says, "How can each day be more beautiful than the last?"

I have no answer.

EDGE OF A CLIFF
(DAY 75)

At breakfast two days later, at an auberge on the outskirts of Landry, we watch three older men at the bar drink some sort of liquor before going to work—or maybe they are just getting off work. I don't know, but it's fun to watch them being jovial at eight in the morning. Perhaps I should have joined them in a drink.

Three hours later, I'm balancing on a large spruce tree trunk. Jim is ahead, jumping gracefully from trunk to trunk. The trail is supposedly somewhere below this jumble of downed logs. The loggers have been here recently, but they have not finished their job.

We have come across logging operations before, and the loggers have usually done an excellent job of rerouting the trail around the activity.

About a kilometer back, we saw GR5 waymarks heading west. We followed them up for a bit, then they ceased and we were met with a divergence of several different trails. We had no idea which way to go. Frustrated, we checked GAIA and the guidebook again. I read the section over and over. It did not say anything about climbing higher.

So, we went back to the beginning of the logging road and followed it by climbing up and over downed trees.

It is slow going for me. I put my hands down on a log to help me move from one to another. Sap sticks to my hand. We continue for fifteen minutes.

"This is not right. There's a thirty-meter drop-off down to a streambed. The logging road is washed away in a mudslide," calls Jim. "It looks like we could potentially crawl down and back up the other side, but I see no sign of the trail across the streambed."

I join him and look across the washout. There are just more logs that look like a pile of matchsticks.

I consult GAIA again trying desperately not to get sap on my phone. The trail seems to be twenty meters below us. We have been paralleling it but not on it.

Discouraged, we backtrack, scrambling over the logs again, doubling the sap on my hands though I try to rub it off at the same time. I keep checking GAIA. This is where the trail forks off the logging road. I start following a faint path through weeds and blackberry canes. Walking a little further, there is a definite path of sorts. I look at GAIA again. Yes, I'm right on the purple line.

"I found it. Over here," I call to Jim, who has continued to backtrack.

We look for waymarks, but there are none. "Maybe there used to be a waymark on one of the felled trees? Perhaps it is hidden below this pile of tree trunks?" I say.

This is what the guidebook says:

"Turn left along a path that undulates across a forested slope . . . Afterwards, it drops in steep and greasy zigzags as it negotiates breaches in rugged cliffs."

What are "greasy zigzags"? Does that mean you can fall off the zigzags because they are slippery? I can't wait for "breaches in rugged cliffs."

We follow the faint path, climbing down along the rugged cliffs. I put one of my hiking poles away so I can use my hand to help haul myself down and around significant outcroppings. With my right hand on the crumbling yellow rock, I reach my left leg out as far as I can to get to the next step. I'm sweating even though it is not warm. My heart is beating faster than it should be.

"Are you sure this is right?" I ask Jim as I'm having doubts again.

"Well, the last time I was here, this is the way I went," he says sarcastically. "How am I supposed to know?"

"Maybe we should go back and follow the few waymarks that we saw?" I ask.

"The trail is definitely here. I think they may have rerouted it up and around. But we are already a third of the way to where we join a woods road."

"Yes, I can tell that someone has been on this trail earlier today or yesterday," I say trying to reassure myself.

This is the dance Jim and I still play. I'm nervous about what is ahead. I want to take the safe route. Jim always wants to push ahead.

Six years ago, I had a turning point.

"Let's do New Frontier," Jim had stated more than asked. He pointed with his ski pole to a hidden tunnel in the spruce woods that dropped steeply down the forested ridge. The clouds were gray, threatening more new snow and making it hard to see depth in the flat light.

New Frontier is one of those "trails" that is not on the map. We were on a narrow ski trail with eight inches of new snow at our local ski area, Mad River Glen. MRG is not your ordinary ski area. They do not allow snowboarders, and the lifts are not high-speed quads, which makes for fewer skiers on the mountain trails. Jim is devoted to the mountain. He was the chair of the board of directors of the skier-owned co-op. We have skied there since Kate and Sam were little. Kate raced on the ski team, and Sam played on the freestyle team.

Jim had been skiing all morning in the fresh snow with his pals. I stayed home in the morning to work and joined him later. "Lower Antelope is all skied out, and so is Lift Line. In here is fresh power," he spouted excitedly, still living on adrenaline from the morning skiing.

I was quiet, wondering, *Do I really want to do this? Am I up to it today?*

"You can ski this. It's tight trees for the first few turns, and then it opens up to a glade area," he cajoled, knowing I was hesitant.

My legs are fresh. I should be able to do this. Last weekend I skied the waterfalls of Paradise with confidence and ease, I told myself. "Okay, let's go. But don't go too far ahead of me. I have not done this trail before," I pleaded.

Jim ducked under the gnarled spruce branches. I saw his purple pants take one turn, and he was out of sight down the fall line into the unknown. I took a deep breath. *Shoulders down the hill. Look between the trees, not at the trees, light on your feet . . . turn, turn, turn.* I made the first turn, but on the second turn, I turned my shoulders into the hill to slow myself down. My helmet snapped a sharp branch as I came to a stop, face-to-face with a malign evergreen. *Fuck, it is steep in here.* Fear shook my legs. Anger at myself and at Jim coursed through my body, competing with my pulse rate. *At fifty-one, why do I still follow him? I should know better by now. Am I the only one who does stupid stuff like this?*

I pointed my skis downhill again and followed his tracks to the next turn. Again, I over-turned into the hill and couldn't get my skis pointing downhill. I was in survival mode. *Just get me out of these woods alive.*

One more turn, and there he was with a big smile. "See, this part is more open."

I was swearing under my breath. "It does not look more open to me," I said with resentment edging my words. "Let's just keep going," I said.

He skied off. I followed in his tracks but didn't feel in the flow. It was just too steep for me to make quick turns.

Then the trail contoured for a bit, and I relaxed for a few breaths. Jim stopped at the top of a small cliff. "I forgot about this part. But you can do it. Come in at an angle and then hop down to the landing like this." he said as he gracefully dropped four feet and landed between two trees. He skied further off to make room for my landing. Then he turned to watch.

Fuck. Fuck. Fuck. I'm not proud of my swearing, which I learned from my father. I've tried to stop but failed. I started at puberty and continued every month during PMS. As the zombie-spirit hormones of perimenopause and menopause flowed through my body, I swore more often but in no particular pattern. Besides the swearing, my body was adjusting to a new normal— no more cyclical hormonal swings, which I had finally gotten used to. Now there was just a dull, flat-line feeling.

I couldn't make my body do what I needed her to do, which was jump gracefully off the short cliff. My shifting body and my anger at myself and at my husband were tangled like a knotted rope. And I was body-shaking scared.

Six years before, I qualified for and ran the Boston marathon, which had been a lifelong goal, so I was no couch potato. I've skied my whole life. I could do this.

I angled my skis off the ice-covered rocks and aimed for the powdery snow below, gave a push, and held my breath. I landed on the uphill ski with my leg straighter than it should have been. I forgot to bend my knees enough when I hit the snow. My right leg trailed behind, and the binding released my boot as I crumpled into a pile. Tears welled up and rolled into the snow. My body shook. My left shoulder was sore from the impact. At least I could still wiggle all my toes.

"Are you okay?" Jim called up from below.

"No, I'm not okay. Nothing is broken, but I'm pissed. Fucking pissed at you for taking me into this hellhole! I'm pissed at myself for following you. Pissed at the world." I screamed back at him, releasing more tears, more emotions.

Slowly I pulled myself up, snapped my boot back into my binding, and pushed off through the woods.

I cried softly, releasing sadness. The slope was gentler now. Six more turns, and we merged with one of the main trails. I knew where I was.

"Okay, let's go do a simpler run now," said Jim, realizing his mistake.

"No. I'm done. I'm going home," I said without eye contact.

A few years later, when I trained to become a Teacher of Mindful Self-Compassion, I engaged in an exercise where we were supposed to dredge up a difficult time when we were suffering. The ski event came to my mind. After identifying the difficult emotions, grief, and anger, I placed my hand on my heart as I had learned. I tenderly said, "I'm feeling sad that my body is changing. Do I even want to keep pushing my limits? Sadness, because I feel like Jim sometimes loves skiing more than he loves me. He is more excited and happier when skiing with his friends than when he is with me. Skiing used to be a fun family sport. I'm sad that Kate and Sam have skied off into their own lives. They have left me with the 'Ski Maniac.' [That is what we called Jim when he would get us all out of bed early to get first tracks.] Am I to become a ski widow? How much do I even like skiing? Do I want to be with this man for the last third of my life?" Emotions, thoughts, and insights came tumbling out. I sat with them and wrote about them.

When I got home to Harvard from the training, I sat with Jim on the couch in the kitchen. "I learned so much, and it was just what I needed. I can't wait to teach this transformational work. Stuff came up about you and me. Sometimes I feel that you love skiing more than you love me. And it hurts." I paused, my throat tight. "And I'm not going to try to keep up with you anymore. If and when we move to Vermont, I will ski when and where I want to," I stated calmly.

He hugged me and said, "I can see why you might feel that way because I do love skiing. It makes me feel alive. But I love you and will always love you."

Now, struggling on this "greasy" trail, I think of all the adventures we have been on and how we've always made it. The challenge is to discern ordinary nervousness from the kind of deep gut feeling that is my psyche's way of signaling danger. While I'm not nearly as tense and fearful as on Brévent, my inner voice is getting louder.

What is it about the difference between men and women? In my experience, the women I know are more cautious in general than the men I know. Women want to preserve life. Men like the feeling of being on the edge. Whether this is due to genetics or society, I don't know. Jim is more comfortable and invigorated on a sharp edge—the sharper the better for him. I'm happiest on a blunt knife where I can keep the end of the handle in sight. I like to know all the risks and escape routes up front.

This is why the GR5 has been so perfect. The GR5 has been steady and mostly very reliable. I'm grateful for all the people in all the villages and hiking clubs along the way who keep the trail in such good shape. They repaint the waymarks every year or two. They cut the trees that have fallen across the trail. They rebuild where the trail has washed out. Back in the Vosges, we passed three men with chainsaws and pickaxes who had been cleaning up the trail. I could not thank them enough. "*Merci beaucoup, merci beaucoup.*"

I recheck GAIA and see that we have passed the section where the logging road washed out into the streambed. So, it can't get any worse, I tell myself. I listen to my intuition with my tough-woman skin on.

We continue on the greasy zigzags and reach the part protected by a cable. This turns out to be no harder than the last thirty minutes. But I think they should cable all the greasy zigzags.

At last, we are up on a narrow, flat, wooded area contouring the ridge. The land to the left drops off 200 meters, but the trees help me feel protected. And there, directly in front of me on a spruce trunk, is a waymark—it feels like a kiss from my mother.

"Let's eat up here on this ridge," says Jim just as I'm about to say the same thing.

We find a three-foot band of soft moss, and Jim sits with his feet hanging off the edge of the cliff. We can hear and see the river churning along the base of the cliff. I ponder the odds that the ground beneath Jim will crumble and give way on precisely this day. I keep my mouth shut.

I lean against a tree and peer between the hemlock branches at the view. These breathtaking vistas never get old: emerald-covered mountain slopes dotted with alpine farms. In the distance, rock peaks striped with snow in the north-facing eroded striations. These views sink into my soul.

I'm not afraid of the Alps anymore. I thought crossing the Alps meant climbing up and over the striated peaks. But this wonderful GR5 guides me between the mountains. It's the best of all worlds. We see and hear the peaks, but we walk between them. We don't conquer them. We respect them and leave them to themselves.

In the United States, the trails always head to the summits. This is true in the White Mountains, the Green Mountains, and the Rockies. To be fair, many of the peaks in the Alps do have summit trails too. But here the path from col to col between the summits is a gentler way of experiencing the spectacular heights. Americans are focused on conquering, Europeans on experiencing.

Honestly, I thought Jim would want to ascend some of the peaks. But he has never mentioned it. He is content with our walk. He is tired at the end of the day. He has dropped the armor of hardcore and relaxed into the flow of the GR5. I also thought when Margo and Todd were hiking with us, he would want to push ahead with them. But he walked with me. He has mellowed as I have gotten stronger. The magic of the GR5 has brought us closer.

This new concept to walk around the mountains is the path of least resistance. If the Alps flooded, it's the path the water would take. I like this new way of walking on the path of least resistance. It feels feminine to me, being in the flow and following the curves around the mountain. The masculine way is straight and direct—up and over. Why don't we have paths that flow around the mountains in the United States? I'd love to see footpaths flow around the flanks of the Green Mountains and pop into small towns for food and shelter. Maybe when I get home, I'll work on that.

PLEASURE FOUND
(DAY 76)

The next day is an auspicious day with deep blue skies and snow-capped jagged peaks; we are in the heart of the Alps. We both know what is going to happen, but we don't speak of it.

Instead of taking a day off, as this is our tenth day walking in the Alps, we decide to divide a long day into two short days. Today we will walk eight kilometers into Vanoise National Park.

Snowmelt waters cascade down over the rock walls of the valley. We stop in the shade of larch trees—the rebel conifers that shed their needles in the fall. I use the fresh green boughs of the larch to frame the jubilant waterfall across the valley as I take photo after photo. Three gigantic falls grace the valley.

As we climb higher and round a bend, we enter another magnificent valley with a lake holding each mountainside in its place.

At the outlet of the calm lake, we lie on stubbly grass with our heads on our packs and lunch. We don't usually eat reclining, but this is our relaxation day, and we are going to soften. Slowly I chew the leftover rock-hard bread like the cows we have seen chewing their cud. A mother duck and her five ducklings swim close to the shore, pulling up tender grass growing in the shallows. These baby ducks seem small for July 10, but the snow around the lake probably just melted a month ago. I wonder where the nest is. The ducklings must be a week old. Hopefully, they will grow up fast enough to fly out before the snows fall again in September. Still, I wonder where the ducks go for the winter. North to Lake Geneva or south to Italy or Africa?

By the time we finish our lunch, we are not alone. Three families have joined our grassy spot on the edge of the alpine lake. These national park trails are used heavily. The refuge we stayed at last night was at a trailhead with a visitor center. This is the perfect day hike into the high Alps with children. Even though these are French people and it is their park, I feel a little possessive of our trail. We are not used to so many people. We walk the last kilometer along the edge of the lake to the refuge at the head of the lake. The trail is underwater in places. The snowmelt raised the height of the lake and flooded the trail. We dodge large boulders and wander along, seeking the white-and-red rectangles painted on the boulders.

The refuge looks tiny in this massive landscape with towering snow-covered mountains watching overall. The main building is built into the rubble of the mountain. We follow the tall owner as he leads us inside, passing through the cramped dining room and into the bunk room that sleeps twenty. Inside, we place our packs on bunks at the back near a window that lets in a bit of light. The refuge owner says they will be more than half full tonight.

Out on the sunny terrace, an herb stand like a bookcase is built at the end of a table featuring *menthe*, *romarin*, *persil*, and *thym*. It must be a short growing season at this elevation. The growing of herbs hints that dinner will be extra seductive tonight.

On the table, plastic containers, pots, and pans dry in the sun. The plastic containers look like they are for cheese making. I look around, and sure enough, there are two cows out in the pasture.

We sit at one of the worn picnic tables and ask the owner what they have for dessert. He returns with a glass bowl holding *fromage blanc* with raspberry sauce. "*Voilà*," he says, placing it between us with two small spoons. "The *fromage blanc* was made this morning."

It's divine. The creamy substance dissolves on my tongue and floats down my throat while the pungent sweet raspberry sauce ushers it along. I feel like I'm eating the essence of the mountainside, the crisp sunny alpine air, and the vibrant green tender grasses all at once.

A nap energy wraps around my shoulders. But I don't want to lay down in the dark of the bunk room.

"Let's walk up behind the refuge. There is a secondary trail leading up into that col," says Jim, pointing west. "We can find a place out of the wind in the sun and take a nap." A smile dances on his lips.

He has read my mind. He wants to go up and away, off the trail to have trail sex.

This has been one of our teasings along the adventure. When I first proposed walking the GR5, I wanted to make it a little more enticing to him, and I said, "We can have trail sex. I promise we can have trail sex at least once."

We have been on the trail seventy-six days, and we have not had sex on the trail yet. Yes, we have had bed sex in the hotels at our regular pace.

In my thirties I called sex "making love," because that sounded so romantic. But love is made when you paint the trim on the windows together, when you share the last oatmeal chocolate chip cookie, and when you listen and hear the other during an argument. Sex is slow and urgent, fiery and soft, guidance and exploration, buzzing and releasing. Sex is a physical pleasure shared. Love is multilayered glue that fluctuates in its bonding ability.

We have both thought about trail sex at different times. When we had a horizontal lunch in a just-cut hayfield in Luxembourg, Jim proposed it. I vetoed it because I was worried people might walk by. No one walked by, but luckily we did not do it, because we got three ticks from just lying there. But here, I'm not thinking about the ticks. Today might be the day.

We pack our string bags with water bottles, puffy coats, and iPads for reading after the "nap." We climb above the refuge. The side trail follows a raging stream cut deep into the bedrock. We can no longer see the refuge. The trail continues up a vast open alpine cirque to the top of a col about a kilometer away. We look up to the left off the trail, searching for a flat spot for our "nap." We start climbing up off the trail. It looks like there could be a flat spot on the nearest ridge.

We get to one rise but find no flat area. Three marmots stand upright, watching us with fascination from a distance. These brown furry animals have been our companions for the last week. They are similar to prairie dogs, which live in colonies, but marmots build their burrows in rock piles. The clownish rodents are entertaining to watch as we walk along. They wrestle, chase, and frolic on the side of the trail until we walk too close. Then they make a high pitched whistling sound and all disappear into their borrows. But today they don't seem to mind that we are here.

Climbing higher, Jim calls, "This looks good." I come up to the rise and see a sloping flat area. Jim spreads his string pack and puffy out on the tufts of grass. I do the same. We lie there with our sun hats over our faces. Higher up on the col, a man is walking down the trail. We can't do anything now until he has stepped out of sight. We are so far away and off the trail, I'm not sure he could tell what we were doing anyway, but I'm not an exhibitionist. It's okay that the marmots, the bees, and the hawks will be watching.

Fifteen minutes later, when the man has walked out of sight, we put on a show for the birds, the bees, the marmots, and ourselves. The cool alpine air brushing parts of my body that do not see the sun adds heightened sensuousness to our moves. These body parts sing out loud and praise the sun in our ivory tower on the side of a mountain.

And the nap afterwards with our bodies entwined is blissful. We never read our books.

WALKING BY MYSELF (DAY 80)

I n the early morning light, the walk down between soaring snow-covered peaks is wondrous.

Last night we stayed at the highest mountain refuge, Refuge du Col de la Vanoise, at an elevation of 2,515 meters, on the GR55. That is not a typo. We've been on the GR55 for three days. The GR55, nicknamed "the high route," cuts through high peaks, while the GR5 travels lower, winding through villages. We, of course, picked the high route. This route through the mountains has been used since the Bronze Age, 2000 BCE to 500 BCE. We found the snowy trail well packed and did not sink down into the snow. However, we used our spikes for one steep pitch that was edged in giant sharp rocks 150 meters below. A friend from college and her husband had joined us, and again it was joyous to have friends for two days to share our adventure and speak English with. Joyce and I talked and talked as we walked, catching up on family and friends, and sharing our dreams and wishes. She is one of those friends who, even when we have not spoken for six months, we always pick up right where we left off. I was energized by talking with Joyce, like nectar for a bee.

Joyce and Dave left this morning, heading north, and we continued south. I was sad to see them go but also a little relieved to be just the two of us again, which surprised me. My women friends are an essential part of my life, infusing it with joy. However, I can feel life shifting. I'm at peace walking in partnership.

As we come off the first high precipice, we see below a large, long lake, Lac des Vaches. Even from up high, we see a strip of stepping-stones in the shallow lake. The guidebook says it is like walking on water the way the trail follows a rock slab causeway. I spot one person, a speck, moving along the stepping-stones.

As we approach the lake, yellow puffy clouds holding the morning light reflect on the surface, creating the effect of two heavens.

We meet the speck just as he finishes walking on water. Skis strapped to his pack form a teepee above his head. I ask him where he was planning on skiing. He answers with a thick French accent, "If there is still enough snow in the snowfields above the mountain refuge, then I will ski there."

"There is lots of snow on the north-facing slopes. We didn't see any other skiers, but we saw climbers and ice climbers. Good luck and have fun," says Jim, looking longingly back up at the col.

We begin walking on the water. Looking ahead, the lake becomes an infinity pool, the silent water merging with the azure air. We walk into the yellow clouds.

At the end of the lake, the slope of the landscape shifts drastically, marking the edge of the hanging valley. Over the lip, a raging white stream of water surges over rocks and plunges with gravity's force. The volume of water cascading down is much more than the volume flowing out of the shallow lake. Hidden underground waterways must feed into this torrential stream as the land falls away. Every molecule of water is in white motion, backlit from the sun. The contrast between the tranquil water above and the dynamic water here is dramatic and truthful, like the difference between walking as a couple and walking with friends. A life flowing between tranquility and spirited enthusiasm ushers me on.

Following the path of the water, we patter down the mountainside, crossing under chairlifts and gondolas. Many families trek uphill. Some are prepared for long day hikes with packs. Others pant and move very slowly, as if they have never been to the Alps before and are not going to make it to the top of the next ridge, their foreheads glistening with sweat. Today is July 14, Bastille Day—French independence day—which marks the beginning of the French summer holiday. From here on out we will see more and more people on holiday.

In a few hours we arrive in the village of Pralognan on the valley floor. Since we only have two more hours of walking, we decide to visit the tourist office and check email. As the office is just closing for lunch, we sit outside on the granite entrance steps and use their Wi-Fi. With our backs against the building, we have a view of the pedestrian street, and in the background is a jagged peak with a waterfall running down its face like a crying baby emoji.

"Shit, shit," says Jim in a low voice, a scowl imprinted on his brow as he hunches over his iPad. My heart races.

"What is it? What's wrong?" I ask, not wanting the answer. My thoughts flicker to the worst—one of our parents sick or dead, and we would have to leave the trail.

"My email got hacked. I can't tell if they got into bank logins." He leans closer to the iPad.

Breathing out a sigh, I say, "Oh no. Can I do anything to help? I'll change my bank passwords."

"This is going to take me a while."

I change my passwords and check email, Instagram, Facebook, and then skim the *New York Times*. Five days ago, we spent a few hours in a tourist office and finished making reservations all the way to the end of the trip. Some of the refuges are getting filled up. We even booked an Airbnb in Nice for four days of rest on the beach before flying home. If all goes as planned, our last day of walking will be August 1. We are taking a risk in making all the reservations ahead because if something happens, we will have a lot to change, but by now we are confident in our walking pace and timing. There are not many big towns in the Alps, so we are only taking one day off in Briançon five days from now. Toward the end of the trail there are some long stages. Again, we are going to split two of the longer days into four short days of walking. Part of me would like to keep going and have more time on the beach, but I also do not want the walking to end.

Thirty minutes later, I ask, "How is it going?"

"I still can't tell exactly what they have and have not gotten into. I'm going through and changing all my passwords. And I've sent a few emails to the bank. But the banks are closed because it's Saturday. I've got about fifteen more minutes to work."

It's times like this that we feel vulnerable being away from regular life, even though most of our life can be managed online now.

Twenty minutes later we walk out of town, following a wooded road on the edge of a campground overflowing with holiday camper vans and colorful tents. The road climbs gradually, following the valley floor and the river that created the valley.

I walk ahead, lost in thoughts. Jim is agitated, but there is nothing I can do.

Suddenly, he calls, "Wait up. I need to go back. I remembered a few more things I need to do to make sure everything is secure. We are not going to have service or Wi-Fi tonight or tomorrow, so I need to get it done now." He pauses and rubs his forehead. "Do you want to come with me or go ahead to the refuge?"

I'm silent for a minute mulling the question. Do I want to go ahead by myself? Jim waits patiently.

"I'll go ahead. I want to keep walking. Also, it looks like we might have rain this afternoon, and I don't want to get soaked. The clouds up ahead are getting darker. How long do you think it will take you?"

"I have to walk back half an hour to town, then an hour of work at the longest, and then two hours of walking to the refuge. So, it's one thirty now. I should get to the refuge about five." He pauses. "I think I made that reservation, so it should be in my name. See you at five o'clock."

We don't discuss what will happen if we need to reach each other during this time. Using my phone, I can call locally if I have cell service, but his phone can only communicate if there is Wi-Fi.

This is one of the few times we have hiked apart.

All along the GR5, I have felt safe and never scared by creepy people. Some women and men walk by themselves the whole time. We met a nineteen-year-old Canadian woman who was walking the Alps part of the GR5 by herself. She camped and stayed in refuges. I admire people who enjoy walking by themselves, but I prefer not to be alone.

Now I'm alone. As I walk up the trail, I see fewer and fewer people. Along the river, there are a few intermittent cabins nestled in the shadows, most of them unoccupied. Outside a cabin on the other side of the river, a family lounges in chairs. They will not be out long. The dark clouds I'm walking towards are coming this way. In a few hours, the summer people will be huddled in their cozy cabin.

The tops of the tall, dark evergreens sway, along with their shadows. Coolness brushes my cheek. I pick up my pace, glad to be walking on a broad gravel road through the woods instead of a narrow path. The shadows would be too close. I travel in the middle of the road evading the sinister shadows.

Eventually, the road crosses over the river and enters a car park overflowing with holiday visitors. The rain begins to spatter the dusty dirt. Families dash to their cars.

At the other end of the car park, the trailhead disgorges a stream of families and couples walking quickly past me. I feel like I'm walking against an agitated crowd fleeing a bomb scare.

I pull out my raincoat from the middle of my pack and eat a small handful of almonds. I feel self-conscious by myself when everyone is in groups on this holiday. The rain and wind bring along the cold, so I pull out my neck warmer to use as a hat.

I'm the only one heading up the trail. I don't have a car to go to. I feel different, alone, and exposed. I have a strong desire to go with the crowd, to be a part of the crowd. I try to convince myself that I'm strong. *You are an independent woman. Walking alone should not be so fraught. But I'm scared. Since I'm walking and scared that makes me brave. But I don't feel brave. Maybe this is what brave feels like?*

The further up I walk, the fewer people I see. The car park down below must be almost empty now. The walkers are back in town preparing to celebrate Bastille Day after their shortened walking day.

I climb higher and higher on smooth trails, emerging into open pastures, leaving the dense forest below. The mountains slopes come down to meet me in the base of the U-shaped valley. Avalanches have washed down the slopes, bringing giant boulders and crumpled trees of destruction. I hear the cows' bells before I see them grazing on the steep green slopes that ascend to rocky cliffs. Even the cows prefer to be with other cows, not separated and alone.

Up ahead is a collection of stone buildings. One is a restaurant. If this were a warm sunny afternoon, the terrace would be a beautiful place to drink beer or lemonade after a walk in the mountains. I contemplate going in and having some tea or hot chocolate but decide to keep moving. One good thing about being on my own is that I don't need to confer or compromise with anyone.

The thunderheads blacken and increase their pace. I turn and look back north. I see where Jim probably is down at the end of the valley. I hope he is done defending us from cyberattacks and beginning to walk. Facing south I see no buildings. Somewhere up ahead is my refuge, tucked away in a side valley.

As I walk, my senses are alert, my backbone rigid. *What am I listening for? Am I creating my agitations, or are they real? If I walked alone for a few days, would I get used to it and relax? How do you just trust that it will all be fine?*

I have learned to trust that our journey will be what it will be. But being alone is different: no one to confer with, no one to evaluate with, and no one to lean on.

This afternoon is confirming that I prefer walking in companionship. I love the word *companionship*. The suffix *ship* feels cozy, as if we are contained and protected. The Latin prefix *com* means friend or fellow, and *panis* means bread, so literally the word means "bread fellow" or messmate. And that is exactly who we are. We eat bread together on our little ship cruising across Europe. *Where is my bread mate?*

I come up to a rise and see a flag off to the left. Next to the trail is a wooden sign: "Refuge du Roc de la Pêche." I've made it to the refuge. I should feel complete relief, but I still need to negotiate check-in.

Two fairy-tale looking stone buildings flank a large stone terrace out front. The lower building off to the right is a humungous stone barn that drops off the slope. The roof, too, is stone. How do they make these large buildings with stone roofs? The slate is three times as thick as any slate we see at home. The massive stones are uneven rectangles, made by hand using rudimentary tools. They are encased in lichen and green moss along their gray edges, showing their age. A gray dog sits like a queen upon the roof, looking off to the mountains, protecting her barn.

I find the entrance and enter an organized mudroom: a row of pegs, a place to hang walking poles, a place for walking boots, a long bench, and a wall of cubbies with colorful Crocs and shoes to borrow. I hang up my poles, pull out my Allbirds shoes, and place my damp walking shoes on a rack beside four other pairs.

The next room is warm with a crackling fire in the stone fireplace. A polished wooden bar runs along the back wall and then opens up to a dining room. In the center of the room hangs a beautiful chandelier with copper deer silhouettes around each electric candle. It reminds me of one we saw in a castle in Luxembourg and gives the refuge a hunting lodge feel. Indeed, many of these refuges were private hunting lodges years ago.

A sturdy woman with dyed-blond hair stands at the desk by the large window overlooking the windswept terrace. I explain that I want to check in and that my husband will arrive in a few hours. She raises her eyebrow and gives me a funny look. But it could be that my French is causing her confused expression.

She says, "Follow me. I'll show you to your room. Dinner is at seven."

She leads me down some stairs to the dank lower level. We walk by five closed doors with the names of flowers on them instead of numbers. She opens "Edelweiss." Inside the utilitarian room are wooden twin beds and a small room with a shower and a sink.

I unpack, wash my muddy socks and shirt, and shower. I'm excited to see a heated towel rack. I turn it on extra high and cram as many damp clothes on it as possible.

As I hang my clothes, someone pushes open the door. Jim, I think. How did he get here so quickly? But it's a woman who got the wrong flower door. She apologizes in French and flees.

It's three thirty. Jim should be here in an hour and a half. I breathe deeply. My natural inclination is to worry. Rationally I know if I can find the refuge, he can find it. What is it about me and many mothers who worry? I feel like a border collie who is always trying to keep the herd together. When the pack is apart, I get agitated. I lie on the bed and try to get lost in my book.

My legs are not tired like other days, as I have only walked eighteen kilometers. I switch to the guidebook: twenty-one kilometers tomorrow. It's a steep climb up to Col de Chavière, the highest point on the GR55, 2,796 meters. And then we have a long walk down to Modane. The book says, "A steep and convoluted descent through the forest."

Just as I begin to doze off, the door opens. It's Jim. The worry and agitation float out the window. It's not that he is my savior; I can walk by myself. But to have a bread mate on this walk is something I choose.

PART SEVEN

THE SOUTHERN ALPS

CHERRY EARRINGS
(DAY 82)

I recall the day when we took the ferry across Lac Léman to the village of Yvoire, where we argued about where to eat lunch. After lunch we walked the touristy streets waiting for the bus. I was in search of a new pair of earrings. I lost one in the Jura, and Yvoire was my first opportunity to shop.

I have not been much of a shopper on this trip; materialism is too heavy to carry.

I first saw the cherry earrings in a gallery; it was love at first sight. They lay on dark gray velvet in a glass case. They looked like brushed silver or stainless steel, but when the gallery owner placed them in my hand, I knew they were something different. They floated in my hand. She said they were aluminum. *Cool, I've never seen or felt earrings made from aluminum.* I held them up to my ears and looked in the mirror. They looked even better on me than on the gray velvet. They were more than two inches long. One cherry, two leaves, and a stem formed a triangle. I flipped over the delicate white price tag: 230 euro. I let out a sigh. *Almost $300.*

I handed them back to the woman and walked to another glass case looking for smaller earrings that would be more functional for walking but did not find any.

I could have gone earringless for the rest of the walk, but I like wearing a little jewelry. I'm wearing a gold bangle that

Jim gave me twenty years ago and my engagement and wedding rings. Jewelry helps me feel feminine on the trail.

I searched a few more shops and eventually found a pair of nestled hoops. I put them on and wore them out of the store.

We had an hour to kill before the bus to Thonon-les-Bains, so we hung out at the tourist office using their internet. As I worked on my food coaching newsletter, I wondered what people thought of me in my dirty walking clothes, greasy hair, and backpack. We were far from the trail. The people wandering around Yvoire had just disembarked from air-conditioned tour buses in shiny clean city clothes. I didn't fit in here.

Interrupting my thoughts, Jim said, "I'm going to walk around town some more." *Where was he going?*

Now, more than two weeks later, it is July 16—my birthday. Last night, France won the World Cup, and this town, Modane, went wild. We watched the scene play out from our second-floor hotel window. The locals celebrated the win by honking horns and setting off firecrackers. They danced through the streets playing music. Some drove their cars slowly, singing and waving massive flags out the window. It was like a parade organized by toddlers, full of passion but on the edge of recklessness.

This morning we're in a small, dingy dining room with no windows. Breakfast is laid out on the table, self-serve. I make my caffè latte with sugar. The sliced meats are curled around the edges and the sliced cheeses dried out. I take a croissant and two containers of yogurt. There is no fruit or eggs. I also take a few slices of baguette. *Not a very exciting breakfast for my birthday.*

I carry my plate back to the table and sit down. Above my place setting is a small box with a squished gray bow. Jim smiles and says, "Happy Birthday."

Slipping the ribbon off, I slowly lift the gray top. The beautiful cherry earrings from Yvoire are nestled in white tissue paper.

I put them on and lean over my mediocre breakfast to kiss Jim. I love them and how Jim can be lavish at just the right time.

"There is a haiku on the back of the card," Jim says.

I flip over the business card from the gallery and there, in Jim's distinctive scrawl, blue smeared words making up five, seven, five:

Cheery, creative, wise
Adventurous, loving, strong
Cerise, mon cheri

When I read the words the first time, I read them quickly and did not take them in. Or could not take them into my heart as I was focused on the earrings. When I read the haiku again at home while unpacking, I realize how well he knows me and how much he listens and cares. The haiku becomes more precious than the earrings.

At the table he asks, "Did you know I went back to get them?"

What do I say? Do I lie and say no this is a total surprise and how wonderful?

I tell him the truth. "I had an inkling that maybe you went back but I was not positive, and I'm so glad you did. They are perfect," I say fingering the smooth metal. "And I love them because they will always remind me of all the cherries we ate. Thank you, sweetie. You are so sweet."

"Now you have to carry them. They have been so heavy weighing down my pack," he says with a playful smile.

"They're too fancy to wear walking, I'll take them off." I place them carefully back in the box. I find the perfect protective place in my pack for them.

BIRTHDAY BROWNIES
(DAY 82)

Later the same day, after seventeen kilometers of ascending 1,500 meters of elevation, we sit in the crowded Refuge du Thabor dining room just above Col de la Vallée Étroit. Jim and I claim the end of a table against the wall. Our hot teas steam, emitting hints of mint, and our iPads are ready for reading. Small clusters of people chat in French, play cards, or read. Most are drinking tea or beer. It is gloomy outside, and the windows rattle with each blast of wind. It's July 16, but it feels like November 16.

For the second time I'm reading a book called *Mountain Lines* by Jonathan Arlan that I first read while planning. It's a memoir about his walk through the Alps on the GR5 when he was a novice hiker in his twenties. The first time I read it, it bolstered my tentative belief that I could walk across the Alps. I figured if a guy who had never done any hiking could do it, then I could too.

The book is structured like a journal. Arlan used the same guidebook that we are using, so we stay in many of the same refuges. As we move through the Alps, a few times a week, I read his descriptions of where we are and where we're headed. He has become our shadow guide.

This afternoon I start reading about his time at Refuge du Thabor. Because he had not made a reservation there was no room for him, so he set up his tent, but a storm came through in the late afternoon. He decided to pack up and move on to the next refuge three hours away. Usually, I just read a few days ahead, but today I get carried away and keep reading. He is in Ceillac, where we will be in five days. He describes a group of older women in their sixties and seventies who are staying at a refuge. He is very impressed with their walking. He writes, "No one inside appeared to be under the age of sixty-five, the place felt more like an old folks' home than a rest stop for hikers."

I look around this refuge and, except for two adult children of an older couple, everyone but Jim and me is sixty-plus with gray hair. And we are not far from sixty. I begin to laugh out loud. I reread the sentence. He feels like he is in a retirement community instead of a mountain refuge. Yes, it is true. I laugh again. People turn to look at me. I can't stop laughing. I reread the sentence to Jim. He has read the book and laughs too. But not as hard as I do.

I continue reading about a very steep descent. But I've noticed that Arlan is either a bit cautious or he embellishes how hard the trail is to make the book more dramatic. Either that or I'm a rock-star hiker now and am intimidated by little.

I enjoy his writing style, and I admire his courage to walk five weeks through the Alps when he has never hiked before.

We have another three hours until dinner. I'm hungry but not for nuts and chocolate. Or is it boredom? Sometimes when we get to a refuge early and have a long time to wait for dinner, that is the hardest part of the day. I check in with my physical hunger, and I am hungry.

This morning at ten thirty, Jim pulled out raspberry and blackberry tarts for a special birthday pastry break, so I should not complain because I've had a treat. However, I had envisioned a beautiful French chocolate torte for my birthday. And I had hinted loudly about it yesterday and earlier today. Jim had tried to find one this morning, but the tarts were all he came up with.

No French chocolate torte for my birthday. And no shower tonight. Ironically this refuge is the only one where we have stayed at that does not have hot showers. Truthfully, I don't care about a hot shower on my birthday. I do care about not having a fancy chocolate torte.

Jim knows I'm hungry. Because of the crowded space, it is difficult for people to move about the room, so one of the caretakers acts as a waiter. Jim orders another tea for himself and a chocolate brownie for me.

The brownie arrives warm but on a cold plate. I wish Jim would sing "Happy Birthday." But why would he think of that? For all the years we have been together, neither of us has wanted a public fuss about birthdays. We usually celebrate at home where we do sing joyously and celebrate. We have never been fond of the restaurant tradition where all the wait staff prance out singing. Maybe it's our stuffy New England upbringing.

But today I would like everyone to sing "Happy Birthday." I do not care if it is in French or English. Maybe I feel a strong connection to these walkers. Maybe turning fifty-eight at a mountain refuge in France needs to be celebrated publicly. Perhaps I'm missing my family to celebrate with. They cannot call today because there is no internet. I did talk with Kate and Sam yesterday, and they wished me happy birthday then.

Maybe because I'm feeling strong at fifty-eight in this retirement community, I want to be celebrated.

How is Jim supposed to know what I want?

After being married twenty-seven years, how do I tell my husband I've changed and I want people to sing "Happy Birthday" to me? *Who is this new me?* I don't even know myself.

The brownie is made from a mix. The warm chocolate and sugar give me a hit of indulgence, but it would taste better with people singing to me.

At dinner we chat with a Dutch couple who are walking the GR5 through the Alps. They carry camping equipment and set their tent up behind the refuge in the wind and the rain.

They share stories of walking an extended route in Italy last year. At one point they arrived at a campground where Italians camped for the summer. They ended up staying for two weeks just because they liked the people. I admire their carefree attitude about life. Will we ever adventure like that? I'm intrigued by such freedom and spontaneity, but I'm not sure it fits my personality—though I may be changing.

At eight thirty we all say good night. I climb up the rickety bunk bed to the top bunk and settle into my sleeping sheet, wool blanket, and small pillow of disappointment. The cherry earrings are spectacular. The haiku fills my heart. And I'm ready to ask for public singing from the rooftops next year.

VULTURES, LUNGS, AND SECRETS (DAY 90)

"Oh, look, there are two more," says Christoph excitedly, pointing below us. A pair of bearded vultures ride the thermals, spiraling upwards to where we sit, on top of the world at 2,670 meters—Pas de la Cavale. Our legs hang off the edge of the towering cliffs.

Christoph is our best friend these days. We met him five days ago at a refuge. An Austrian living in Germany, he works for a solar cell research consortium. He and Jim have had lots to talk about. In his mid-forties, tall and lanky, he is faster than we are. But he enjoys accompanying us and is intrigued by our long trek. He is walking the five weeks of the Alps. Every summer, for four to six weeks, he takes a different route in Europe.

Perched on the impressive narrow, rocky col, we eat our second lunch, ham sandwiches with potato chips slipped in to add crunch, while watching the vultures play. Tracking vultures allows me to notice the vast space between the lofty mountains. So much of our time is spent looking at the mountains when really what makes the view rapturous is the space between—the void.

The vultures are above and below. Looking down on them, we see off-white with black wingtips; looking up at their undersides, we see the wings are darker, but their bodies buff. They play in the air currents, mesmerizing and relaxing; it's like watching schools of fish. The ease with which the vultures soar is the ease with which we walk now—the most natural thing to do.

Time to move on. We have one more col to walk before getting to the tiny village of Bousieyas.

The trail, carved into the crumbling gray limestone, descends steeply. I concentrate on where to place my feet and my walking poles. Jim and Christoph chat ahead of me, moving more nimbly down the trail to a lovely broad open valley, Salse Morene.

I enjoy my quiet time. To walk in silence through these expansive alpine valleys is blissful. I sink into my meditative pace, where breath and footsteps are in rhythm. My mind melts from subject to subject. *Why isn't Christoph married? Why did my parents have to get divorced? Jim's parents have been married for fifty-nine years; that's a long time. Will Jim and I last that long?* I love Jim more now than when I married him. I need to tell him this.

I have this little pebble of a secret that I've been carrying around for twenty-eight years. I was not madly in love with Jim when we decided to get married. Now that I look back on it, I loved him, but it was more that; I was ready to get married and have kids. It was time. I was twenty-nine. He was going to be a good provider. Writing that now makes me cringe. He was loyal, solid, and dependable. Growing up in the '60s and '70s, I got a strong message from our culture that I should marry for love, not for convenience. I felt a little guilty that I was not madly in love with him. *What does madly in love even mean?*

I want to tell him that I was not madly in love with him. I want to explain that I love him so much more deeply now. I don't think I can broach this now while we are traveling. There is a part of me that fears that he will take it the wrong way, and we will fight. I can't handle a profound argument here on the trip. We need to stay united. I'll share when we get home and are settled again in Vermont. I feel better now that I have a plan.

Up ahead Jim and Christoph wait at a stream crossing. On the other side, we turn and face where we came from.

"There's where we were two hours ago, on the col watching the vultures. I don't see them anymore. Do you?" Jim asks.

"No, I don't see them. We are headed up to that col now. It does not look as high," I say.

"It's not; it's a little over two kilometers. Col des Fourches. And it has WWII fortifications and nineteenth-century barracks. I read about it last night," says Christoph.

We continue walking. We pass a stone shepherd's hut, the most amazing work of masonry. The irregular shapes of stones are placed so perfectly that they look like they were made for each spot. And maybe they were. The skill of stonecutter and puzzle placer is extraordinary. The stone hut is a masterpiece.

Have Jim and I have been chiseling ourselves to make the perfect shape to fit together? Of course, it is not perfect. Marriage is cutting and shaping ourselves to be individuals that fit well enough together. Finding the balance of being an individual stone and also a part of a solid foundation is the work of marriage.

Now I'm walking ahead and Jim and Christoph are behind, continuing to chat. They are solving the world's problems.

Ascending the last col of the day, I notice that when I'm pushing myself uphill, the inhale is even, but the exhale is more forced. This way my lungs have more time to refill. When I exhale, I can feel the exhaust flow over my lower lip and down across my chin, rustling my chin hairs gently. Yes, I have a few new blond chin hairs since menopause.

When I push harder, the airflow out increases, but I can't keep the pace up for long. Some days I push a bit and then ease off. Other days I stay at that perfect pace where I just barely notice.

I think of my rib cage as golden gates that protect my lungs and heart. My lungs and heart are the most critical organs in my body because they fuel my body with oxygen. My lungs take in the oxygen, and my heart distributes the oxygen to all the different body parts, especially my legs. The GR5 gifts top-quality oxygen. Yes, breathing is something I do most of the time without thinking. But walking day after day allows me to notice how the entire system works. I appreciate and love my heart and lungs for supporting my powerful body.

But I have an irrational fear. My father's side of the family is bigger and stockier. My mother's side of the family is stick thin. My sister and brother are thin. I inherited my father's side of the family's body type. His sister, my aunt Minty, always struggled with her weight. People have always told me I look like her. We both have round faces. What scares me is Aunt Minty died of lung cancer at age seventy-two even though she never smoked a day in her life. I fear dying of lung cancer because I am so much like her.

I want to take the fear out and hold it gently with compassion, so I do. I don't want it to bloom into anything significant. *Just be with the fear, irrational or not.* I want to kiss the fear and blow it away into this expansive landscape, so I do.

Maybe I don't need to carry the fear any further, so I won't.

I'm walking the mountain-scape with Jim, and I'm walking the heart-scape with myself. I find both good company.

FLASH OF CHOICE
(DAY 93)

Two days ago, we said good-bye to Christoph for the last time as we stood under a roof waiting for a downpour to stop. He was heading on to the GR52, which heads into the Italian Alps. It's a longer route but prettier. Jim and I decide to stay on the GR5 and end in Nice because we have not been able to get reservations in the refuges on the GR52 and we are loyal to our trail.

Four weeks into the Alps, the landscape has less vegetation and more rocks, if that is possible. Sheep, not cows, graze beside the trail. The sheep can survive on less vegetation. A few days ago, we walked by a large flock with a shepherd sitting above them, watching over. It could have been a scene from two thousand years ago. But when I looked closely, his head was down, and he was staring at his iPhone. Jim and I had a belly laugh over this ancient way of life adapting to the present.

Sometimes the sheep are guarded by large white dogs called *pastous*, with no humans around. Signs and the guidebook tell us not to cut through the flock and not to approach or pat the dogs. The other day two pastous charged us, barking endlessly. The uncertainty of the attack made my heart pound as we slowly moved off to avoid the animals.

Now that I've passed this flock, I'm relaxed and fall into the flow of walking. We have about three hours of uphill this morning. Jim is behind me.

I take a deeper breath than I need, filling my lungs, diaphragm, and airway. The scent of rock and blue expanse enters my lungs. All the yoga classes and meditation classes I've taken over the years were an exploration of breathing. When I was in those classes with my thumb over one nostril, practicing alternate nostril breathing and finally getting the hang of it, I did not have any epiphanies. It felt interesting at the time, but I was never sure why I was learning it. I see now all that practice and focus was for this—to be present with my breathing.

Fun and energizing, my breath is my companion. I take a breath and exhale as much as I can. I pull my belly inward, contracting my muscles to push every ounce of air out. If I were not moving uphill, I could push even more out. But I feel lightheaded, so I relax my stomach muscles, and the alpine air surges in, expanding my lungs like a purple birthday balloon. My breath and I play with the air, moving it inside and outside of my body so much that I become the air. I become the air that fills the valley and brims over the basin walls; the air that rises in spiraling thermal currents; the air that forms the distant cotton clouds.

I stop and look back from where we came this morning. The peaks this far south are spattered with small patches of snow on their rock faces. Looking down the valley, I see the sinuous creek we walked alongside through the green. The ridge I'm on with my back to the sun casts a shadow below where I walked ten minutes before. I see my strong detailed shadow with her backpack perched on the ridge. Jim's shadow joins mine on the ridge, and we comment on the speck of the stone shepherd's hut we passed forty-five minutes ago. Jim sits to adjust his sock and stretch out his toes, as they still bother him. It never seems to get bad enough to stop, but some days are worse than others.

The high pitch of a marmot whistle nudges me to keep moving up the trail. The grasses are short from grazing. Forget-me-nots, purple thistle, and buttercups add inspiration and depth to the green carpet.

Left foot, right foot. The pattern moves on forever, matched perfectly with my inhale and exhale. In, out, in, out. The transition from physical pace to ethereal pace is faster every day of walking. As I climb higher and breath deeper, layers of consciousness peel away, exposing fragments of thoughts.

A thought flashes between inhale and exhale. *What would life be like without Jim?* Inhale. *We've known each other for thirty years.* Exhale. *I'm going to live for another thirty years, hopefully.* Inhale. *Do I want to spend the rest of my life with him?* Exhale. *Perhaps it's time to be on my own?*

Flashes of thoughts continue to spew.

I know just the other day I realized how much more in love I am with Jim, but still these thoughts come and I do not judge them.

Would I be lonely by myself? There is a certain freedom that comes from living on your own. And I do enjoy solitude. Now would be the perfect time to do it. I'm still vibrant enough to start again. At seventy or eighty, it might be too difficult. Though I'm sure there are badass seventy- and eighty-year-old women who start again. I need to hear their stories.

I certainly know lots of single female friends. I could survive. *Would I thrive?*

I have one friend who is so happy to be married. She thinks it would be a drag to be single at this point in her life. She feels like they have made it this far, so she should keep going.

Why do these flashes invade my mind? Am I supposed to appreciate Jim more than I do? I do sometimes take our relationship for granted. Mostly, I've been jubilant on this adventure. We are working as a couple in unique ways. And the day that I walked by myself was not as much fun as walking with Jim. I love walking alone together the way we do.

Maybe in our marriage, we can be more alone together. What would that look like? My parents took many of their vacations separately. My mother went to Italy to paint, and my father went to the jungle to band birds. Jim's parents do everything together. There are many ways to be a couple.

What is our path?

There is something deeper about these flashes of thought. *Maybe the divine is inviting me to choose again? Choose Jim again. The first time I chose him was to form a family. This time I would be choosing Jim for Jim.*

What crazy lives we humans live. Choices to make. It would be easier to be bearded vultures soaring and mating with raw instincts, no thought involved. And maybe that is the path. Tap into my instinct and intuition. I'm going to keep an eye out for waymarks on this path.

I ask a multitude of questions but cannot answer them. *Can I walk with this uncertainty by my side?*

Solitary walking is getting crowded, with *Breath* and *Uncertainty* as my companions.

Two more switchbacks to climb. The path is nicely graded, a smooth up. To the left of the trail, growing in the crevices, are pale violet pansies with a yellow center—the only plant this high up. I laugh out loud. *Pansy* has the offensive connotation of being feminine and weak. But here she is growing and blooming amongst the rocks and harsh wind.

Later I learn that *pansy* is derived from the French word *pensée* meaning *thought*—thoughts growing in the crevices of the slope and in the crevices of my mind and blooming in the alpine air.

I stand on top of the col alone. There are fewer and fewer

people as we move south. I don't understand because these mountains are just as spectacular. Looking south, I see layers upon layers of peaks fading into the horizon. I see into forever.

I love the way the ridges angle down and intertwine like fingers creating the valleys, holding life.

Looking north, I see Jim ambling up the trail. His gray shirt and shorts match the gray of the rock. His blue pack matches the sky. And his rough smile matches my heart.

THE MAGIC HOUR
(DAY 95)

Sadness, power, and gratitude buzz in my body as I move up the trail. Today is our fourth-to-last day with the GR5. It's our last long day—twenty-eight kilometers. Then we'll have two short days, and a half day to Nice, to the water, to the sea, to the end, to the edge of the world. No more land to walk. Some hikers who finish the Appalachian Trail in the United States turn around and walk back north. But I have not read about anyone walking the GR5 south to north. Walking the Alps, the Jura, the Vosges, and then the rolling hills and flats would be anticlimactic and wrong. The magic of the GR5 is the way it builds and builds.

I'm sad that it is almost over. I love walking more and more each day. I feel like I can't hold all the love I have for walking.

But my body has had enough. She is tired. My body hurts from the day before. My shoulder strap digs into my collarbone and the pain feels like the shape of a steel rod. I have a new ache—my left elbow feels like tennis elbow from overusing my poles on the downhill sections. Today I'm using just my right pole. I slide my left hand into my right backpack strap to keep the arm from banging around. The strap acts like a sling. Even with all these pains, I have power flowing through me.

I focus on my breath. In and out. After ninety-five days of walking, I'm still not exactly sure when the first hour of walking becomes the magic hour of walking, but it has to do with the colors and smells intensifying. Though really, it is myself becoming more aware, falling into the flow, and becoming more receptive.

Today I know I've entered the magic phase when I notice the deep purple-blue flowers on the sides of the trail, as if the dirt path is wearing a royal necklace in the filtered morning light that shines through the towering spruce. The purple-blue pops out of the deep green background, demanding, "Look at me, look at me!" This is a flower I have seen almost every day for the last month: a wild geranium. She is cheering me on. She is my friend. She lines the trail going up, up, up.

A bird call vibrates against the spruce trunks and then falls away down the mountainside. The bird calls are one at a time. I listen to the whole song. It's not like a few months ago when there were so many different songs being sung; then it was a symphony. Now there are solos with long silences between.

The spruce fragrance mixed with the soil from the trail enters my nose and is absorbed by the cells in my body and my memory.

The color of the geranium, the song of the bird, and the smell of the earth all combine to form magic. Real magic.

I'm in love with the trail. Even though we have walked on a different part of the GR5 each day, my relationship with her gets thicker and thicker. Each day of walking lays down a new layer of experiences and sensations like a tree accumulating growth rings. We are bonded together.

I'm in love with my life. I'm exuding gratefulness. Gratefulness sweats out my pores. I'm in love with my fifty-eight-year-old body gliding up the trail. My flesh and bones, powered by a flower, a song, and the smell of the earth, arrive on the top of the ridge.

I am free and high on the abundance of beauty. *Could it be I'm longing for deeper love? Longing to crack open my heart and let more love in? Have I kept my heart closed to protect myself?*

I've struggled with opening my heart to others. The old coping skill of building a wall to protect myself is from my shame growing up. I've stripped the wall away before, but life builds the wall back up. Just the way we have been carrying lighter packs so that we can walk longer and with ease, it is time to let go of the wall of protection. By honoring my strength and voice, I do not need the wall. Time to open up and let more love in.

Mothering love came easy to me, like a trail through a meadow, direct and defined. No questions. I would die for my children. My children are the muscle fibers of my heart.

Long-term marriage love is different. It rises and falls like the trail through these mountains—often challenging and exhausting, sometimes easy and joyous. It's hard work. Every day I put on my walking shoes and take it one step at a time.

I'm learning my heart is expandable and infinite, like the vast mountain-scape.

These last few years, as I have shifted away from being hardcore, I have blamed Jim for being too hardcore. I've felt we are too different. But on the trail, I've seen a softer side of Jim that was probably always there, only the wall around my heart did not let in. His softer side has blossomed on the GR5; it is poking through my wall.

An hour later, we sit on an outcropping and eat our second breakfast: coffee éclairs. Far to the west, rain clouds with light sheets of pale rain move slowly. A few drops spatter as the sun shines.

"With the sun and the rain, we may get a rainbow," says Jim, scanning the view. He arches his hand over his eyebrows like a sailor looking out to the horizon. He slides his hand over mine. "Look how you have changed me. I look for rainbows. I'm a rainbow hunter now."

My heart smiles. I flip my hand over and squeeze his. "I don't think I've changed you. The GR5 has changed you," I say, looking into his deep brown eyes. "But since I chose the GR5, I'll take credit."

We don't see a rainbow, but the GR5 has changed us. The trail allowed us the time and space to open and receive—to become our best selves. It's basic spiritual math: Me plus Jim plus the GR5 equals something more than the sum of us.

YELLOW PANTS
(DAY 95)

Later in the afternoon, my calves brush a lavender plant on a ridge that falls steeply off to the left. I reach down, grasp a handful, and crush the purple flowers between my fingers, releasing a fragrance that balances on the ridge. A warm current of air rises up the slope from the valley, diminishing the scent to a whiff of remembrance.

A rolling fog shrouds the views to the south and west—still no sea view. But I can smell the sea. The air is thicker now. Denser. It carries more weight in my nostrils. The rock changes as we climb higher. It is crumbly, white, and chalky. The vegetation continues to be arid. I'm hot, tired, and a little crumbly myself.

I check my phone to see if I have service as I need to text the host of the Airbnb. But before I text, I check to see the location of the Airbnb in Utelle, basically a cluster of buildings upon a precipice.

On the Airbnb app, a red arrow points to the center of the map at Utelle. I can't zoom in. All the other times, when using the app, I could zoom in to see the exact location. I remember that the host sent me his address. I search the thread and put the address into Google Maps.

"This can't be right," I say out loud. The address the host gave me is seven kilometers further down the trail. It is not in a town, just a collection of buildings near the river. I reread our correspondence. I had told him we were walking. He had said that his house was right near the trail. And it is, but not in the town of Utelle. Now that I think about it, I thought it was weird that he had sent me his address because on Airbnb, once you pay for the room, you can find the address on the map. But not this time. *How can I make a mistake like this after more than ninety-five days on the trail?*

Meanwhile, Jim has caught up with me and is sitting in the shade of a pine tree, swigging water. "Jim, we have a problem." We are both tired, not just from today's twenty-five-kilometer day, but all the days. I explain what has happened. Jim is quiet, then, "Well, we can eat dinner and then walk down the seven kilometers."

"I'm not sure I can do that. It might be dark by the time we are walking."

"We have headlamps that we haven't used yet," he says in a flat voice.

I text the host, and I ask him if there are taxis or restaurants near his house. Because if not, we will eat in Utelle and walk down to his home after dinner.

I get a text back quickly. "There are no taxis, but there might be an Uber. There are no restaurants near my house."

I was hoping he would offer to come to pick us up or offer dinner.

I'm irritated at myself for not dealing with this earlier, but how was I supposed to know? I text him back and tell him his address is not on the app the way it should be. He retorts that he sent me the address.

Nothing to do but keep walking.

Maybe we can find a room in the town. It's a Sunday night in the high season of the European summer, but possibly there will be a room. We won't lose much money; the inconvenient Airbnb only cost $54. I stop for a minute and look up rooms in Utelle. I recall when I was making these reservations that all the places were full three weeks ago. I can't believe that they have anything open. But we will try.

Nothing to do but keep walking.

Walking calms me down. But my feet, my back, and my left shoulder all throb. We are climbing very high now along a rocky ridge. There's no vegetation anymore, just rock cliffs dropping off sharply on both sides.

Jim drops back again. His toe must be hurting.

We have not seen anyone else on the trail since this morning. Ivory clouds fill in the voids. The white rocks merge with the clouds, making it easy to plummet off the edge if I don't pay attention. The GR5 is an old mule trail now—just wide enough for a mule. Mule trains carried salt from the Mediterranean inland for preserving food. The footing is sound compared to the path we were scrambling down earlier. I wonder what else the mules carried. And were the mule traders ever scared of walking on the trail alone at the end of the day? Did they worry about where they would sleep at the end of the day? These trails were the primal highways across the Alps.

I wait for Jim at what seems like the top of the col. A small trail goes straight up to the peak, which at this moment is straight up into the clouds, like walking up into a Hollywood heaven.

As Jim arrives, I point to the trail. "Let's just keep going. There will be no view with the clouds."

He nods and silently follows me down the zigzags.

We come to a section of trail that has collapsed down the mountainside in a pile of rubble. A metal bridge spans the collapse—now a thirty-meter cliff—and carries us to where the trail continues. The sound of our walking shoes on the metal bridge is jarring, and echoes off the cliff walls like weariness is echoing in my soul.

Jim perks up. "What a cool bridge."

Shortly after, the clouds blow out, and we see the hill town of Utelle below. The buildings cling to the top of a precipice like a cluster of insects.

Soon we enter the village. Right away, we see one of the hotels. No rooms. They suggest we go to the bar in the central square.

Following the cobblestone paths laced between stone buildings, we enter the town square with the bar and the church on opposite sides. The bartender says there are no hotel rooms, but he may be able to help us. He disappears and returns with a teenage boy dressed in a burgundy polo shirt who does not speak English. We infer that the bartender is telling him to take us somewhere. Then the bartender says that the bar is closing at six thirty because it is Sunday. We promise to be back at six for dinner.

We follow the teenager, who guides us back the way we came for two blocks. He knocks with a strong fist on the door of a pink stucco building with pink roses climbing the wall.

A peppy petite woman with bright yellow pants opens the door. They chatter back and forth for a few minutes.

The young man turns back to us and says, "Yes, a room."

We thank him profusely. He heads back to the bar. The yellow-pants woman goes into the apartment and we tentatively follow.

"No, no," she says, shooing us back out the door. In French she says, "Not here. Follow me, I will take you to the *gîte*." We don't understand her words, but we do understand her flapping arms. We follow her out the door and back towards the center again.

She maneuvers her black high heels across the cobblestones like a general. We have a hard time keeping up. But we will not lose her because of her bright yellow pants and the promise of a room.

As we come to the central square, we wave at the bartender.

The yellow-pants woman stops and talks to the bartender. Again, we can't understand precisely what is being said, but we gather that the yellow-pants woman is giving the bartender a talking-to for not keeping the bar open later for dinner.

If she only knew that we are thrilled to eat at six o'clock.

Finally, she finishes berating the bartender and leads us out under the old city wall to a renovated building, perhaps an old town hall, with ornate inscriptions above the door.

She enters a code, and the door opens with ease. The technology of a coded door on an ancient building makes me smile; old buildings can adapt to the times. Inside is a kitchen with a white metal table that fits ten people. We follow her upstairs to a hot, stuffy dorm room with five bunk beds. Two of the beds have packs and sleeping sheets laid out. She shows us where the gray wool blankets are stored in a cupboard next to the only window.

We leave our packs on one of the bunk beds, staking out our territory, then follow her downstairs. She tells us the beds are sixteen euro apiece. We pay her in cash. She writes down the code to the front door and leaves.

I'm relieved that we have a room in town and don't have to walk seven more kilometers. I text the Airbnb host and tell him we have found a place in town and do not need his. I don't ask for my money back. I'll contact Airbnb tonight and deal with refunds.

After short showers, we head to the bar. As we pass the first outdoor table, I hear my name called. A man I don't recognize in a stiff white shirt is drinking a Perrier. He does not look like a walker.

He says he is Jean, and for a moment I remain clueless. Then it dawns on me: the owner of the out-of-town Airbnb.

"It's nice to meet you," I say. "Thank you for coming but we ended up finding a room in town. I sent you a text about twenty minutes ago."

His head bends down in disappointment, and we apologize for the mix-up.

But in truth, I'm exhausted and hangry, and want to say, "Why didn't you offer us a ride when you texted an hour ago?" I want to say, "If you had set up the app correctly, this would not have happened." Yet he was kind to come retrieve us. Maybe we should have trusted that it would all work out. Instead we fixed our problem by finding another room, and we got to meet the yellow-pants lady.

We thank him again for his trouble and he wishes us *"Bonne journée,"* pays his bill and leaves. Meanwhile the bartender seats us at a table. We order the special, stuffed bell peppers, and two beers.

Just as our dinners are being served, I spot the yellow-pants lady charging across the central plaza still in her high heels with two walkers trying to keep up with her. A man and his adult son with packs on. Potential roommates? I hope they do not snore.

We order chocolate ice cream for dessert. A summer evening close to the sea—seems like a chocolate ice cream kind of night.

Before our ice cream is delivered, the father and son come back and order dinner though it is already six-thirty. I guess the bartender will be late getting home to his Sunday supper.

"Voilà." The bartender places two glass bowls with a scoop of chocolate indulgence in front of each of us. There's that word again: *voilà.* It's my favorite French word. I love the sound and the meaning. *Here it is. Here's your food. Here's your life.* As if the divine feminine is whispering, *What are you going to do with it?*

After ice cream, we stroll to a tiny park with a bench and a few overgrown rosebushes that celebrate the highest point in town. Hazy clouds to the south obscure a view of the Mediterranean. Looking straight down, we can see the deep valley with the river winding through. Somewhere down there is Jean's house, the kind man.

I sit on the bench and look closely at one of the drooping roses. The yellow is faded, and the petals are beginning to fall from the bloom. *What happens when we go home?*

We are on the edge of a town. We are on the edge of an ending. And we are on the edge of a beginning.

We walk back to the central plaza and check to see if the church is open. Jim lifts the handle. Nothing moves. We turn to walk away just as a man across the street rushes towards us. He unlocks the church. He says something in French. We think he is telling us to just pull the door shut when we leave. We nod and say, "*Merci, merci.*"

He walks home across the street.

We turn to face the church. It's brilliant. The door to the church faces west. With the massive wooden door sprung open at this time of day, the yellow sun streams straight in. The brilliance of the gold covering the tall altar, the brilliance of the white carved-marble columns, and the brilliance of the arched ceiling swoons—a massive baroque church glowing in the setting sun. We walk around, breathing in the brilliance. I do not sit to meditate. I turn to look at Jim, who also glows in the brilliant light. *When does yellow become gold?*

WALKING TO THE MED
(DAY 98)

Ninety-eight days is enough time to fall in love with the GR5. She flows in my veins. If Hoek van Holland is my right ear, then my left baby toe is Nice. Today, our last day, we walk the length of my baby toe.

We walk out of the Hostellerie d'Aspremont at 7:50 a.m. The morning air washes over my face. In the square in front of the hostel, a produce vendor is setting up his crates of fruits and vegetables on wooden tables. Part of me wants to buy some fruit for our walk. But he doesn't look ready to make a transaction yet.

Atop a ridge on the way out of town, we spy the Mediterranean again. We saw it twice yesterday. It's still hazy, not the deep blue I keep expecting. To our right, we see a large fanned-out delta merging into the sea. The wide river is flanked by massive industrial parks along its whole length; we are not in the Alps anymore. Nice is the seventh largest city in France. Around 350 BCE, Greeks of Marseille founded a permanent settlement and called it Nikaia, after Nike, the goddess of victory.

The sprawl of the city is laid out in front of us. We will descend this ridge then have about two hours of walking through the city to reach the sea.

I'm excited to get to the water. I want to float. I want to stop moving. But I'm also anxious about where my life will lead next.

I tell myself to be in the present. *Notice the trail and the dust. Enjoy these last ten kilometers to the sea.*

As we walk down the ridge, losing sight of the Mediterranean, we enter an old olive grove; the neglected trees with overgrown, tangled branches have no form. Empty chip bags and soda cans are caught in the dried weeds around the trees—the first trash we have seen. It pierces my heart. We pass by a barrel with a GR5 waymark on it, where the garbage should be.

Now we see more and more walkers out for a morning stroll with their dogs. I used to be a morning walker. But now I'm a Walker with a capital *W*.

Oops, I'm not in the present. I've gone off on a thinking trail. Time to get back to the actual trail. The olive grove has morphed into a run-down park. Picnic tables and more trash barrels not in use.

Out of the park and onto a paved street, still walking downhill.

The houses are small and rustic, but a few blocks further on the walls around the houses grow higher and higher, which means the homes must be getting bigger and bigger.

Vibrant coral bougainvillea flows over white stucco walls. Palm trees tower over the walls too, announcing once again we are not in the Alps. We could be in Florida, except that it is not flat. Fancy ornate wrought-iron gates keep the unwanted out. Down, down, down, we meander on the winding road.

Eventually, the road comes to an intersection edged with fancy shops sporting colorful awnings. We spot a patisserie, and, without a word, we walk into the shop. It's crowded and cramped with men in designer loafers sans socks, and women wearing sparkly sandals over painted-pink toenails. I want to take my pack off so I don't bump anyone. They stare at us. I wonder, *Do we smell? Even though we have been washing our socks, underwear, and shirts every night, do we smell?* My backpack is a faded purple now. My purple plaid sun shirt is gray from today's dust and yesterday's dirt. We don't fit in with this loafer-wearing crowd.

Apricot pasties in hand, we seek a spot to sit. But there are no benches. We saunter slowly, savoring our pastries. Pastries will never again taste this divine. Two halves of a fresh apricot the color of the setting sun glisten under a light syrup. The fruit tang counteracts the sweetness of the custard and the flaky, paper-thin pastry ripples with butter.

As I take my next-to-last bite, I notice a deep apricot-colored rosebush growing up and over a granite wall. The rosebush is so abundant and exuberant that I move to the edge of the sidewalk so as not to get caught by the thorns. Roses, pastries—I'm going to miss them all.

Now, we are surrounded by larger buildings: white apartment buildings, hospital complexes, and community centers. Dads push sleeping babies in strollers down the hill. I wonder where they are going.

The sidewalks are full; we dodge and weave. Somewhere amid this bustle there is a park where the GR5 ends. But from all the books and blogs I've read, no one ever stops at the park; they keep going to the sea. Graffiti decorates the walls of buildings here and there. We must have passed the park because I don't see any more waymarks. *Good-bye, waymarks. Thanks for guiding us all these kilometers.*

The streets are broad now, wide enough to have an electric train run up the middle. We could jump on the streetcar and get a ride for the last kilometer. Can you imagine walking all this way and then taking a train the last kilometer?

My legs are not sore or tired. This is not a long walk. However, there is an overall tiredness in my body, as if my Eveready battery is not ever ready anymore. There is a dull heaviness in every cell of my body, and at the same time there is a little spark of excitement for the sea.

We are now in an expansive plaza, Place Masséna. Black-and-white checkerboard marble tiles extend to the pastel neoclassical buildings. People move in every direction, though we still walk south. Without a glance, we pass the Fountain of the Sun with a statue of Apollo, my focus on a line of giant palm trees marking the Promenade des Anglais that edges the Mediterranean.

We wait at three crosswalks to cross the busy streets. Now the wide cement boardwalk. Finally, the brilliant blue of the Mediterranean is squarely in front of us, stretching out to the unbroken horizon. But my eyes keep staring at all the people on the beach. Hundreds of people of all colors enjoy the beach and the water for as far as I can see, looking east and west. We are alone in a crowd of bathing tourists.

There are places to pay for a beach chair and umbrella. But we don't want that. I scan the beach looking for our entrance to the sea. To the west, there is space. We walk for half a block, then down the stairs to the gray-pebbled beach.

I'm used to the golden sandy beaches of Massachusetts. I have read that this beach is rocky, but still, the pebbles surprise me. With each step on the pebbles, we sink in. It's awkward walking. The trail has been sturdy, but this is loose and wobbly.

We walk to the edge of the water between a woman sunbathing and a mother watching her young son play in the small waves.

We are as close to the water as we can get while still keeping our packs dry from the lapping waves. I sit beside my pack and remove my shoes, socks, and sun hat. Jim asks two Belgian guys if they will take a video of us. I can't find my bathing suit buried at the bottom of my pack so I decide to baptize my walking garments.

"Are you ready?" Jim asks, taking my hand. I long to gallantly walk into the water like a goddess entering her sea. I've imagined this moment so many times, but instead, we stagger across the pebbles like an old couple, our feet tender from months swaddled in woolen socks and hiking shoes.

My right foot enters the water first. It's warm—bathwater warm. Ankle deep. Knee deep. And just before waist deep, we pull our hands apart and dive in. The alluring water surrounds me and holds me. Coming up for air, I taste the intensity of the salty water on my lips and feel the sting at the corners of my eyes. I stand and extend a thumbs up to the camera. We made it. I made it. We made it. Victory. I'm numb with no feelings—or so many feelings swimming around inside I feel none of them. I let the salty warm molecules cradle my worn-out body.

Jim retrieves his camera from the Belgians and then goes back in the water.

I sit on the hot pebbles next to our backpacks, trying to take it all in. Trying to sort out how I feel. I decide to record a video. I talk about how anticlimactic the whole morning has been. There are thousands of people, but we don't know a soul. And no one cares that we have just finished walking 2,289 kilometers. I'm feeling small but at the same time larger than this scene. It's been a profound, joyous journey, and it is over. I begin to cry. Tears spill out: simple tears, strong tears, partnership tears. I stop the video but not the crying.

Maybe these walking tears are composed of the water I drank from the North Sea. The water from the North Sea and the Mediterranean meet on my cheek. Salt and salt come together. North and South come together. Jim and I come together.

EPILOGUE

HOME

Not long after returning to Vermont from our epic journey, Jim and I are folding laundry in our tiny guestroom. The late afternoon sun streams through the west window, bathing the small room in gold.

"How was your solo hike today?" Jim asks. "That's your third hike of the week."

"It was great—I feel so strong still. I would never have attempted that hike by myself before the GR5. I powered up Mad River then had to slow my pace so I wouldn't run out of energy for the other three summits. I am strong."

"I thought you didn't like hiking alone," Jim says.

"I actually love it now. I wouldn't want to camp by myself, but I love walking solo. I fell right into the zone." *Calm and contentment flowed through my veins, the smell of the spruce energizing me and the alpine wind gently cleansing me.*

"I'm glad. It's kind of funny how we've swapped positions: when the kids were growing up you were surrounded by friends because I was so busy working. Now I have all these mountain biking and skiing buddies while you are content to hike and walk by yourself."

"I miss the GR5. My body aches to keep walking. I miss the simplicity of walking every day. The sight of the path leading onward is profound joy to me."

Jim drops the shirt he is folding, steps to me, and wraps his arms around me. "I miss it too," he whispers in my ear.

Tears flow and get matted in my hair as my face nestles into his shoulder. "People keep telling us it was the trip of a lifetime. And I don't want it to be the trip of a lifetime because I want more trips—but maybe it really *was* the trip of a lifetime."

Jim holds me tighter. Then he steps away and picks up a pair of socks to roll.

I pause, remembering a moment on the trail. *This is the time.* "I have something that I want to talk to you about," I say.

"Oh no, now that we've done the trip, you're ready to get rid of me," Jim jokes. He picks up a shocking yellow biking shirt and begins to fold it.

"No." I pause and swallow. "Remember way, way, back when we were dating? We had been dating for two and a half years, and I kept pushing you to get married. But you know, this is hard for me to say." My heart is beating faster. I feel like I'm pushing myself too fast. My face is flushed. I take a breath and exhale slowly. "There has always been this pebble of doubt. I was not fully in love with you. It was more that I was ready to settle down." I backtrack a little to make it not so harsh. "I did love you. I just was not madly in love with you, if you know what I mean?"

Jim takes a deep breath and exhales slowly, mirroring my exhalation. He drops the biking shirt back in the pile. I can't read his body or his face. He suddenly looks tired and paler. I'm nervous but not scared. I need to share this truth. I want to open my heart, fully, honestly to him.

"I love you so much more now. I'm totally in love with you now," I tell him in a calm, clear liquid voice. The fragrance of cedar and laundry detergent wafts between us while the dust suspended in the sunbeams waits for a response.

"I'm so relieved you said that. I feel the exact same way." He pauses, and a smile grows on his face. "I'm so much more in love with you now too. Thank you for telling me," he says in a quiet voice.

I exhale now with compassion for myself, for Jim, and for our relationship. We both step forward and embrace as the rest of the laundry lies in a tangle on the bed. He whispers in my hair, "I love how our love keeps evolving."

Walking is never far from my thoughts these days. I listen to a podcast about walking in Japan. The host talks about tourists wanting to climb iconic Mt. Fuji. But to really see Mt. Fuji, he says, you should climb a neighboring mountain. Only the perspective of removal allows you to truly witness its beauty, shape, and uniqueness. Walking the GR5, I now realize, has allowed me the distance to see the beauty, shape, and uniqueness of my marriage to Jim.

All that late fall and early winter, I notice the dried beech leaves blowing across the snow. Beech leaves stay attached to the trees for a long time, especially the young trees. They don't let go the way most leaves fall to the forest floor in October. When beech leaves finally release, there is usually snow on the ground here in Vermont. This was something I had not noticed the first winter, maybe because I was so engrossed in planning our trip. But now that we have returned, I see the tan papery leaves roll along the top of the white snow, playing and dancing in the wind. I notice them when I climb into my car to go to the grocery store. I notice them when I'm on the single chair at Mad River Glen. And every time I see the papery leaves skittering across the snow, a little energy inside of me sparks, *Pay attention, pay attention.* Though, I cannot figure out what I'm supposed to pay attention to.

I ask a friend who is an intuitive. She tells me, "For me the leaves are nature's reminder of the cycle of life. We are meant to embrace the process of things coming to an end or even dying in order to make space for the new. The snow is your blank canvas from which the new will emerge."

Her words make perfect sense to me. I need to let go of grieving the GR5. I will always have it in my heart. But it's over.

For the past five months, I have been trying to rekindle my coaching business in a new place. And I realize it's not just a new physical place but an unfamiliar spiritual place where I find myself in the aftermath of this grand adventure.

The white snow represents the blank page. One way to keep the story of my love affair with the GR5 alive is to write it down. Could this be the new beginning? Because I'm dyslexic, I'd never thought I could write a book. Yet haven't I just learned that when I take small steps every day, I can walk cross an entire continent?

All along the GR5, we followed the white-and-red waymarks. In life, there are waymarks too, but we don't often see them. The papery beech leaves rolling on the white snow are my waymarks.

Now I see. Small steps are essential and powerful.

You hold my story in your hands.

ACKNOWLEDGMENTS

Walking the GR5 was easier than writing it. Gratefully, I had many supporters to guide me along the writing trail.

Hellie Swartwood and Linda Foster listened to my stories for over twenty years as we ran early in the mornings in all weather, fostering my storytelling skills. Their respect, friendship, and love gave me the courage to become the woman I am.

First thanks goes to Laura Martineau for believing in me throughout the process. She was my first reader, biggest cheerleader, and brilliant editor.

Thank you to Mima Tipper and Jayne Becker for their valuable critique, wisdom, and support.

Special heartwarming gratitude goes to the women in my two writing groups: Penny Dickson, Lois Wisman, Marcia Croyle, Robin Benziger, and June Anderson for being at my side every step of the way.

I'm particularly grateful to Camilla Sanderson and Jodi Paloni for providing insightful feedback and editorial help.

Catherine Drake, Bunny Merrill, Sherry Sidoti, Jessica Bennett, Annika Holtan, Candace Nelson, and my sister, Sarah Raymond, were careful and gracious readers.

To Brooke Warner, publisher at She Writes Press, Shannon Green, my project manager, and Susie Chinisci, copy editor: I send deep gratitude to these amazing women, whom I am honored to work with.

Thanks to my mother, Tess Raymond, who taught me by example about unconditional LOVE.

Gratitude and love to my children, Kate and Sam for reading, supporting and encouraging me. And to Sam for creating the map.

Finally, thank you, Jim, for being you. For walking with me through the jungle of drafts and revisions. For sharing your journal, which offered different details than mine. For supporting me through the publishing process. Our love has grown stronger through this process. Let's keep walking through life together.

ABOUT THE AUTHOR

Photo credit: Kathryn Costello

Kathy Elkind is a long-distance walker, writer, and eater. She is a Teacher of Mindful Self-Compassion. She can be reached at www.kathyelkind.com. Along with her husband she has walked the GR5, the Andalusian Coast to Coast Walk in Southern Spain, and parts of the Cammino Materano in Italy. Kathy lives in the Mad River Valley of Vermont, in Fayston.

SELECTED TITLES FROM SHE WRITES PRESS

She Writes Press is an independent publishing company
founded to serve women writers everywhere.
Visit us at www.shewritespress.com.

Travel Mania: Stories of Wanderlust by Karen Gershowitz. $16.95, 978-1-64742-126-7. After flying to Europe at seventeen, Karen Gershowitz became addicted to travel and adventure—and went on to visit more than ninety countries. In these engaging stories, she reflects on the amazing ways in which travel has changed her life.

Rudy's Rules for Travel: Life Lessons from Around the Globe by Mary K. Jensen. $16.95, 978-1-63152-322-9. Circle the twentieth-century globe with risk-taking, frugal Rudy and his spouse Mary, a catastrophic thinker seeking comfort. When this marriage of opposites goes traveling, their engaging stories combine laugh-out-loud humor with poignant lessons from the odyssey of a World War II veteran.

Searching for Family and Traditions at the French Table, Book One by Carole Bumpus. $16.95, 978-1-63152-896-5. Part culinary memoir and part travelogue, this compilation of intimate interviews, conversations, stories, and traditional family recipes (*cuisine pauvre*) in the kitchens of French families, gathered by Carole Bumpus as she traveled throughout France's countryside, is about people savoring the life they have been given.

She Rode a Harley: A Memoir of Love and Motorcycles by Mary Jane Black. $16.95, 978-1-63152-620-6. After escaping an abusive marriage, Mary Jane finds love with Dwayne, who teaches her to ride a Harley; traveling together, they learn to be partners, both on and off the road, until Dwayne gets cancer. Without him, Mary Jane once again must learn to live on her own—but she'll never be the same again.

Brave(ish): A Memoir of a Recovering Perfectionist by Margaret Davis Ghielmetti. $16.95, 978-1-63152-747-0. An intrepid traveler sets off at forty to live the expatriate dream overseas—only to discover that she has no idea how to live even her own life. Part travelogue and part transformation tale, Ghielmetti's memoir, narrated with humor and warmth, proves that it's never too late to reconnect with our authentic selves—if we dare to put our own lives first at last.

Finding Venerable Mother: A Daughter's Spiritual Quest to Thailand by Cindy Rasicot. $16.95, 978-1-63152-702-9. In midlife, Cindy travels halfway around the world to Thailand and unexpectedly discovers a Thai Buddhist nun who offers her the unconditional love and acceptance her own mother was never able to provide. This soulful and engaging memoir reminds readers that when we go forward with a truly open heart, faith, forgiveness, and love are all possible.